Rome

DIRECTI

WRITTEN AND RESEARCHED BY

Martin Dunford

ADDITIONAL RESEARCH BY

Katie Parla and Flo Austin

NEW YORK • LONDON • DELHI

www.roughguides.com

RMA PRO
TRES TVOS
CLAVES REGNI
DILIGO TE
NC VNA FIDE

Contents

Introduction to Rome

Rome is the most fascinating city in Italy, which arguably makes it the most fascinating city in the world. An ancient place, packed with the relics of over two thousand years of habitation, you could spend a month here and still only scratch the surface. Yet it is so much more than an open-air museum: its people, its culture and its food make up a modern and vibrant city that would be worthy of a visit irrespective of its history. As a historic place, it is special enough, but as a contemporary European capital, it is utterly unique.

◂ Trajan's Column and SS Nome di Maria

Rome's eras crowd in on top of one another to a remarkable degree: there are medieval churches atop ancient basilicas and palaces, houses and apartment blocks that incorporate fragments of Roman columns and inscriptions, and roads and piazzas that follow the lines of ancient amphitheatres and stadiums. It's not an easy place to absorb on one visit, and you need to take things slowly, even if you only have a couple of days here. Most of the sights can be approached from a number of directions, and part of the allure of Rome is stumbling across things by accident, gradually piecing the city together, rather than marching around to a timetable. It's best to decide on a few key attractions (check out our Ideas section) and see where your feet take you – don't be afraid to just wander.

◂ Roman snacks

When to visit

It's possible to visit Rome at any time. However, you should, if you can, avoid coming in July or August, when it's very hot and most Romans are on holiday. May, June and September are the most comfortable months weatherwise – warm but not unbearably so, and not too humid. April and October can be nice too – the city is less crowded, outside Easter, and days can still be warm. The winter months can be a good time to visit, but bear in mind that the weather can be rainy and while you'll find everything pleasantly uncrowded, a lot of attractions will have reduced opening hours.

Certainly, you'd be mad to risk your blood pressure in any kind of vehicle, and the best way of getting around the city centre is to walk. The same goes for the ancient sites, and probably the Vatican and Trastevere quarter too – although for these last two you might want to jump on a bus or a tram going across the river. Keep public transport for longer hops – down to Testaccio, Ostiense or EUR, or to the catacombs and the Via Appia Antica, and of course for trips outside the city: to Ostia Antica, Tivoli, or to the beach at Anzio.

However you get around, the atmosphere is like no other city – a monumental, busy capital and yet an appealingly relaxed one, with a centre that has yet to be consumed by chainstores and multinational hotels. Above all, there has perhaps never been a better time to visit: Rome has recently been hauled into the twenty-first century. Museums, churches and other buildings that had been "in restoration" as long as anyone can remember have reopened, and some of the city's historic collections have been re-housed. Plus, the city's cultural life has been enhanced, with frequent open-air concerts, a new film festival, and initiatives like September's

▾ Speeding past Piazza Venezia

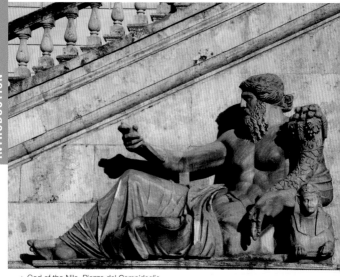

▲ God of the Nile, Piazza del Campidoglio

"Notte Bianca" helping to restore Roman pride. Transport, too, is being tackled, with the construction of a third metro line and various other initiatives – although it will be some time before these reach fruition.

Whether all this will irrevocably alter the character of the city remains to be seen – the enhanced crowds of visitors, spurred on by the growth of cheap flights in recent years, are certainly having a go. But for now, at least, there's definitely no place like Rome.

▼ Priests outside the Vatican City

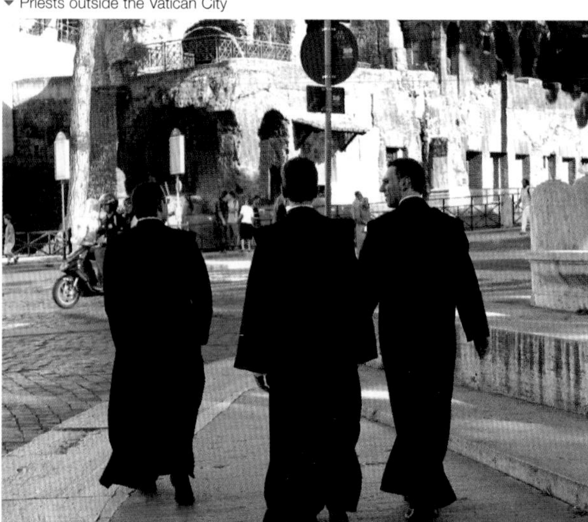

Rome
AT A GLANCE

CENTRO STORICO

It's easy to lose a sense of direction in Rome's historic centre, but you're so likely to come across something interesting it hardly matters.

▲ Piazza Navona, centro storico

CAMPO DE' FIORI AND THE GHETTO

Centring on the square and its market, this is a bustling neighbourhood of tiny streets and secluded piazzas that sits next to Rome's diminutive, crumbling old Jewish

ANCIENT ROME

The main concentration of Rome's ancient sites is just south of the city centre, focusing on the Forum, Palatine Hill, and, of course, the Colosseum.

◄ Swiss Guards, Vatican City

VATICAN CITY

It's not much like visiting a sovereign state, but you shouldn't leave town without seeing St Peter's or the wonders of the Vatican Museums.

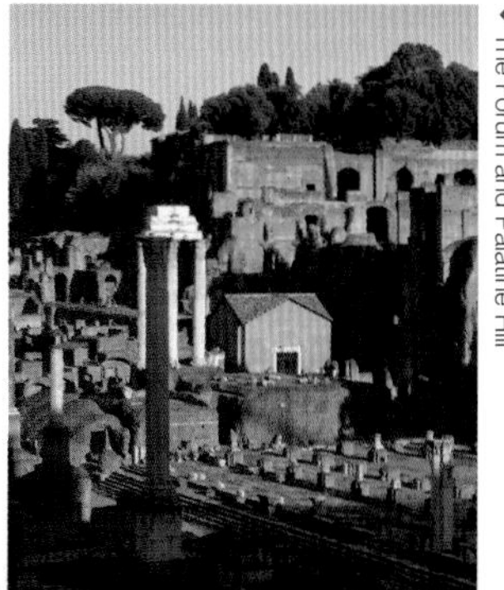

◄ The Forum and Palatine Hill

▲ The Spanish Steps

PIAZZA DI SPAGNA AND THE TRIDENTE

The Spanish Steps and the square below are the heart of tourist Rome, and the surrounding Tridente area, stretching either side of Via del Corso up as far as Piazza del Popolo, holds many of the key sights and the city's smartest designer shopping.

MONTI

Between the Colosseum and Termini, this nineteenth-century district of small hilly streets sandwiched between the city's busiest thoroughfares is one of the city centre's most up-and-coming areas – full of appealing small bars and restaurants.

TESTACCIO AND SOUTH OF THE CENTRE

There's lots to see in Rome's southern neighbourhoods, from the funky, foody and clubby district of Testaccio to Via Appia Antica and the catacombs on the city's semi-rural edges.

TRASTEVERE AND THE JANICULUM HILL

On the west bank of the Tiber, Trastevere still has a village-like atmosphere, despite the tourists, as well as some of the city's best food and nightlife. The Janiculum Hill, just above, offers great views over the city and is one of the best places to get your bearings.

▼ Looking down from the Janiculum Hill

Ideas

The big six

Rome is stacked with more big-name sights than any other city, and it's hard to reduce the city to six must-see attractions. Yet while any list will depend on where your interests lie, there are a number of places so key to the city's history, and so memorable, that it would be a pity to miss them out, even on one visit.

▼ The Vatican Museums

Home to the largest, richest and most dazzling collections in the world.

P.170 ▸ THE VATICAN CITY

▼ Museo Nazionale Romano

There are great collections of Roman artefacts elsewhere in the city, but you'll find the finest in this museum's two main locations: Palazzo Altemps and Palazzo Massimo.

P.76 & P.131 ▸ THE CENTRO STORICO & THE QUIRINALE, TERMINI AND AROUND

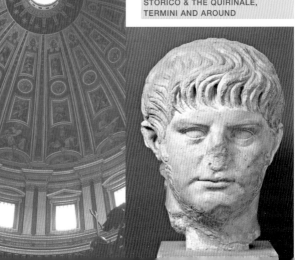

▼ The Roman Forum and Palatine Hill

The heart of Western civilisation for centuries, and a timely reminder that no great power lasts forever.

P.106 & P.108 ▸ THE FORUM, COLOSSEUM AND AROUND

▼ The Colosseum

So iconic, it would be wrong to ignore it.

P.109 ▸ THE FORUM, COLOSSEUM AND AROUND

▲ Museo e Galleria Borghese

An amazing building that's home to some of the best Bernini sculpture, as well as one of Rome's finest picture galleries.

P.148 ▸ THE VILLA BORGHESE AND NORTH OF THE CENTRE

▲ St Peter's

The principal seat of the Catholic church is as large and overbearingly magnificent as you might expect.

P.168 ▸ THE VATICAN CITY

Fountains

Like most Italian cities, Rome's old centre is defined by its piazzas, and these in turn are often characterised by their fountains. Some are simple and easy to miss, others are rearing, outsized monstrosities. They punctuate your strolls around the city centre, their waters providing a soothing respite from the noise and traffic.

▲ Fontana di Tritone

Bernini's spluttering Triton fountain marks the centre of one of the city's busiest road junctions.

P.124 ▸ THE QUIRINALE, TERMINI AND AROUND

Fontana delle Tartarughe

Perhaps the city's cutest fountain, on one of Rome's most secret squares.

P.87 ▸ CAMPO DE' FIORI, THE GHETTO AND AROUND

Fontana di Trevi

Rome's most famous fountain, tucked away in the city's backstreets and most rewarding when stumbled on by surprise.

P.97 ▸ THE TRIDENTE

Fontana dei Quattro Fiumi

The grandest and most Baroque of Bernini's Roman fountains is the centrepiece of Piazza Navona.

P.73 ▸ THE CENTRO STORICO

Fontana della Barcaccia

Bernini's father's unique legacy to the city – a boat beached on Piazza di Spagna.

P.92 ▸ THE TRIDENTE

Ancient Rome

Everyone who visits Rome wants to see the sights of the ancient city, and these are easy enough to find – they literally litter the city centre. The area richest in interest is centred on the Forum and Colosseum, and could keep you busy for a couple of days. But take some time to see more offbeat sights, like the ruins of Ostia Antica, outside Rome, and the amazing Ara Pacis Augustae, now housed in a brand-new purpose-built museum.

▲ Ostia Antica

The ruins of Rome's ancient port are some of the most atmospheric and complete you will find anywhere, and well worth the brief trip out by train.

P.183 ▸ DAY-TRIPS

▲ Ara Pacis Augustae

This marble block was sculpted in 13 BC to celebrate the subjugation of Spain and Gaul. One of the most revealing and naturalistic pieces of Roman carving you'll find, now housed in a gleaming modern structure.

P.97 ▸ THE TRIDENTE

▼ The Pantheon

An amazing building even in its time, but all the more incredible now given how completely it has survived.

P.69 ▸ THE CENTRO STORICO

▼ Largo di Torre Argentina

Major junction where the traffic winds around the remains of four Republican temples – now home to a large colony of cats.

P.82 ▸ CAMPO DE' FIORI, THE GHETTO AND AROUND

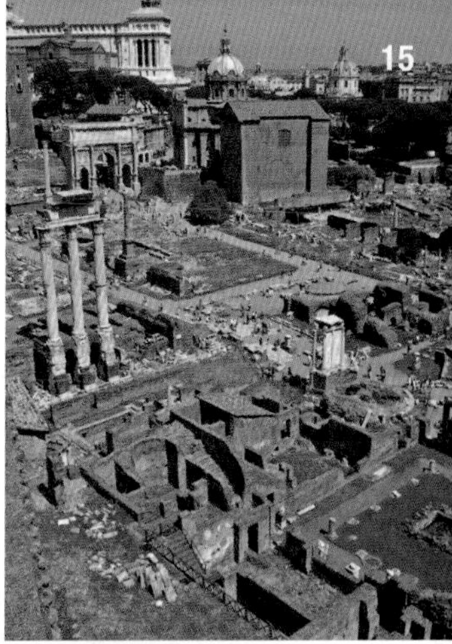

▲ The Roman Forum

The heart of the city during the days of the Roman Republic and, although barely recognizable now, it's one of the city's most evocative ancient sites.

P.106 ▸ THE FORUM, COLOSSEUM AND AROUND

▲ Colosseum

The most photographed of Rome's monuments, but deservedly so – it has provided the blueprint for virtually all sports stadiums since.

P.109 ▸ THE FORUM, COLOSSEUM AND AROUND

Churches

Rome is home to some of the earliest churches in the Christian world – a reflection of its role as birthplace and headquarters of the Catholic Church. Some of the oldest are conversions of ancient ruins; others follow the shape and floorplans of Roman basilicas. They are often beautifully plain buildings, with colourful Cosmati floors and apse mosaics, although some were remodelled during the Baroque era and don't feel ancient at all. Later churches tend to be solidly Baroque in style, and are often treasure-houses of art.

▼ Santa Maria sopra Minerva

The city's only Gothic church, and worth a visit just for that – as well as its various art treasures.

P.70 ▸ THE CENTRO STORICO

▼ San Giovanni in Laterano

Rome's official cathedral, and the former headquarters of the Catholic Church.

P.141 ▸ MONTI AND SAN GIOVANNI

▲ **San Pietro in Vincoli**

A beautifully plain church, home to one of Michelangelo's greatest sculptures.

P.136 ▸ MONTI AND SAN GIOVANNI

▶ **San Clemente**

This ancient Roman church is the best place to appreciate the city's multi-layered history.

P.143 ▸ MONTI AND SAN GIOVANNI

▲ **Santa Maria Maggiore**

One of the great Roman basilicas, and a treasure-trove of art and history.

P.137 ▸ MONTI AND SAN GIOVANNI

▼ **San Luigi dei Francesi**

Visit the French national church in Rome to see some amazing early paintings by Caravaggio.

P.71 ▸ THE CENTRO STORICO

Mosaics

Beautiful mosaics from different eras can be seen all over Rome. The best of the ancient examples are in the Palazzo Massimo, although you can also see them *in situ* at the Baths of Caracalla and Ostia Antica. Mosaics were subsequently used to decorate the early churches, often with gold leaf added to give a shimmering effect. The art form also survived into the modern era, when it was used by Mussolini to decorate parts of his Foro Italico sports complex.

▲ Santa Maria in Trastevere

The mosaics here show a solemn arrangement of saints around Christ and Mary.

P.158 ▸ TRASTEVERE AND THE JANICULUM HILL

▲ Palazzo Massimo

These Roman mosaics and frescoes are probably the city's finest and give you a great idea of day-to-day life in acient times.

P.131 ▸ THE QUIRINALE, TERMINI AND AROUND

▲ Foro Italico

The mosaics at Mussolini's monumental sports centre were intended to celebrate the strength of a new Roman empire.

P.152 › THE VILLA BORGHESE AND NORTH OF THE CENTRE

► Santa Prassede

The Chapel of Saint Zeno here has ninth-century mosaics which reflect the daylight beautifully.

P.140 › MONTI AND SAN GIOVANNI

▼ Santa Pudenziana

The mosaics of the Apostles are an expressive marvel.

P.137 › MONTI AND SAN GIOVANNI

Green Rome

Visiting Rome is essentially an urban experience but there are green spaces – even right in the centre – that offer the chance to cool off and relax between sights. The Villa Borghese is the most extensive park, containing a host of different attractions, but you should consider exploring less obvious locations such as the botanical gardens in Trastevere, the Villa Celimontana or the gorgeous Vatican Gardens.

▲ **Orto Botanico**

Rome's peaceful botanic gardens are a lovely spot for a stroll.

P.160 › TRASTEVERE AND THE JANICULUM HILL

▲ Villa Celimontana

A pleasant park on the Celian Hill – a good spot for a picnic after seeing the Colosseum.

P.111 ▸ THE FORUM, COLOSSEUM AND AROUND

▲ Vatican Gardens

Only visitable on a tour, but worth planning ahead to see.

P.130 ▸ THE VATICAN CITY

▼ Pincio Gardens

Laid out in the nineteenth century, these formal gardens give fine views over the domes of central Rome.

P.95 ▸ THE TRIDENTE

▼ Villa Borghese

The city centre's largest open space by far. There's plenty to see and do, including galleries, a zoo and bikes to hire.

P.147 ▸ THE VILLA BORGHESE AND NORTH OF THE CENTRE

Viewpoints

As a city built on hills, Rome provides all sorts of aspects from which to view its sea of domes, piazzas and patches of green punctured by ruins. The landmarks are easy enough to pick out if you know what you're looking for, but just as exciting if you don't. In fact, heading up to one of these viewpoints is the first thing you should do on arrival – it's great for orientation but also totally inspiring.

▲ Aventine Hill

Perhaps the best views of St Peter's and the Vatican are to be had from the top of Aventine Hill on the other side of the river.

P.111 ▸ THE CELIAN AND AVENTINE HILLS AND SOUTH OF THE CENTRE

▼ Janiculum Hill

Of all Rome's hills, this one, just to the west of the city centre, gives the fullest panorama of Rome's domes and towers.

P.161 ▸ TRASTEVERE AND THE JANICULUM HILL

▼ Spanish Steps

Tourist Central, but also a great place from which to take it all in without making too much effort – the whole of Rome's centre is spread out before you.

P.94 ▸ THE TRIDENTE

▲ Il Vittoriano

Many people's favourite view of Rome, because it's the one place from which you can't see the Vittoriano monument itself.

P.61 ▸ PIAZZA VENEZIA AND THE CAPITOLINE HILL

▼ St Peter's

It's worth the climb up the dome to see this classic panorama.

P.168 ▸ THE VATICAN CITY

Roman food

Roman cooking is traditionally dominated by the earthy cuisine of the working classes, with a little influence from the city's Jewish population thrown in. Pasta is important, and you'll find all sorts served in restaurants (spaghetti is probably the most popular – it stands up well to gutsy Roman sauces). Offal dishes are staples in the more traditional restaurants. Whatever and wherever you eat, it's very hard to eat badly, even in the busy tourist areas. Here are six of the best specialities and some suggestions on where to enjoy them.

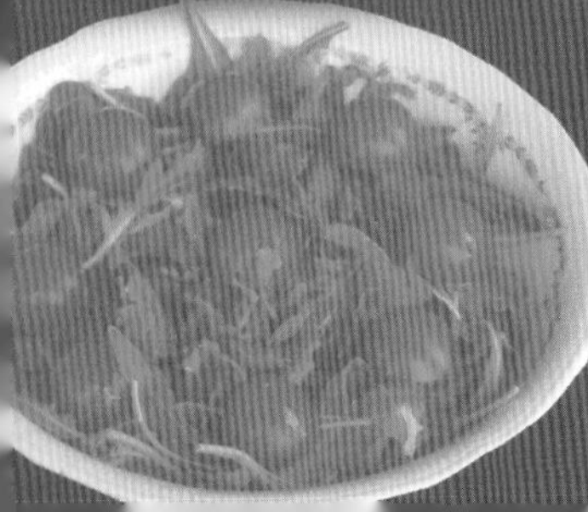

▲ Carciofi alla Giudea/Fiori di Zucca

Flattened artichokes and courgette flowers, both deep fried in batter – delicious, and about as Roman as you can get.

P.89 ▸ DA GIGGETTO

▲ Pasta alla Carbonara

Pasta with beaten eggs, bacon and pecorino cheese, you'll find this dish everywhere.

P.79 ▸ ENOTECA CORSI

▼ Pizza

Roman pizzas are delicious, but have a style of their own, with a thinner and crispier base than you'll find elsewhere in the country.

P.121 ▸ DA REMO

▲ Coda alla Vaccinara

Oxtail stewed with tomato and celery – a delicious feature on the menus of Rome's more traditional restaurants.

P.121 ▸ CHECCHINO DAL 1887

▶ Abbacchio al Forno

Lamb roasted to tender perfection with rosemary, sage and garlic.

P.101 ▸ OTELLO ALLA CONCORDIA

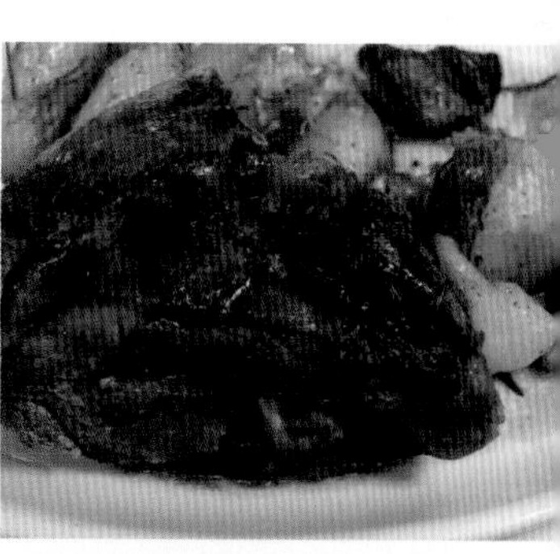

▼ Bucatini Cacio e Pepe

Hollow pasta tubes with lots of black pepper and pecorino cheese – simple and delicious.

P.163 ▸ DA LUCIA

Museums and galleries

It's likely that you'll be spending a fair amount of your time in Rome's museums and galleries, and there's certainly a dazzling amount to choose from, even without including the Vatican Museums – see p.000. There are two broad categories: those based on the collections of Rome's famous families (often including work by the city's Renaissance masters), and galleries that gather together the cream of the city's archeological finds, from both the Etruscan and Roman eras.

▼ Villa Giulia

A staggering assortment of Etruscan art, housed in the cleverly restored Renaissance villa of Julius II.

P.151 ▸ THE VILLA BORGHESE AND NORTH OF THE CENTRE

▼ Capitoline Museums

Two amazing galleries – one displaying Roman sculpture, the other Roman sculpture and Italian art.

P.65 ▸ PIAZZA VENEZIA AND THE CAPITOLINE HILL

▼ Museo e Galleria Borghese

Fabulous Bernini sculpture and one of Rome's best picture galleries, housed in the Borghese family villa.

P.148 ▸ THE VILLA BORGHESE AND NORTH OF THE CENTRE

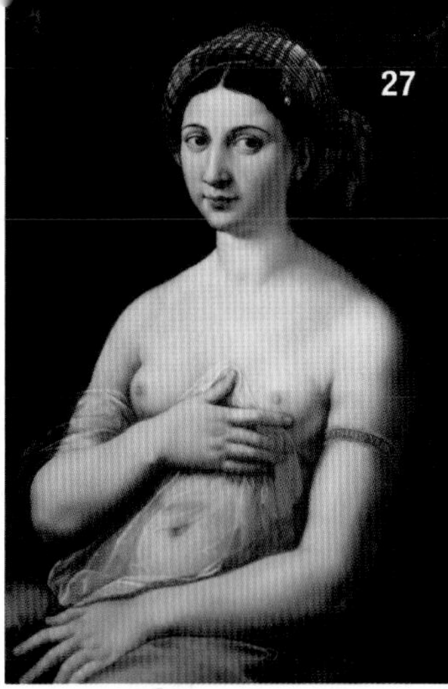

▲ Galleria Nazionale d'Arte Antica (Palazzo Barberini)

The Barberini palace is worth a visit in its own right, but it also houses one of the city's best collections of Renaissance and Baroque art, including Raphael's *La Fornarina*.

P.125 ▸ THE QUIRINALE, TERMINI AND AROUND

▼ Museo Nazional Romano

The museums of ancient Rome in the Palazzo Altemps and Palazzo Massimo are two of the city's unmissable attractions.

P.76 & P.131 ▸ THE CENTRO STORICO & THE QUIRINALE, TERMINI AND AROUND

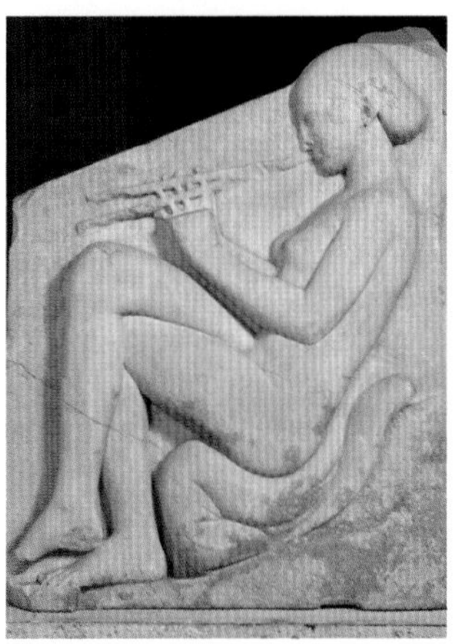

▲ Galleria Doria Pamphilj

The best and most intimately displayed of Rome's private art collections.

P.67 ▸ THE CENTRO STORICO

Shopping

You may wonder where to start when it comes to shopping in a big, chaotic city like Rome. In fact it's more appealing than you might imagine, thanks to the many pedestrianized shopping streets and colourful markets, most of which are in the city centre. Most importantly, Rome is yet to be overrun by the large chainstores and shopping malls that blight many European city centres, and many shops are small family-run affairs.

▲ Via Condotti

The main spine of Rome's designer shopping quarter.

P.92 ▸ THE TRIDENTE

▲ Via dei Coronari

Rome's antique row, lined with shops selling everything from Renaissance chests to 1960s Italian coffeepots.

P.75 ▸ THE CENTRO STORICO

▲ Porta Portese market

Still one of the best flea markets in Europe.

P.155 ▶ TRASTEVERE AND THE JANICULUM HILL

▼ Via del Corso

Main Street Rome, with all the clothing and shoe chains you would expect.

P.67 ▶ THE CENTRO STORICO

▲ Piazza di Campo de' Fiori

This centrally located fruit and veg market has been around for centuries and still takes place every morning.

P.83 ▶ CAMPO DE' FIORI, THE GHETTO AND AROUND

Bars

Italians aren't big drinkers, and most of Rome's bars are functional daytime haunts in which to consume a coffee and a sandwich. Nonetheless you'll find plenty of places that are conducive to an evening's drinking; indeed, there's an Irish pub on virtually every corner, and quite a number of appealing Italian haunts where the emphasis is on night – rather than day – life.

▼ Bar della Pace

Once Rome's coolest watering-hole, this remains one of the city's most central and appealing bars for an evening aperitif.

P.80 ▸ THE CENTRO STORICO

▼ Jonathan's Angels

Heavily decorated bar that draws an interesting mix of locals and tourists.

P.81 ▸ THE CENTRO STORICO

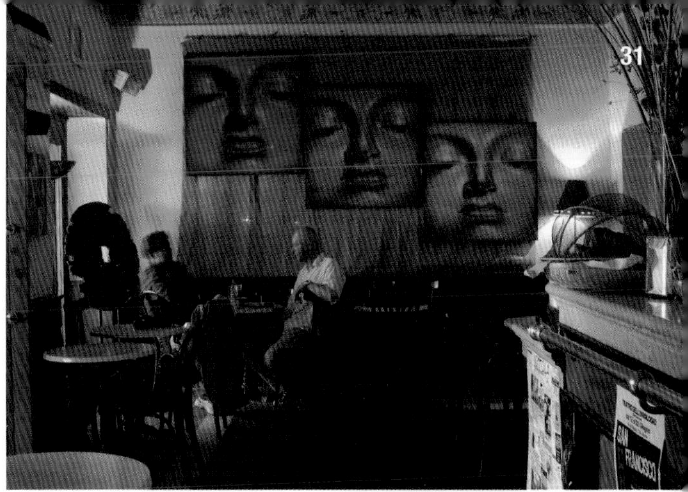

▲ Bar del Fico

Popular and pleasant bar in a busy part of the centro storico whose terrace is great for people-watching.

P.80 ▸ THE CENTRO STORICO

▶ Bartaruga

Trendy bar (named after the turtle fountain nearby) furnished with all sorts of Rococo paraphernalia.

P.90 ▸ CAMPO DE' FIORI, THE GHETTO AND AROUND

▼ Vineria

Long the haunt of Rome's nightclubbing demi-monde, and still going strong.

P.91 ▸ CAMPO DE' FIORI, THE GHETTO AND AROUND

Kids' Rome

Italians love children. Don't be surprised by how much attention people pay your kids here; peeking into buggies and helping you up and down steps is quite normal, as is giving up seats for you and your child on public transport. This in itself can make Rome a good place for a family holiday, although many sights hold a special appeal for children.

▲ Colosseum

Children (especially boys) are often fascinated by the gory past of the Colosseum, and they'll particularly like the *centurioni* who loiter outside for photocalls.

P.109 ▸ THE FORUM, COLOSSEUM AND AROUND

▼ Time Elevator

An entertaining virtual trip through the history of the city.

P.98 ▸ THE TRIDENTE

▲ Bocca della Verità

Kids love the fact that the "mouth of truth" never lies.

P.88 ▸ CAMPO DE' FIORI, THE GHETTO AND AROUND

▼ Museo della Civiltà Romana

Engaging museum with a huge model of ancient Rome – very evocative for both kids and adults.

P.120 ▸ THE CELIAN AND AVENTINE HILLS AND SOUTH OF THE CENTRE

▼ Bioparco

Recently hauled into the modern age, this city centre zoo has a great range of animals and an increasingly strong emphasis on conservation.

P.150 ▸ THE VILLA BORGHESE AND NORTH OF THE CENTRE

Hotels

Rome has plenty of decent, good-value hotels in nice locations, as well as lots of over-priced dross. In recent years, meanwhile, thanks to the arrival of a crop of self-consciously cool designer hangouts, Rome has caught up with the rest of Europe. If you want to do the city in style, look no further.

▲ **Daphne**

Perhaps the best of Rome's cheaper options.

P.193 ▸ ACCOMMODATION

▲ Hotel de Russie

The hotel of choice for the beautiful people, worth looking into just for its amazing lobby. Or settle for a cocktail in its courtyard garden.

P.194 ▸ ACCOMMODATION

▼ Hotel d'Inghilterra

Right in the heart of Rome's most elegant quarter, with exquisite rooms in palatial premises.

P.194 ▸ ACCOMMODATION

▼ Radisson SAS

The harbinger of the city's designer hotels, and still up there with the best.

P.195 ▸ ACCOMMODATION

Coffee and ice cream

Most Romans start their day in a café or bar, bolting down a coffee and a pastry, and there are some great places to do just this. But cafés also provide more substantial snacks throughout the day, such as panini, *tramezzini* (ready-made sandwiches with mixed fillings) and sometimes pizza and other hot snacks. Remember in most cafés your bill will be cheaper if you stand by the bar rather than take a seat at a table. Italian ice cream (*gelato*), meanwhile, is justifiably famous; for real quality you should go to a *gelateria*, where the range is a tribute to the Italian imagination and flair for display.

▲ Palazzo del Freddo di G. Fassi

Lovely old-fashioned ice-cream parlour.

P.144 ▸ MONTI & SAN GIOVANNI

▼ Caffè Sant'Eustachio

You get great coffee everywhere in Rome, but this place is considered by some diehards to serve the city's best.

P.77 ▸ THE CENTRO STORICO

▲ Giolitti

Rome's most famous *gelateria*, and although maybe past its best, the variety and atmosphere is second to none.

P.77 ▸ THE CENTRO STORICO

▼ Bernasconi

Tiny bar with great coffee and a very good selection of sweets and pastries – the *cornetti alla crema* are superb.

P.89 ▸ CAMPO DE' FIORI, THE GHETTO AND AROUND

▲ Il Gelato di San Crispino

Around the corner from the Trevi Fountain, some claim this is Rome's best ice cream.

P.100 ▸ THE TRIDENTE

The Vatican

The Vatican Hill is one of the original seven hills of Rome, and its location as the supposed site of St Peter's crucifixion has helped ensure its status as the centre of the world's most popular Christian faith – Catholicism. The Vatican City (Holy See) has been a sovereign state since 1929, and is visited by thousands of pilgrims and tourists keen to explore its staggering wealth of art and architecture.

▲ Castel Sant'Angelo

This Roman mausoleum has been used as prison and papal fortress, and now provides slightly lighter relief from the rest of the Vatican.

P.165 ▸ THE VATICAN CITY

▼ Museo Pio-Clementino

You can safely miss out most of the Vatican's many museums as long as you take in this one, home to the cream of its classical statuary.

P.170 ▸ THE VATICAN CITY

▲ Sistine Chapel

The Capella Sistina's ceiling and *The Last Judgement* on the wall behind together make up arguably the greatest masterpiece in western art, and the largest body of painting ever planned and executed by one man – Michelangelo.

P.174 ▸ THE VATICAN CITY

▲ The Pinacoteca

The cream of the Vatican paintings and, as such, as great a gallery as you'll find.

P.175 ▸ THE VATICAN CITY

▲ The Raphael Rooms

The frescoes here, most of them painted by Raphael, are one of the highlights of the Italian Renaissance, second only to the Sistine Chapel in their achievement.

P.172 ▸ THE VATICAN CITY

▶ St Peter's

The monuments and memorials of St Peter's, not to mention the sheer scale of the building, deserve a visit in their own right.

P.168 ▸ THE VATICAN CITY

Famous Romans

Every city has its icons, but none more so than Rome, which can lay claim to an array of household names stretching back over two thousand years. Ours is an entirely subjective list and you could easily put together your own as you tour the city.

▲ Julius II

As patron of Raphael and Michelangelo, Giuliano delle Rovere, or Julius II, left a legacy of art that is arguably the greatest of all the popes.

P.173 ▸ THE VATICAN CITY

▼ Augustus

The first Roman emperor, Augustus presided over Rome's great imperial years.

P.97 ▸ THE TRIDENTE

▼ Francesco Totti

Rome's favourite son, playing for the city's favourite football team.

P.153 ▸ THE VILLA BORGHESE AND NORTH OF THE CENTRE

▲ Mussolini

Not a Roman by birth, but Il Duce will forever be associated with his rule from Rome during the Thirties and the war years – in particular his breast-pumping speeches from the Palazzo Venezia balcony.

P.61 ▸ PIAZZA VENEZIA AND THE CAPITOLINE HILL

▲ Valentino

Arguably the most "Roman" of Italy's current designers. Check out his shop on Via Condotti.

P.92 ▸ THE TRIDENTE

▼ Caravaggio

The ne'er-do-well painter's works can be found all over the city, including this supposed self-portrait (as Bacchus) in the Galleria Borghese.

P.149 ▸ THE VILLA BORGHESE AND NORTH OF THE CENTRE

Statues

Whether they're inside a museum or exposed to the elements, Rome's statues always manage to make you stop and pause. Some tell a story or are representative of a particular era, others are simply beautiful examples of sculpture. Wherever you on almost every piazza and street) take time to linger and see what they can tell you about the history of the city.

▼ The Elephant Statue

Bernini's elephant and obelisk illustrates the fact that strength should support wisdom.

P.70 ▸ PIAZZA VENEZIA AND THE CAPITOLINE HILL

▼ Pasquino

This battered torso was one of Rome's "talking statues", a focus for satirical comment during the Renaissance.

P.73 ▸ THE CENTRO STORICO

▲ The Dying Gaul

One of the finest statues in the Palazzo Nuovo's great collection.

P.65 ▸ PIAZZA VENEZIA AND THE CAPITOLINE HILL

▲ Marcus Aurelius

This equestrian statue of the emperor was placed on the Piazza del Campidoglio by Michelangelo. The piazza now contains a copy: the original is in the Capitoline Museums' new wing.

P.64 ▸ PIAZZA VENEZIA AND THE CAPITOLINE HILL

▼ The She-wolf

This symbol of Rome's beginning can be found in the Palazzo dei Conservatori, in the Capitoline Museums and just off Piazza del Campidoglio.

P.65 ▸ PIAZZA VENEZIA AND THE CAPITOLINE HILL

▼ The Laocoön

Perhaps the most famous piece of Roman sculpture ever found.

P.171 ▸ THE VATICAN CITY

Palaces

Rome's great palaces tell the story of the city's richest and most influential families. These were the people who commissioned much of Rome's great architecture, sponsored her artists and, of course, provided most of the Vatican's popes over the years. Nowadays, many of their former homes are open to the public as museums or galleries.

▲ Palazzo Spada

The home of one Cardinal Spada is perhaps best known for its ingenious Borromini trompe l'oeil tunnel.

P.86 ▸ CAMPO DE' FIORI, THE GHETTO AND AROUND

▲ Palazzo del Quirinale

The residence of the Italian president, now open once a week.

P.128 ▸ THE QUIRINALE, TERMINI AND AROUND

◀ Villa Farnesina

This Trastevere mansion was home to the banker and Renaissance big shot Agostino Chigi, who employed Raphael to do the decorating.

P.160 ▸ TRASTEVERE AND THE JANICULUM HILL

▼ Palazzo Barberini

There are reminders of the Barberini family everywhere, and their palace is one of the largest and most sumptuous in the city.

P.125 ▸ THE QUIRINALE, TERMINI AND AROUND

▲ Palazzo Farnese

Perhaps the city's most elegant palace, home to the French embassy, whose Carracci murals are one of the city's must-sees.

P.85 ▸ CAMPO DE' FIORI, THE GHETTO AND AROUND

▲ Palazzo Venezia

Now the site of a museum of arts and crafts, this palace was also home to Mussolini's fascist government.

P.61 ▸ PIAZZA VENEZIA AND THE CAPITOLINE HILL

Literary Rome

Rome has produced its fair share of Italian literary greats. But many of the writers associated with the city are, in fact, foreigners who travelled here in search of inspiration and romance. Here are a few of the locations that remember writers who left a lasting mark on the city.

▲ Keats-Shelley House

Where Keats breathed his last, and these days a shrine to the poet and the English Romantic movement.

P.92 ▸ THE TRIDENTE

▲ Protestant Cemetery

The last resting-place of Keats, Italian politico Gramsci, American Beat poets and many other Godless literary types.

P.115 ▸ THE CELIAN AND AVENTINE HILLS AND SOUTH OF THE CENTRE

▼ Baths of Caracalla

It was while sitting among these ruins that the poet Shelley was moved to write his poem *Prometheus Unbound*.

P.114 ▸ THE CELIAN AND AVENTINE HILLS AND SOUTH OF THE CENTRE

▲ Casa di Goethe

The German poet and dramatist lived here on Via del Corso for two years.

P.96 ▸ THE TRIDENTE

▼ Rosati

Once the main gathering place for Rome's left-wing writers and activists.

P.102 ▸ THE TRIDENTE

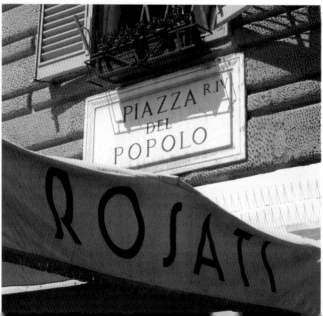

Piazzas

The life of any Italian city is dominated by its piazzas – airy open spaces where people congregate, strut and pose, drink a coffee and watch the world go by. Rome's piazzas vary hugely: some are simple traffic hubs, others large squares laid out along the lines of ancient Roman ruins or impeccably planned open spaces flanked by uniformly elegant period buildings.

▲ Piazza di Spagna

The heart of tourist Rome, and of its swanky shopping district.

P.92 ▸ THE TRIDENTE

▲ Piazza Santa Maria in Trastevere

The centre of Trastevere's villagey neighbourhood, popular at night with everyone from tourists to disaffected youth and local families pushing strollers.

P.158 ▸ TRASTEVERE AND THE JANICULUM HILL

▲ Piazza del Popolo

If you're coming to Rome for the first time, try to approach the centre from the sweeping oval of Piazza del Popolo.

P.95 ▸ THE TRIDENTE

▲ Piazza del Campidoglio

Laid out by Michelangelo, this is Rome's most ordered and elegant open space.

P.64 ▸ PIAZZA VENEZIA AND THE CAPITOLINE HILL

▼ Piazza di Campo de' Fiori

The city centre's most earthy, happening square, home to a lively market in the morning, and the best of Rome's nightlife come the evening.

P.83 ▸ CAMPO DE' FIORI, THE GHETTO AND AROUND

▼ Piazza Navona

If anywhere can be said to be the heart of Rome, this is it.

P.72 ▸ THE CENTRO STORICO

Underground Rome

Rome is a city of layers, and much of its history lies beneath the surface. There are temples, roads, rivers and houses beneath its streets, many of which have yet to be excavated – those areas that have are often only sporadically open to the public. The following highlights were all open at the time of writing.

Mithraic Temple

Located under the church of San Clemente, this was the site of bull worship in ancient times.

P.143 › MONTI AND SAN GIOVANNI

▲ **Catacombs of San Calisto**

One of several underground Christian burial grounds around the edges of the city centre.

P.119 ▸ THE CELIAN AND AVENTINE HILLS AND SOUTH OF THE CENTRE

▼ **The Vatican Necropolis**

Plan ahead far enough in advance and you can visit the remains of the first St Peter's under the current church and view what may be the saint's tomb.

P.169 ▸ THE VATICAN CITY

▼ **Mamertine Prison**

This dank space under the church of San Pietro in Carcere was where St Peter was held by the Romans.

P.66 ▸ PIAZZA VENEZIA AND THE CAPITOLINE HILL

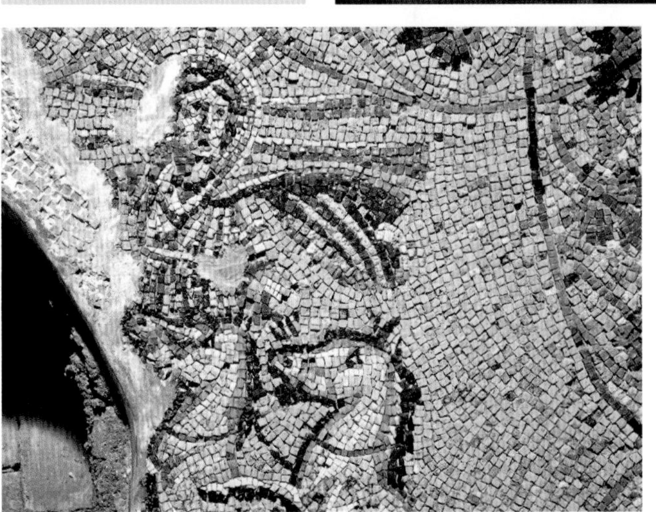

Hills of Rome

Rome's famous seven hills – the Capitoline, Palatine, Quirinale, Esquiline, Viminale, Aventine and Celian – continue to define the look and feel of the city centre.

▲ Palatine

Where Rome was founded, according to the legend of Romulus and Remus.

P.108 ▸ THE FORUM, COLOSSEUM AND AROUND

▲ Capitoline

The heart of the Roman Republic, and the origin of the modern city.

P.63 ▸ PIAZZA VENEZIA AND THE CAPITOLINE HILL

▼ Esquiline

A slum quarter in ancient Roman times and a mixed bag today, but with plenty to see, not least the basilica of Santa Maria Maggiore.

P.136 ▸ MONTI AND SAN GIOVANNI

▲ Quirinale

The first of Rome's hills to be colonized during Renaissance times, and now home to the presidential palace among many other attractions.

P.124 ▸ THE QUIRINALE, TERMINI AND AROUND

▼ Aventine

Home to the poor of ancient Rome, and the wealthy in modern times.

P.111 ▸ THE CELIAN AND AVENTINE HILLS AND SOUTH OF THE CENTRE

▲ Celian

A relatively peaceful escape from the nearby city centre's bustle.

P.111 ▸ THE FORUM, COLOSSEUM AND AROUND

Baroque Rome

If any one period can be said to define Rome, it's the Baroque, an era of flamboyance and drama in art and architecture that grew out of the Catholic Church's need to re-establish itself during the Counter-Reformation. There are Baroque sculptures, fountains and churches all over Rome, and many churches from previous periods have been redecorated in Baroque style.

▲ **The Rooms of St Ignatius**

Pozzo's trompe l'oeil corridor here is the era at its cleverest and most fanciful.

P.83 ▸ THE CENTRO STORICO

▲ **Piazza San Pietro**

Bernini's colonnaded piazza is pure, theatrical Baroque.

P.168 ▸ THE VATICAN CITY

▲ The Gesù

As the centre of the Jesuit movement, this church set the benchmark for all Baroque churches to come.

P.82 ▸ CAMPO DE' FIORI, THE GHETTO AND AROUND

▲ Ecstasy of Santa Theresa

Bernini's saucy statue (in the church of Santa Maria della Vittoria) is perhaps the city's most dramatic piece of Baroque art.

P.129 ▸ THE QUIRINALE, TERMINI AND AROUND

▲ Bernini and Borromini

The city's two greatest Baroque architects and sculptors, whose works compete for space throughout the city, pitch in at the Palazzo Barberini with two very different staircases.

P.125 ▸ THE QUIRINALE, TERMINI AND AROUND

◀ San Carlo alle Quattro Fontane

Borromini's clever use of space makes this a one of the most ingenious churches of the Baroque era.

P.128 ▸ THE QUIRINALE, TERMINI AND AROUND

Rome on film

Given that Rome is such a visual city, and the fact that the Italian film industry is based right outside, it's hardly surprising that the city has featured as the backdrop in so many movies. Here's a few of our favourites.

▼ Belly of an Architect

Peter Greenaway's film uses the city's landmarks – especially Palazzo Venezia and the Pantheon – as a brooding backdrop to a man's disintegration.

P.69 ▸ THE CENTRO STORICO

▼ La Dolce Vita

The classic film of Swinging Sixties Rome. Unfortunately the police aren't keen on you recreating the Trevi Fountain scene.

P.97 ▸ THE TRIDENTE

▲ Gladiator

Not actually filmed in Rome, but as close to the blood and gore of the Colosseum as you're likely to get.

P.109 ▸ THE FORUM, COLOSSEUM AND AROUND

◄ Roman Holiday

Audrey Hepburn and some fine 1950s Roman locations – such as the Spanish Steps (shown here) – make a great combination.

P.94 ▸ THE TRIDENTE

▼ The Talented Mr Ripley

Great locations on Piazza Mattei and elsewhere.

P.87 ▸ CAMPO DE' FIORI, THE GHETTO AND AROUND

CLEMENS XII PONT MAX
AQVAM VIRGINEM
COPIA ET SALVBRITATE COMMENDATAM
CVLTV MAGNIFICO ORNAVIT
ANNO DOMINI MDCCXXXV PONTIF VI
PERFECIT BENEDICTVS XIV PON MAX

Places

Piazza Venezia and the Capitoline Hill

For many people the modern centre of Rome is Piazza Venezia – not so much a square as a road junction, but a good central place to start your wanderings, close to both the medieval and Renaissance centre of Rome and the city's ancient ruins. Flanked on all sides by imposing buildings, it's a spot you'll find yourself returning to time and again: it's the best landmarked open space in Rome, the great white bulk of the Vittorio Emanuele monument marking it out from anywhere else in the city. Behind lie the Piazza del Campidoglio and the Capitoline Hill, one of the first settled and most central of Rome's seven hills.

Palazzo Venezia

Via del Plebiscito 118. Tues–Sun 8.30am–7.30pm; €4. Forming the western side of the piazza, Palazzo Venezia was the first large Renaissance palace in the city, built for the Venetian Pope Paul II in the mid-fifteenth century and for a long time the embassy of the Venetian Republic. More famously, Mussolini moved in here while in power, occupying the vast Sala del Mappamondo and making his declamatory speeches to the huge crowds below from the small balcony facing on to the piazza. Nowadays it's a venue for great temporary exhibitions and home to the **Museo Nazionale di Palazzo Venezia** – a museum of Renaissance arts and crafts, with a lot of fifteenth-century devotional works from central and northern Italy, some beautifully displayed bronzes and rooms full of weapons and ceramic jars from an ancient monastic pharmacy. You can also walk out to the palace's upper **loggia** for a view over the palm-filled courtyard – the gardens are some of the prettiest in Rome.

San Marco

Daily 8.30am–noon & 4–7pm; closed Mon am & Wed pm. Adjacent to the Palazzo Venezia on its southern side, the church of San Marco is a warm, cosy basilica, one of the oldest in Rome. Originally founded in 336 AD on the spot where the apostle is said to have lived, it was rebuilt in 833 and added to by various Renaissance and eighteenth-century popes including Pope Paul II, who added the graceful portico and gilded ceiling. The apse mosaic dates from the ninth century and shows Pope Gregory IV offering his church to Christ.

Vittorio Emanuele Monument

Daily 9.30am–6.30pm; free. The rest of the buildings on Piazza Venezia pale into insignificance beside the marble monstrosity rearing up across the street from San Marco – the Vittorio Emanuele Monument or

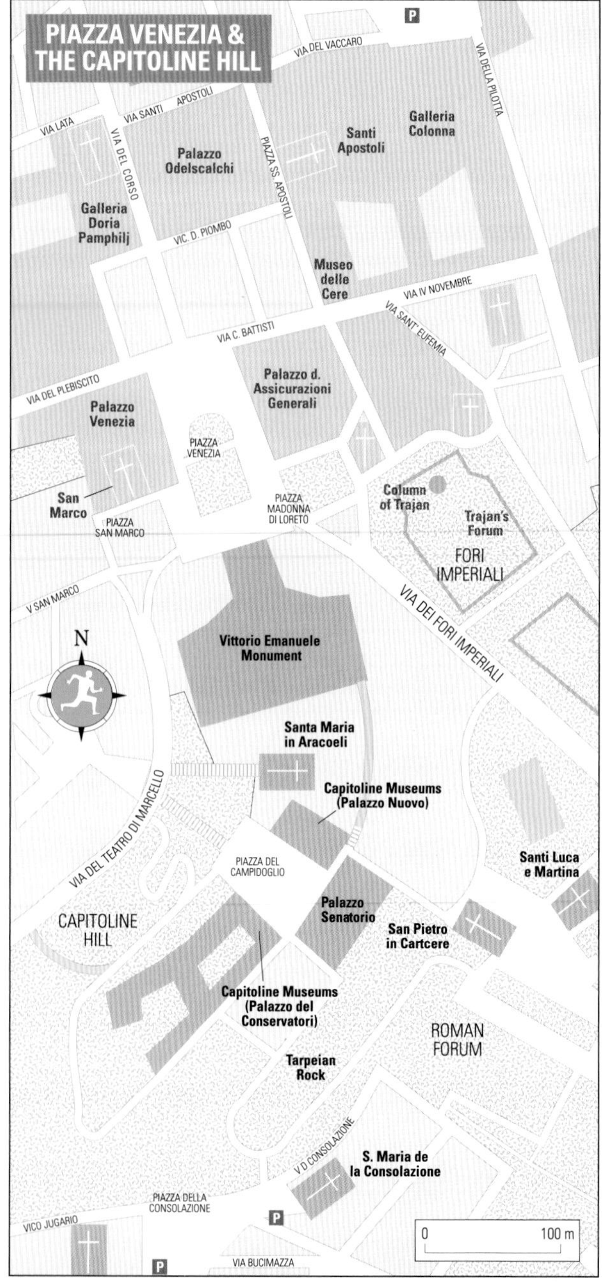
PIAZZA VENEZIA &
THE CAPITOLINE HILL
VIA DEL VACCARO
VIA DELLA PILOTTA
VIA SANTI APOSTOLI
VIA LATA
VIA DEL CORSO
Palazzo Odelscalchi
PIAZZA SS. APOSTOLI
Santi Apostoli
Galleria Colonna
Galleria Doria Pamphilj
VIC. D. PIOMBO
Museo delle Cere
VIA IV NOVEMBRE
VIA SANT' EUFEMIA
VIA C. BATTISTI
VIA DEL PLEBISCITO
Palazzo Venezia
Palazzo d. Assicurazioni Generali
PIAZZA VENEZIA
San Marco
PIAZZA SAN MARCO
PIAZZA MADONNA DI LORETO
Column of Trajan
Trajan's Forum
FORI IMPERIALI
V SAN MARCO
VIA DEI FORI IMPERIALI
N
Vittorio Emanuele Monument
Santa Maria in Aracoeli
Capitoline Museums (Palazzo Nuovo)
VIA DEL TEATRO DI MARCELLO
PIAZZA DEL CAMPIDOGLIO
Santi Luca e Martina
Palazzo Senatorio
CAPITOLINE HILL
San Pietro in Cartcere
Capitoline Museums (Palazzo del Conservatori)
ROMAN FORUM
Tarpeian Rock
V D CONSOLAZIONE
S. Maria de la Consolazione
PIAZZA DELLA CONSOLAZIONE
VICO JUGARIO
0
100 m
VIA BUCIMAZZA
P

▲ IL VITTORIANO

"Vittoriano", erected at the turn of the nineteenth century as the "Altar of the Nation" to commemorate Italian Unification. Variously likened in the past to a typewriter and, by American GIs, to a wedding cake (the white marble used will never mellow with age), it's now open after years of closure, and it's great to clamber up and down the sweeping terraces and flights of steps that, before, you could only gaze at from the street (you can now also take the elevator – €7). There are things to see inside – not least the large Museo di Risorgimento, and the Complesso del Vittoriano, which hosts temporary art exhibitions – but it's the outside that's best, centring on an enormous equestrian statue of Vittorio Emanuele II and providing a route through to Piazza del Campidoglio behind. The views of the city are fabulous, most of all perhaps because it's the one place in Rome from which you can't see the Vittoriano.

The Capitoline Hill

The real pity about the Vittorio Emanuele Monument is that it obscures the view of the Capitoline Hill behind – once, in the days of Imperial Rome, the spiritual and political centre of the Roman Empire. Its name derives from its position as the "caput mundi" or "head of the world", and its influence and importance resonates to this day – words like "capitol" and "capital" all derive from here, as does the word "money", which comes from the temple to Juno Moneta that once stood nearby and housed the Roman mint. These days the Capitoline forms a tight, self-contained group of essential attractions, with the focus on its pair of museums and the church of Santa Maria in Aracoeli. It is much more connected to the rest of the city than it once was, with paths connecting with the Vittoriano in one direction and down to the Roman Forum in the other.

Santa Maria in Aracoeli

Daily 9am–12.30pm & 3–6.30pm.

The church of Santa Maria in Aracoeli crowns the highest point on the Capitoline Hill and is built on the ruins of a temple to Juno. Reached by a flight

▲ SANTA MARIA IN ARACOELI

of 124 steps up the Aracoeli Staircase, erected in 1348, it's a steep climb to the top, but the church is worth it: it's one of Rome's most ancient basilicas, known for its role as keeper of the so-called "Bambino", a small statue of the child Christ, carved from the wood of a Gethsemane olive tree. The statue is said to have miraculous healing powers and was traditionally called out to the sickbeds of the ill and dying all over the city, its coach commanding instant right of way through the heavy Rome traffic. The Bambino was stolen in 1994, but a copy now stands in its place, in a small chapel to the left of the high altar.

Piazza del Campidoglio

Next door to the Aracoeli Staircase, the smoothly rising ramp of the Cordonata leads to Piazza del Campidoglio, one of Rome's most perfectly proportioned squares, designed by Michelangelo in the last years of his life for Pope Paul III. Michelangelo died before his plan was completed, but his designs were faithfully executed – balancing the piazza, redesigning the facade of the Palazzo dei Conservatori and projecting an identical building across the way, the Palazzo Nuovo. These buildings, which have recently been completely renovated, are home to the Capitoline Museums (see opposite); both are angled slightly to focus on Palazzo Senatorio, Rome's town hall. In the centre of the square Michelangelo placed an equestrian statue

▼ PIAZZA DEL CAMPIDOGLIO

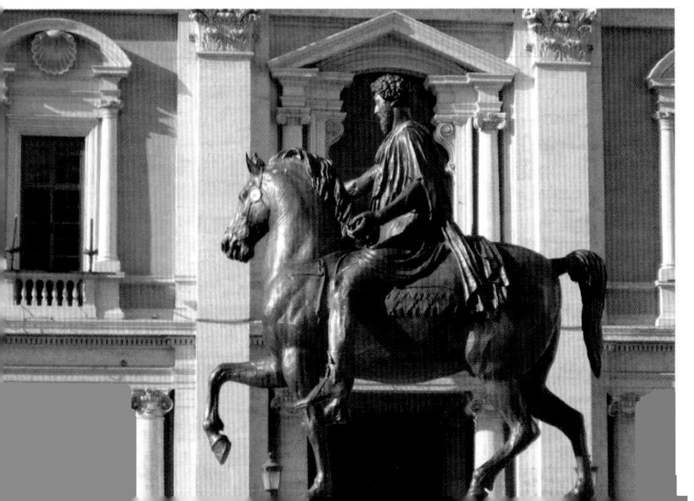

of Emperor Marcus Aurelius (now a copy), which had previously stood outside San Giovanni in Laterano; early Christians had refrained from melting it down because they believed it to be of the Emperor Constantine (the first Roman ruler to acknowledge and follow Christianity).

The Capitoline Museums

Tues–Sun 9am–8pm; €6.50, €8.50 for joint ticket with Centrale Montemartini (see p.116). Valid 7 days; Ⓦwww.museicapitolini.org. If you see no other museums of ancient sculpture in Rome, try to at least see the Capitoline Museums, which are perhaps the most venerable of all the city's collections. They're divided into two parts – the Palazzo dei Conservatori and the Palazzo Nuovo – and you should try to see both rather than choosing one. Tickets are valid for a day so you can fit in each museum with a break in-between, perhaps for a stroll around the Roman Forum. The **Palazzo dei Conservatori** is the larger, more varied collection, with some ancient sculpture as well as later pieces and an art gallery. Inside, the centrepiece of the first floor, the Hall of the Orazie e Curiaze, is appropriately decorated with giant, late sixteenth-century frescoes depicting legendary tales from the early days of Rome. Check out the corner room, which contains the so-called *Spinario*, a Roman statue of a boy picking a thorn out of his foot, and, next door, the sacred symbol of Rome, the Etruscan bronze she-wolf nursing the mythic founders of the city, before moving on to the airy new wing, where the original statue of Marcus Aurelius, formerly in the square outside, takes centre stage, alongside a giant bronze statue of Constantine – or at least its head, hand and orb – and a rippling bronze of Hercules. Behind are part of the foundations and a retaining wall from the Capitoline's original temple of Jupiter, uncovered during the work for the new wing.

The second-floor *pinacoteca* holds Renaissance painting from the fourteenth to the late seventeenth centuries – highlights include a couple of portraits by Van Dyck and a penetrating *Portrait of a Crossbowman* by Lorenzo Lotto, a pair of paintings from 1590 by Tintoretto – a *Flagellation* and *Christ Crowned with Thorns*, and a very fine early work by Lodovico Carracci, *Head of a Boy*. In one of the two large main galleries, there's a vast picture by Guercino, depicting the *Burial of Santa Petronilla* (an early Roman martyr who was the supposed daughter of St Peter), and two paintings by Caravaggio, one a replica of the young *John the Baptist* which hangs in the Palazzo Doria-Pamphilj, the other an early work known as *The Fortune-Teller*.

The **Palazzo Nuovo** across the square – also accessible by way of an underground walkway that takes in good views of the Forum just below – is the more manageable of the two museums, with some of the best of the city's Roman sculpture crammed into half a dozen or so rooms. Among them are the remarkable, controlled statue of the *Dying Gaul*, a *Satyr Resting*, the inspiration for Hawthorne's book *The Marble Faun*, and the red marble *Laughing Silenus* – along with busts of Roman emperors and other famous names: a young Augustus, a cruel Caracalla, and the

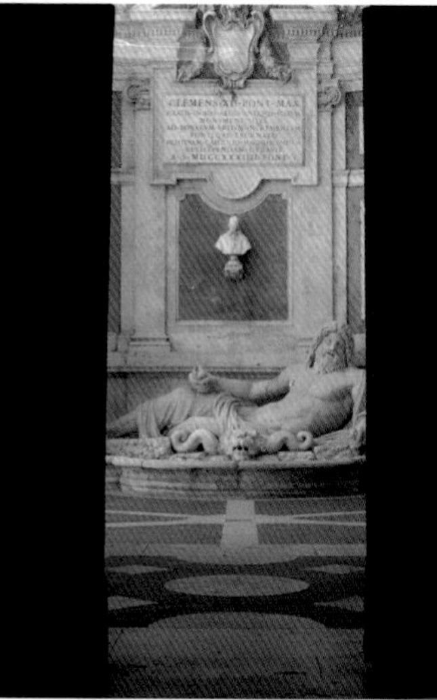

▲ MARFORIO, PALAZZO NUOVO

centrepiece, a life-sized portrait of Helena, the mother of Constantine, reclining gracefully. Also, don't miss the coy, delicate *Capitoline Venus*, housed in a room on its own.

The she-wolf and Tarpeian Rock

Just off the Piazza del Campidoglio, the statue of Romulus and Remus suckling the she-wolf provides one of Rome's most enduring images. Beyond is the Tarpeian Rock, from which traitors were thrown in ancient times – and which now gives excellent views over the Forum.

San Pietro in Carcere and the Mamertine Prison

Daily 10am–7pm; donation expected for the prison.

Steps lead down from the Tarpeian Rock to the little church of San Pietro in Carcere – built above the ancient Mamertine Prison, where spies, vanquished soldiers and other enemies of the Roman state were incarcerated, and where St Peter himself was held. Steps lead down into the murky depths of the jail, where you can see the bars to which he was chained, along with the spring the saint is said to have created to baptize other prisoners. At the top of the staircase, hollowed out of the honeycomb of stone, is an imprint claimed to be of St Peter's head as he tumbled down the stairs (though when the prison was in use, the only access was through a hole in the ceiling). It's an unappealing place even now, and you won't be sorry to leave – through an exit cunningly placed to lead you through the gift shop.

The centro storico

The real heart of Rome is the centro storico ("historic centre"), which makes up most of the triangular knob of land that bulges into a bend in the Tiber. This area, known in ancient Roman times as the Campus Martius, was outside the ancient city centre, a low-lying area that was mostly given over to barracks and sporting arenas, together with several temples, including the Pantheon. Later it became the heart of the Renaissance city, and nowadays it's the part of the town that is densest in interest, an unruly knot of narrow streets and alleys holding some of the best of Rome's classical and Baroque heritage and its most vivacious street- and nightlife. It's here that most people find the Rome they have been looking for – a city of small crumbling piazzas, Renaissance churches and fountains, blind alleys and streets humming with scooters and foot-traffic. Whichever direction you wander in there's something to see; indeed it's part of the appeal of the centre of Rome that even the most aimless ambling leads you past some breathlessly beautiful and historic spots.

Via del Corso

Named after the races that used to take place along here during Renaissance times, Via del Corso is now Rome's main shopping street and most central artery. It's home to a mixture of upmarket boutiques and chain stores that make it a busy stretch during the day but a relatively dead one come the evening. Running north–south from Piazza del Popolo to Piazza Venezia, it divides the city centre in two: the western side gives on to the dense streets of the centro storico and to the east, the swish shopping streets that converge on Piazza di Spagna.

Galleria Doria Pamphilj

Via del Collegio Romano 2. Mon–Wed & Fri–Sun 10am–5pm; €8, including audio guide in English; private apartments tours every 30min 10.30am–12.30pm; €3.50; Ⓦwww.doriapamphilj.it. The Palazzo Doria Pamphilj is among the city's finest Rococo palaces; the Doria-Pamphilj family have long been one of Rome's most illustrious, and still own the building and live in part of it. They were also prodigious collectors of art, and inside, the Galleria Doria Pamphilj constitutes one of Rome's best late-Renaissance art collections. The first part of the gallery is made up of a series of private apartments, furnished in the style of the original palace. But it's the picture gallery that's of most interest, its paintings – mounted in the style of the time – crammed in floor-to-ceiling. Just inside there's a badly cracked bust of *Innocent X* by Bernini, which the sculptor apparently replaced in a week

with the more famous version down the hall, where he appears to have captured the pope about to erupt into laughter. In the same room, Velázquez's famous painting of the same man is quite different, depicting a rather irritable character regarding the viewer with impatience. There is also perhaps Rome's best concentration of Dutch and Flemish paintings, including a rare Italian work by Bruegel the Elder, a highly realistic portrait of an old man and the fabulously ugly *Moneylenders and their Clients* by Quentin Matsys, and a Hans Memling *Deposition*. Other highlights include Carracci's bucolic *Rest during the Flight into Egypt*, painted shortly before the artist's death, two paintings by Caravaggio – *Repentant Magdalene and John the Baptist* – and *Salome with the head of St John*, by Titian. All in all, it's a marvellous collection of work, displayed in a wonderfully appropriate setting.

Sant'Ignazio

Daily 7.30am–12.30pm & 4–7.15pm. The Jesuit church of Sant'Ignazio was dedicated to the founder of the Society of Jesus after his death and canonization. It's worth visiting for its marvellous Baroque ceiling by Andrea del Pozzo, showing St Ignatius being welcomed into Paradise by Christ and the Virgin, a spectacular work that creates the illusion of looking at the sky through open colonnades. Pozzo also painted the ingenious false dome in the crossing (a real dome was planned but was deemed too

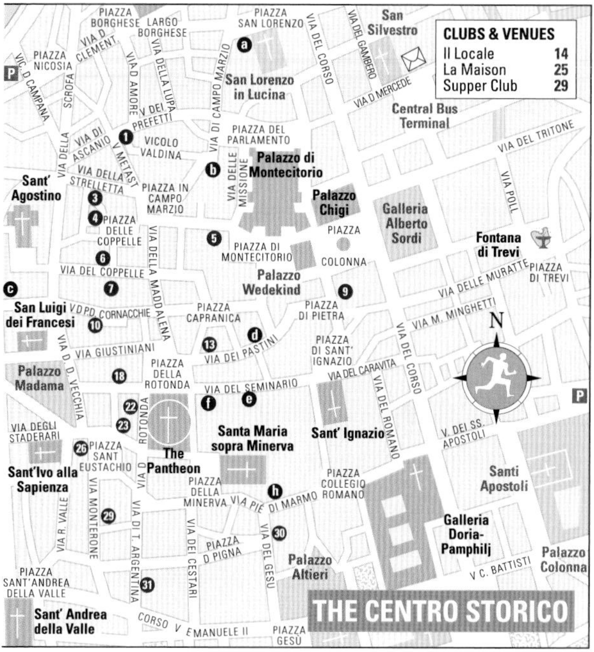

THE CENTRO STORICO

CLUBS & VENUES	
Il Locale	14
La Maison	25
Supper Club	29

▲ PIAZZA SANT'IGNAZIO

expensive). Stand on the disc in the centre of the nave to get the full effect of this trompe l'oeil masterpiece.

The Pantheon

Mon–Sat 8.30am–7.30pm, Sun 9am–6pm; free. One of the centro storico's busiest sights, the Pantheon is easily the most complete ancient Roman structure in the city, and along with the Colosseum, visually the most impressive. Though originally a temple that formed part of Marcus Agrippa's redesign of the Campus Martius in around 27 BC – hence the inscription – the building was rebuilt by the emperor Hadrian and finished around the year 125 AD (it has since been consecrated as a church). It's a formidable architectural achievement

▲ THE PANTHEON

even now, and inside you get the best impression of the engineering expertise of the time: the diameter is precisely equal to its height (43m), the hole in the centre of the dome – from which shafts of sunlight descend to illuminate the musty interior – a full 9m across. Most impressively, there are no visible arches or vaults to hold the whole thing up; instead they're sunk into the concrete of the walls of the building. It would have been richly decorated, the coffered ceiling heavily stuccoed and the niches filled with the statues of gods. Now, apart from the sheer size of the place, the main object of interest is the tomb of Raphael, between the second and third chapel on the left, with an inscription by the humanist bishop Pietro Bembo: "Living, great Nature feared he might outvie Her works, and dying, fears herself may die." The same kind of sentiments might well have been reserved for the Pantheon itself.

Santa Maria sopra Minerva

Mon–Sat 7am–7pm, Sun 8am–7pm. Piazza della Minerva is home to the rose-windowed medieval church of Santa Maria sopra Minerva. This is Rome's only Gothic church, and worth a look just for that, although it's also one of the city's art-treasure churches, crammed with the tombs and self-indulgences of wealthy Roman families. Of these, the Carafa Chapel, in the south transept, is the best known, holding Filippino Lippi's fresco of *The Assumption*. The children, visible in the foreground here, are portraits of the young future Medici popes, Leo X and Clement VII – both of whose tombs lie either side of the main altar. Look also at the figure of *Christ Bearing the Cross*, just in front, a serene work that Michelangelo completed for the church in 1521. Outside, the diminutive **Elephant Statue** is Bernini's most endearing piece of work: a cheery elephant trumpeting under the weight of the obelisk he carries on his back – a reference to Pope Alexander VII's reign and supposed to illustrate the fact that strength should support wisdom.

Sant'Ivo alla Sapienza

Mon–Fri 8.30am–5pm, Sat & Sun 9am–noon. Between the Pantheon and Piazza Navona, the rather blank facade of the Palazzo della Sapienza cradles the church of Sant'Ivo alla Sapienza – from the outside at least, one of Rome's most impressive churches, with a playful facade designed by Carlo Borromini. Though originally built for the Barberini pope, Urban VIII, the building's construction actually spanned the reign of three pontiffs. Each of the two small towers is topped with the weird, blancmange-like groupings that are the symbol of the Chigi family and the central cupola spirals helter-skelter-fashion to its zenith, crowned with flames that are supposed to represent the sting of the Barberini bee, their family symbol. Inside, too, it's very cleverly designed, impressively light and spacious given the small space the church is squeezed into, rising to the tall parabolic cupola.

San Luigi dei Francesi

Daily except Thurs pm 8.30am–12.30pm & 3.30–7pm. The French national church of San Luigi dei Francesi is worth a visit, mainly for the works by Caravaggio it numbers amongst its collection. In the last chapel on the left are three paintings: *The Calling of St Matthew*, in which Christ points to Matthew, who is illuminated by a shaft of sunlight; *St Matthew and the Angel*, showing the visit of an angel as the apostle writes the Gospel; and *The Martyrdom of St Matthew*. Caravaggio's first public commission, these paintings were actually rejected at first, partly on grounds of indecorum, and it took considerable reworking by the artist before they were finally accepted. Despite that, they are among the artist's finest works.

Sant'Agostino

Daily 7.45am–noon & 4–7.30pm. The Renaissance facade of the church of Sant'Agostino is not much to look at from the outside, but a handful of art treasures might draw you in. Just inside the door, the serene statue of the *Madonna del Parto*, by Sansovino is traditionally invoked during pregnancy, and

▲ SANT'IVO ALLA SAPIENZA

is accordingly surrounded by photos of newborn babes and their blissful parents. Further into the church, Raphael's vibrant fresco of *Isaiah,* is on the third pillar on the left, beneath which is another work by Sansovino, a craggy *St Anne, Virgin and Child*. But the biggest crowds gather around the first chapel on the left, where the *Madonna di Loreto*, painted in 1605 by Caravaggio, is a characteristic work of what was at the time almost revolutionary realism, showing two peasants praying at the feet of a sensuous Mary and Child, their dirty feet and scruffy clothes contrasting with the pale, delicate feet and skin of Mary.

Piazza di Montecitorio and Piazza Colonna

Piazza Montecitorio takes its name from the bulky Palazzo di Montecitorio on its northern side, home since 1871 to the lower house of the Italian parliament – the building itself is a Bernini creation from 1650

▲ COLUMN OF MARCUS AURELIUS

(open the first Sun of each month 10am–6pm; free). Just beyond, Piazza Colonna fronts on to Via del Corso and is flanked on its north side by the late sixteenth-century Palazzo Chigi, official residence of the Prime Minister. The **Column of Marcus Aurelius**, which gives the square its name, was erected between 180 and 190 AD to commemorate military victories in northern Europe, and (like the column of Trajan that inspired it) is decorated with reliefs depicting scenes from the campaigns.

Piazza Navona

The western half of the centro storico focuses on Piazza Navona, Rome's most famous square – a pedestrianized oval that is as picturesque as any piazza in Italy. Lined with cafés and restaurants and often thronged with tourists, street artists and pigeons, the best time to come is at night, when the inevitably tourist-geared flavour of the place is at its most vibrant, with crowds hanging out around the fountains watching the buskers and street artists or clocking the scene while nursing a pricey drink at a table outside one of the bars. The square takes its shape from the first-century AD Stadium of Domitian, the principal venue of the athletic events and later chariot races that took place in the Campus Martius, and until the mid-fifteenth century the ruins of the arena were still here, overgrown and disused. It was given a facelift in the mid-seventeenth century by Pope Innocent X, who built most of the grandiose palaces that surround it and commissioned Borromini to re-design the church of Sant'Agnese in Agone (daily 9.30am–12.30pm & 4–7pm) on the piazza's western side.

▼ PIAZZA NAVONA

▲ FONTANA DEI QUATTRO FIUMI

Fontana dei Quattro Fiumi

One of three fountains that punctuate Piazza Navona, the Fontana dei Quattro Fiumi is a masterpiece by Bernini, built in 1651. Each figure represents one of what were considered at the time to be the four great rivers of the world – the Nile, Danube, Ganges and Plate – though only the horse, symbolizing the Danube, was actually carved by Bernini himself. The fountain is topped with an Egyptian obelisk, brought here by Pope Innocent X from the Circus of Maxentius.

Pasquino

It's easy to miss the battered marble torso of Pasquino, even in the small triangular space of Piazza Pasquino (you'll find him in the corner), just west of Piazza Navona. Pasquino is perhaps the best known of Rome's "talking statues" of the Middle Ages and the Renaissance, upon which anonymous comments on the affairs of the day would be attached – comments that had a serious as well as a humorous intent, and gave us the word "pasquinade".

Museo di Roma

Piazza San Pantaleo 10. (Tues–Sun 9am–7pm; €6.50; ⓦ www.museodiroma.comune.roma.it. The eighteenth-century Palazzo Braschi is the home of the Museo di Roma, which has a permanent collection relating to the history of the city from the Middle Ages to the present day. It's a large museum and, to be honest, only sporadically interesting; indeed, the building is probably the main event, particularly the magnificent Sala Nobile where you go in, the main staircase, and one or two of the renovated rooms. But some of the paintings are absorbing, showing the city during different eras. Frescoes from demolished palaces also provide decent enough highlights.

Sant'Andrea della Valle

Mon–Sat 7.30am–noon & 4.30–7.30pm, Sun 7.30am–12.45pm & 4.30–7.45pm. This church has the

▲ SANT'ANDREA DELLA VALLE

distinction of sporting the city's second-tallest dome (after St Peter's), built by Carlo Maderno, and of being the setting for the first scene of Puccini's *Tosca*. Inside, it's one of the most Baroque of Rome's churches and your attention is drawn not only to the dome, decorated with paintings of the *Glory of Paradise* by Giovanni Lanfranco, but also to a marvellous set of frescoes in the apse by his contemporary, Domenichino, illustrating the life of St Andrew. In a side chapel on the right, you may, if you've been in Rome a while, recognize some good-looking copies of not only Michelangelo's *Pietà* (the original is in St Peter's), but also of his figures of *Leah* and *Rachel*, from the tomb of his patron, Julius II, in the church of San Pietro in Vincoli (see p.136).

Museo Barracco

Corso Vittorio Emanuele II 166. Tues–Sun 9am–7pm; €3. The so-called Piccola Farnesina palace, built by Antonio Sangallo the Younger and recently restored, holds the Museo Barracco, a small but high-quality collection of ancient sculpture that was donated to the city at the turn of the century by one Baron Barracco. It contains ancient Egyptian and Hellenistic pieces, ceramics and statuary from the Greek classical period and later Roman items, most notably a small figure of Neptune from the first century BC and an odd, almost Giacometti-like column-sculpture of a very graphically drawn hermaphrodite. The two charming busts of young Roman boys date from the first century AD.

Palazzo della Cancelleria

The grand Palazzo della Cancelleria was the seat of the papal government that once ran the city. The Renaissance architect Bramante is thought to have had a hand in its design and it is a well-proportioned edifice, exuding a cool poise quite at odds with the rather grimy nature of its location. You can't get in to see the interior, but you can stroll into the marvellously proportioned, multi-tiered courtyard, which is a treat enough in itself, although San Lorenzo in Damaso (daily 7.30am–12.30pm & 4.30–8pm), one of the oldest churches in Rome, also forms part of the complex. It was rebuilt with the palace and has since been greatly restored, most recently at the end of the nineteenth century, and has a painting by Federico Zuccaro, *The Coronation of the Virgin*, over the altar, and a twelfth-century icon of the Virgin Mary in a chapel.

Via del Governo Vecchio

Via del Governo Vecchio leads west from Piazza Pasquino through one of Rome's liveliest quarters, the narrow streets noisy at night and holding some of the city's most vigorous restaurants and bars. A little way down on the left, the delightfully small Piazza del Orologio is named after the quaint clocktower that is its main feature – part of the Oratorio dei Filipini, designed by Borromini, which is part of the Chiesa Nuova complex (see below). The followers of St Philip Neri attended musical gatherings here as part of their worship, gifting the language forever with the musical term "oratorio".

Chiesa Nuova

Daily 8.30am–noon & 4.30–7pm. The Chiesa Nuova was founded by St Philip Neri, who tended the poor and sick in the streets around here for most of his life, and commissioned this church in 1577. Neri died in 1595 and was canonized in 1622, and this large church, as well as being his last resting-place (he lies in the chapel to the left of the apse), is his principal memorial. Inside, its main features include three paintings by Rubens hung at the high altar, centring on the *Virgin with Angels*, and Pietro da Cortona's ceiling paintings, showing the *Ascension of the Virgin* in the apse and, above the nave, the construction of the church and Neri's famous "vision of fire" of 1544, when a globe of fire entered his mouth and dilated his heart – a physical event which apparently affected his health thereafter.

Via dei Coronari

Running almost from the Tiber to the top end of Piazza Navona, this is the fulcrum of Rome's antiques trade. Although the prices are as high as you might expect in such a location, there is a huge number of shops (Via dei Coronari itself consists of virtually nothing else), selling a tremendous variety of stuff. A browse makes for one of the city's most absorbing bits of sightseeing.

Santa Maria dell'Anima

Daily 9am–1pm & 3–7pm. Just off Via dei Coronari, the German national church in Rome is a richly decorated affair, almost square in shape, with a protruding main sanctuary flanked by Renaissance tombs. The one on the right, a beautiful, rather sad concoction, is that of the last non-Italian pope before John Paul II, the Dutchman Hadrian VI, who died in 1523, while at the far end, above the altar, you can just make out a dark and glowing *Virgin with Saints* by Giulio Romano.

Santa Maria della Pace

Tues–Sat 8.30am–noon & 4–8pm, but notoriously erratic. The church of Santa Maria della Pace dates from the late fifteenth century, although its facade and portico were added a couple of hundred years later by Pietro da Cortona. Inside, you can see Raphael's frescoes of various sibyls above the Chigi chapel (first on the right), executed in the early sixteenth century, although the opening times are decidedly erratic. If the church is closed, look in instead on the attached *chiostro del Bramante*, finished in 1504, a beautifully proportioned two-tiered cloister that is nowadays given over to temporary art exhibitions.

Palazzo Altemps

Tues–Sun 9am–7pm; €7, includes Palazzo Massimo, Terme Diocletian, Crypta Balbi, valid 3 days. Just across the street from the north end of Piazza Navona, the beautifully restored fifteenth-century Palazzo Altemps now houses the cream of the **Museo Nazionale Romano**'s aristocratic collections of Roman statues. Among treasures too many to mention, there are two, almost identical renderings of Apollo the Lyrist, a magnificent statue of Athena taming a serpent, and, in the far corner of the courtyard, a shameless Dionysus with a satyr and panther. Upstairs, the Painted Views Room, so-called for the bucolic scenes on its walls, has a fine statue of Hermes; the Cupboard Room, next door, named for its fresco of a display of wedding gifts against a floral background, has a wonderful statue of a warrior at rest, the *Ludovisi Ares*, restored by Bernini in 1622, and a sensitive portrayal of *Orestes and Electra*, from the first century AD by a sculptor called Menelaus – his name is carved at the base of one of the figures. Beyond, one room retains a frieze telling the story of Moses as a cartoon strip, with each scene displayed by nude figures as if on an unfurled tapestry, while in the room itself there is a colossal head of Hera, and – what some consider the highlight of the entire collection – the famous Ludovisi throne: an original fifth-century BC Greek work embellished with a delicate relief portraying the birth of Aphrodite. There's also the Fireplace Salon, whose huge fireplace, embellished with caryatids and lurking ibex – the symbol of the Altemps family – looks onto the *Suicide of Galatian*, apparently commissioned by Julius Caesar to adorn his Quirinal estate and an incredible sarcophagus depicting a battle in graphic, almost visceral sculptural detail. Without question one of Rome's best collections of classical art.

▼ PALAZZO ALTEMPS

Shops

Arsenale

Via del Governo Vecchio 64. Mon 3.30–7.30pm, Tues–Sat 10am–7.30pm. This large store is one of many good boutiques along this funky stretch, with great dresses by the owner Patrizia Pieroni and lots of other stuff by small independent designers.

Campo Marzio Penne

Via Campo Marzio 41. Daily 10am–1pm & 2–7pm. Small shop dedicated to ultra-cool pens and writing accessories, briefcases and pencil cases.

Il Gancio

Via del Seminario 82/83. High-quality leather bags, purses and shoes, all made right here on the premises.

Ai Monasteri

Piazza delle Cinque Lune. Cakes, spirits, toiletries and other items, all made by monks.

Moriondi & Gariglio

Via Pie di Marmo 21/22. Mon–Sat 9.30am–1pm & 3.30–7.30pm. Just a short walk from the Pantheon, this is perhaps the city centre's most sumptuous and refined hand-made chocolate shop – great for exquisitely wrapped gifts.

Pellicano

Via Seminario 93. Ezio Pellicano only sells one thing: ties, made by Ezio himself or his daughter. You can buy any of the hundreds you see on display, or you can choose from one of the many rolls of material and have your own made up in about a week.

Teichner

Piazza San Lorenzo in Lucina 17. Good all-round foodstore and deli with stocks of the kind of Italian goodies you want to take home with you.

Vacanze Romane

Via dei Pastini 18a. Upmarket gift shop with fun and often kitsch souvenirs of Rome.

Cafés and snacks

Camilloni

Piazza Sant' Eustachio 54, Tues–Sun 8.30am–midnight. Rivals *Caffè Sant'Eustachio* – see below – for Rome's best coffee, and serves great cakes too.

Cremeria Monteforte

Via della Rotonda 22. Tues–Sun 10am–11pm. This *gelateria* is a tiny treasure hidden in the shadow of the Pantheon. Their speciality, a Sicilian slush called *cremolato* comes in ten flavours.

Gran Caffè La Caffetteria

Piazza di Pietra 65. Daily 7.30am–10pm. Bureaucrats flock to this Neapolitan café from the nearby Parliament: the pastries are imported from Naples daily, and the espresso is among Rome's best. Good for lunch too.

Giolitti

Via Uffici del Vicario 40. This *gelateria* is an Italian institution, and once had a reputation – now lost – for the country's top ice cream. It's still pretty good, however, with a choice of seventy flavours.

Pascucci

Via di Torre Argentina 20. This café specialises in *frullati* – fresh fruit whipped up with ice and milk. The ultimate Roman refreshment on a hot day.

Caffè Sant'Eustachio

Piazza Sant'Eustachio. Just behind the Pantheon you'll find what many feel is Rome's best coffee, as well as a good line in coffee-based sweets and cakes.

▲ PASCUCCI

La Tazza d'Oro

Via degli Orfani 84/86. Straight off Piazza del Pantheon, this place is well named, since it is by common consent the home of one of Rome's best cups of coffee, and sinfully rich *granita di caffè,* with double dollops of whipped cream.

Lo Zozzone

Via del Teatro Pace 32. Mon–Fri 9am–9pm, Sat 10am–11pm. This Rome legend, just around the corner from Piazza Navona and with outside seating, serves the best *pizza bianca* in town, filled with whatever you want, as well as lots of delicious *pizza al taglio* choices.

Restaurants

Da Alfredo e Ada

Via dei Banchi Nuovi 14 ☎06.687.8842. Weekdays only, lunch and dinner. There's no menu, and precious little choice, at this city-centre stalwart, at which Ada presides over an appreciative clientele of regulars, serving up pasta starters, followed by whatever they happen to have cooked that day. €16 for three courses, including half a litre of wine.

Armando al Pantheon

Salita de' Crescenzi 30. ☎06.6880.3034. Closed Sat pm and all day Sun. Unpretentious surroundings and moderately priced hearty food in this long-standing staple close by the Pantheon.

Il Bacaro

Via degli Spagnoli 27 ☎06.686.4110. Mon–Fri 12.30–2.30pm & 8–11.30pm, Sat 8–11.30pm. This tiny restaurant has a small, focused menu featuring a good and interesting selection of antipasti and *primi*, and main courses focusing on meat, particularly beef.

Da Baffetto

Via del Governo Vecchio 114 ☎06.686.1617. Daily 7pm–midnight. A tiny, authentic pizzeria that has long been a Rome institution, though it now tends to be swamped by tourists. Amazingly, it's still good value, and has tables outside in summer, though you will always have to queue. Especially good bruschette (toasted hunks of bread with savoury toppings).

Il Convivio da Troiani

Vicolo dei Soldati 31 ☎06.686.9432. Closed Mon lunch, all day Sun; otherwise open lunch and dinner. Beautiful restaurant with tables set out in three vaulted rooms, and food that is adventurous and exquisite – and expensive. Perfect for a special night out, but you'll have to book.

Le Cornacchie

Piazza Rondanini 53 ☎06.6819.2096. Classic Roman dishes served on this quiet piazza bang in the centre of the city. The cooking is good, the service fast and the prices moderate: €8–9 for a *primo*, €10–15 for a *secondo*.

Cul de Sac

Piazza Pasquino 73 ⓣ06.6880.1094. Daily noon–4pm & 7pm–12.30am. Busy, long-running wine bar with an excellent wine list, a great city-centre location with outside seating, and decent food. One of the best centro storico locations if you don't want a full meal.

Enoteca Corsi

Via del Gesù 87–88 ⓣ06.679.0821. Lunch only, closed Sun. Tucked away between Piazza Venezia and the Pantheon, this is an old-fashioned Roman trattoria and wine shop where you eat what they happened to have cooked that morning. Very cheap, and a real taste of old Rome.

Da Franceso

Piazza del Fico 29 ⓣ06.686.4009. Mon & Wed–Sun 7pm–1am. Not just pizzas in this full-on pizzeria in the heart of trendy Rome – though they're delectable enough – but good antipasti, *primi* and *secondi* too. The service can be slapdash, but the food and atmosphere are second to none.

▲ CUL DE SAC

Maccheroni

Piazza delle Coppelle ⓣ06.6830.7895. Mon–Sat 12.30–3pm & 8pm–midnight. A friendly restaurant that enjoys a wonderful location on this quiet piazza right in the heart of the centro storico. Inside is spartan yet comfy, while the outside tables make the most of the pretty square-cum-intersection. The food is good, basic Italian

▲ ENOTECA CORSI

fare, affordably priced and cheerfully served.

Myosotis

Via della Vaccarella 3–5 ☎06.686.5554. Mon–Sat 12.30–2.45pm & 8–11pm. Upmarket restaurant tucked away off a small square in the heart of the centro storico. Great food in an elegant environment – a fine place for a posh night out.

Obikà

Via dei Prefetti 26 ☎06.683.2630. Daily 10am–midnight. The ultra-modern interior and pleasant outside terrace on secluded Piazza Firenze are home to the world's first restaurant specializing in mozzarella: here it's served with everything from tomatoes to salami to anchovies and much more. There are a few salads and pasta dishes on offer too, but cheese is the main thing, and as such it's a great place for lunch, though not perhaps dinner. Dishes start at about €8.

Riccioli

Piazza della Coppelle 10 ☎06.6821.0313. Daily except Sun 5pm–2am. This swish, modern restaurant does great sushi, oysters and other seafood, and its funky bar leads the way till late in this busy square in the heart of old Rome.

Da Tonino

Via del Governo Vecchio 18–19 ☎06.333.587.0779. Closed Sun. There are no menus in this unmarked centro storico favourite, so usually they'll just tell you what they've got that day – basic Roman food, always freshly cooked, and always delicious, although the service can be a bit slow.

Bars

Anima

Via Santa Maria dell' Anima 57. Tues–Sun 10pm–3am. This late-night bar-club is kitted out in post modern-meets-The Flintstones chic and offers an assortment of elegant snacks to go with your cocktails as DJs spin house, funk and drum & bass beats.

Bar del Fico

Piazza del Fico 26/28. Daily 8–2am. One of several long-standing hot spots in the area, with a pleasant terrace that's heated in winter.

Fluid

Via del Governo Vecchio 46/47 ☎06.683.2361. Über-trendy and usually ultra-crowded bar and club whose labyrinthine interior sports a watery theme. Don't go till late.

Jonathan's Angels

Via della Fossa 18. Daily 1pm–2am. This quirky bar certainly wins the "most decorated" award. Every inch (even the toilet, which is worth a visit on its own) is plastered, painted or tricked out in outlandish style.

Bar della Pace

Via della Pace 5. Daily 10–2am. *The* summer bar, with outside tables full of Rome's beautiful people. Quietest during the day, when you can enjoy the nineteenth-century interior – marble, mirrors, mahogany and plants – in peace.

Société Lutèce

Piazza Montevecchio 17. Daily 6pm–2am. One of the most self-consciously cool bars in the centre of Rome, where patrons

▲ BAR DELLA PACE

sip cocktails late into the night in a whitewashed interior hung with abstract art. An *aperitivo* buffet is included in the drink price.

Clubs and venues

Il Locale

Vicolo del Fico 3 ⓣ06.687.9075. Tues–Sun 10.30pm–2.30am. Located close to Piazza Navona, this popular joint enjoys a lively, if not chaotic, atmosphere, with English and American alternative bands and Italian folk-rock. Not the trendsetter it once was, but still a fun, central venue.

La Maison

Vicolo dei Granari 4 ⓣ06.683.3312. Tues–Sun 11pm–3am, until 5am on Fri & Sat. Ritzy club whose chandeliers and glossy decor attracts Rome's gilded youth. Sunday – gay night – is the one to go for, although you'll need to book a table if you want to sit down.

SupperClub

Via de Nari del Fico 3 ⓣ06.687.9075. Tues–Sun 10.30pm–2.30am. An updated version of a debauched Roman banquet – patrons recline on white couches as a masseuse-for-hire makes the rounds and barely dressed performance artists writhe to the DJ's beat.

Campo de' Fiori, the Ghetto and around

This southern slice of Rome's historic core lies between Corso Vittorio Emanuele II (the main thoroughfare that dissects the centre) and the river. It's similar to the centro storico just to the north, its cramped, wanderable streets opening out onto small squares flanked by churches. However, this is more of a working quarter – less monumental, with more functional buildings and shops, as evidenced by its main focus, Piazza di Campo de' Fiori, whose fruit and veg stalls and rough-and-ready bars form a marked contrast to the pavement artists and sleek cafés of Piazza Navona. To the east it merges into the gloomy streets and scrabbly Roman ruins of the Old Jewish Ghetto, a small but atmospheric neighbourhood that nuzzles up close to the city's giant central synagogue, while just north of here lies the major traffic intersection and ancient Roman site of Largo di Torre Argentina.

Largo di Torre Argentina

The busy traffic hub of Largo di Torre Argentina is the site of the ruins of four (Republican-era) temples that now are home to a thriving colony of cats – although it's more a place to wait for a bus than to deliberately linger. You can visit the **cat sanctuary** (daily noon–6pm; Ⓦwww.romancats.com) down the steps on the southwestern corner. As for the **temples**, there are guided tours in English (daily at 5pm, 1hr), although they don't add much to what you can see from the road. On the far side of the square, the Teatro Argentina was, in 1816, the venue for the first performance of Rossini's *Barber of Seville*, not a success at all on the night: Rossini was apparently booed into taking refuge in Bernasconi's pastry shop (see p.89). Built in 1731, it is today one of the city's most important theatres, and is thought to have been built over the spot where Caesar was assassinated.

The Gesù

Daily 6am–12.30pm & 4–7.15pm.

The church of the Gesù was the first Jesuit church to be built in Rome, and has since served as the model for Jesuit churches everywhere – its wide single-aisled nave and short transepts edging out under a huge dome were ideal for the large congregations the movement wanted to draw. Today it's still a well-patronized church, notable not only for its size (the glitzy tomb of the order's founder, St Ignatius, is topped by a huge globe of lapis lazuli – the largest piece in existence) but also for the staggering richness of its interior. Opposite, the tomb of

▲ THE GESÙ

the Jesuit missionary, St Francis Xavier, holds a reliquary containing the saint's severed arm (the rest of his body is in Goa), while the ceiling's ingenious trompe l'oeil, the *Triumph of the Name of Jesus* by Baciccia, oozes out of its frame in a tangle of writhing bodies, flowing drapery and stucco angels stuck like limpets – the Baroque at its most fervent.

The Rooms of St Ignatius

Mon–Sat 4–6pm, Sun 10am–noon; free. Occupying part of the first floor of the Jesuit headquarters, these are basically the restored rooms where St Ignatius lived from 1544 until his death in 1556. There are bits and pieces of furniture and memorabilia relating to the saint, but the true draw is the corridor just outside, decorated by Andrea Pozzo in 1680 – a superb exercise in perspective on a small scale, giving an illusion of a grand hall in what is a relatively small space.

Crypta Balbi

Via delle Botteghe Oscure 31. Tues–Sun 9am–7pm; €4. This corner plot is the site of a **Roman theatre**, the remains of which later became incorporated in a number of medieval houses. There's a ground-floor exhibition that takes you through the evolution of the site in painstaking, sometimes excruciating, detail, with lots of English explanation, but you have to take one of the hourly tours down into the site proper, and try to glean what you can from the various arches, latrines, column bases and supporting walls that make up the cellar of the current building. The real interest is in the close dissection of one city block over two thousand years – an exercise that could presumably be equally well applied to almost any city corner in Rome. On Saturdays there are visits to parts of the site currently under excavation, including a latrine, Mithraic sanctuary and meeting hall.

Piazza di Campo de' Fiori

In many ways Rome's most appealing square, Piazza di Campo de' Fiori is home to a lively fruit and vegetable market (Mon–Sat 8am–1pm), flanked by restaurants and cafés, and busy pretty much all

▼ CAMPO DE' FIORI

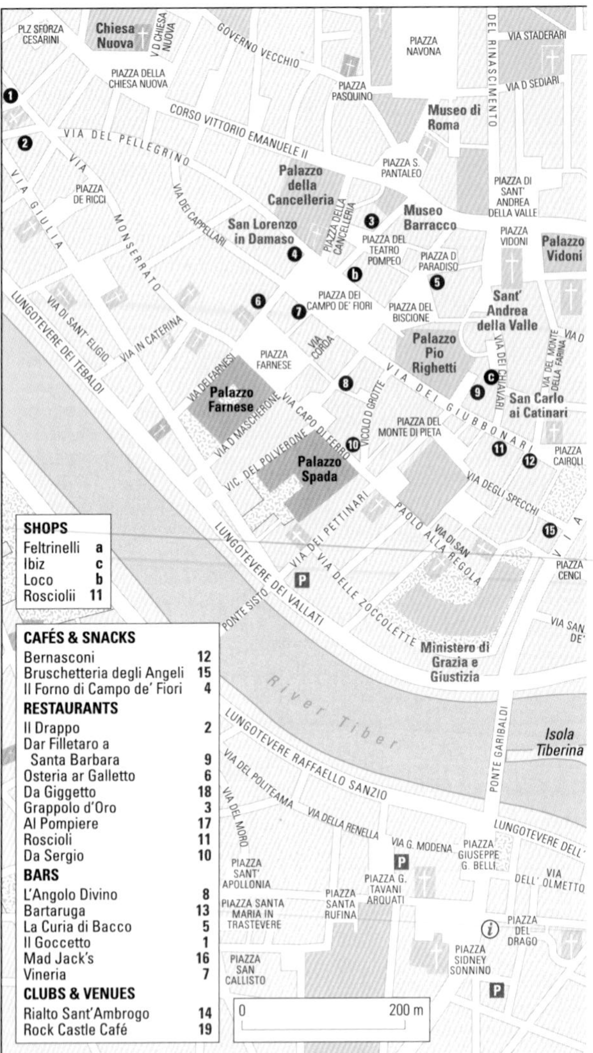

day and night. No one really knows how the square came by its name, which means "field of flowers", but one theory holds that it was derived from the Roman Campus Martius which used to cover most of this part of town; another claims it is after Flora, the mistress of Pompey, whose theatre used to stand on what is now the northeast corner of the square. Later, Campo de' Fiori was the site of the city's cattle market and public executions, the most notorious

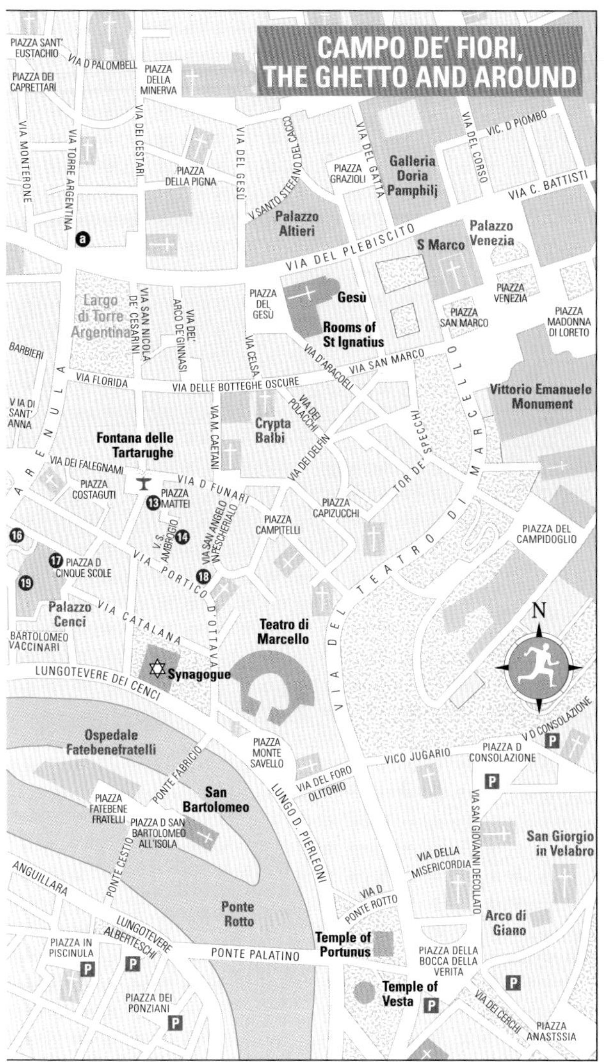

of which is commemorated by the statue of Giordano Bruno in the middle of the square. Bruno was a late sixteenth-century freethinker who was denounced to the Inquisition; his trial lasted for years, and finally, when he refused to renounce his philosophical beliefs, he was burned at the stake.

Palazzo Farnese

Mon & Thurs visits in French or Italian at 3pm, 4pm, 5pm; free; book in advance at Via Giuia 250 on

☎06.6889.2818, or ©visitefarnese @france-italia.it. Just south of Campo de' Fiori, **Piazza Farnese** is a quite different square, with great fountains spurting out of carved lilies – the Farnese emblem – into marble tubs brought from the Baths of Caracalla, and the sober bulk of the **Palazzo Farnese** itself. Commissioned in 1514 by Alessandro Farnese – later Paul III – from Antonio di Sangallo the Younger, the building was worked on after the architect's death by Michelangelo, who added the top tier of windows and cornice. It now houses the French Embassy and holds what has been called the greatest of all Baroque ceiling paintings, Annibale Carracci's *Loves of the Gods*, completed in 1603. Centring on the *Marriage of Bacchus and Ariadne,* this is supposed to represent the binding of the Aldobrandini and Farnese families, and leaps out of its frame in an erotic hotchpotch of cavorting flesh. It's a spectacle of virtuoso technique and perfect anatomy, surrounded by similarly fervent works illustrating various classical themes. Carracci did the main plan and the central painting himself, but left the rest to his brother and cousin, Agostino and Lodovico, and various assistants such as Guido Reni and Guercino, who went on to become some of the most sought-after artists of the seventeenth century. It's a fantastic piece of work, perhaps only eclipsed in Rome by the Sistine Chapel itself; sadly, Carracci, disillusioned by the work, and bitter about the relative pittance that he was paid for it, didn't paint much afterwards, and died penniless a few years later.

Palazzo Spada

Tues–Sun 8.30am–7.30pm; €5; ☎06.855.5952. The Renaissance Palazzo Spada houses a gallery of paintings collected by Cardinal Bernardino Spada and his brother Virginio in the seventeenth century. However, the main feature is the building itself: its facade is frilled with stucco adornments, and, left off the small courtyard is a crafty trompe l'oeil by Borromini – a tunnel whose actual length is multiplied about four times through the architect's tricks with perspective (you have to wait for one of the guided tours – every 45mins – to see this). Inside, the gallery's four rooms aren't spectacularly interesting unless you're a connoisseur of seventeenth- and eighteenth-century Italian painting – of special note, though, are two portraits of Cardinal Bernadino by Reni and Guercino.

Via Giulia

Via Giulia, running parallel to the Tiber, was built by Julius II to connect Ponte Sisto with the Vatican. The street was conceived as the centre of papal Rome, and Julius commissioned Bramante to line it with imposing palaces. Bramante didn't get very far, but the street became a popular residence for wealthier Roman families, and is still packed full with stylish *palazzi* and antique shops; it makes for a nice wander, with features like the playful Fontana del Mascherone to tickle your interest along the way.

Via Portico d'Ottavia

The main artery of Rome's Jewish Ghetto area, Via Portico d'Ottavia leads down to the Portico d'Ottavia, a not terribly well-preserved second-century BC gate, rebuilt by Augustus and dedicated to his sister in 23 BC (summer daily 9am–7pm, winter daily 9am–6pm; free). It used to be the entrance to the adjacent **Teatro di Marcello**, which was begun by Julius Caesar and finished by Augustus, but pillaged in the fourth century and not properly restored until the Middle Ages, when it became a formidable fortified palace for a succession of different aristocratic families. Recently restored, it provides a grand backdrop for classical concerts in the summer.

Fontana delle Tartarughe

A sheltered enclave between Via Portico d'Ottavia and Via del Botteghe Oscure, Piazza Mattei might be recognisable from its role as a set in the 1990s film, *The Talented Mr Ripley*. But it's best known as the site of one of the city's most charming fountains, the Fontana delle Tartarughe, or Turtle Fountain, a delightful late sixteenth-century creation, perhaps restored by Bernini, who apparently added the turtles.

The Synagogue

Sun–Thurs 10am–5pm, Fri 9am–2pm; closed Sat & Jewish holidays; €7.50; Ⓦ www.museoebraico.it.

The Ghetto's principal Jewish sight is the huge Synagogue by the river, built in 1904 and dominating all around with its bulk – not to mention the *carabinieri* who stand guard 24 hours a day outside. The only way to see the building is on one of the short guided tours it runs regularly in English, afterwards taking in the small two-room museum. The interior of the building is impressive, rising to a high, rainbow-hued dome, and the tours are excellent, giving good background on the building and Rome's Jewish community in general.

▲ THE SYNAGOGUE

Isola Tiberina

Almost opposite the Synagogue, the Ponte Fabricio crosses the Tiber to Isola Tiberina. Built in 62 BC, it's the only classical bridge to remain intact without help from the restorers. As for the island, it's a calm respite from the city centre proper, and is mostly given over to Rome's oldest hospital, that of the **Fatebenefratelli**, founded in 1548 – appropriately, it would seem, as the island was originally home to a third century BC temple of Aesculapius, the Roman god of healing. The tenth-century church of **San Bartolomeo** (Mon–Sat 9am–12.30pm & 3.30–6pm, Sun 9am–1pm) stands on the temple's original site and is worth a peep inside for its ancient columns, probably rescued from the temple, and an ancient wellhead on the altar steps, carved with figures relating to the founding of the church, including St Bartholomew himself, who also features

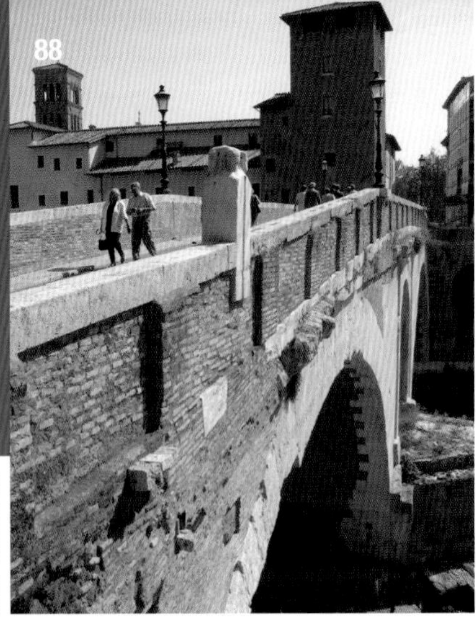

▲ ISOLA TIBERTINA

in the painting above the altar, hands tied above his head, on the point of being skinned alive – his famous and gruesome mode of martyrdom.

Piazza della Bocca della Verità

Further along the river, Piazza della Bocca della Verità has as its focus two of the city's better-preserved Roman temples – the Temple of Portunus and the Temple of Hercules Victor, the latter long known as the Temple of Vesta because, like all vestal temples, it is circular. Both date from the end of the second century BC, and although you can't get inside, they're fine examples of Republican-era places of worship.

Santa Maria in Cosmedin

Daily 10am–5pm. The church of Santa Maria in Cosmedin is a typically Roman medieval basilica with a huge marble altar and a colourful Cosmati-work floor – one of the city's finest. Just outside, and giving the square its name, is the **Bocca della Verità** (Mouth of Truth), an ancient Roman drain cover in the shape of an enormous face that in medieval times would apparently swallow the hand of anyone who hadn't told the truth. It was particularly popular with husbands anxious to test the faithfulness of their wives; now it is one of the city's biggest tour-bus attractions.

Shops

Feltrinelli

Largo Argentina 5. Mon–Fri 9am–9pm, Sat 9am–11pm, Sun 10am–8pm. One of two flagship Rome stores of this national chain, selling books (including English-language), music and stationery.

▲ BOCCA DELLA VERITÀ

Ibiz

Via dei Chiavari 39. Mon–Sat 10am–7.30pm. Great leather bags, purses and rucksacks in exciting contemporary designs made on the premises.

Loco

Via dei Baullari 22. Mon 3.30–8.30pm, Tues–Sat 10.30am–8.30pm. Eccentrically designed shoes, the like of which you won't find anywhere else.

Roscioli

Via dei Giubbonari 21–23. Cheeses, salamis and a very good selection of wine. Food is served at lunch and early evening. Roscioli also has its own bakery across the street at Via dei Charivari 34.

Cafés and snacks

Bernasconi

Piazza Cairoli 16. A great family-run *pasticceria*, with *sfogliatelle* to die for and a host of other goodies. Good coffee too.

Bruschetteria degli Angeli

Piazza Cairoli 2a. Weekdays lunch and dinner, weekends dinner only. Lovely large *birreria* that does a great line in large bruschette with all kinds of toppings to soak up the booze. Lots of other choices, too. Very good and very central. You'll pay €8 or so for a large bruschetta, which is enough for two as a snack.

Il Forno di Campo de' Fiori

Campo de' Fiori 22. Closed Sat eve in summer, Thurs eve in winter. The pizza *bianca* here (just drizzled with olive oil on top) is a Roman legend and their pizza *rossa* (with a smear of tomato sauce) follows close behind.

Restaurants

Il Drappo

Vicolo del Malpasso 9 ☎06.687.7365. Mon–Sat 1–3pm & 7–11.30pm. This Sardinian restaurant just off Via Giulia has been going for years, and attracts large crowds of loyal regulars to sample its fish, seafood and suckling pig, along with wafer-thin flat Sardinian bread. Great Sardo desserts, too.

Dar Filletaro a Santa Barbara

Largo dei Librari 88 ☎06.686.4018. A fish-and-chip shop without the chips. Paper-covered Formica tables (outdoors in summer), cheap wine, beer and fried cod. A timeless Roman speciality, though the service can be offhand.

Osteria ar Galletto

Piazza Farnese 102 ☎06.686.1714. Situated on one of Rome's stateliest piazzas, and just off one of its trendiest, this manages to retain the feel of a provincial trattoria, specializing in traditional Roman cookery with a homely touch. Very good-value, too.

Da Giggetto

Via del Portico d'Ottavia 21a–22 ☎06.686.1105. Though usually very crowded, and mainly with tourists these days, this place still does decent traditional Roman-Jewish fare, featuring deep-fried artichokes, *baccalà* (salt cod), and *rigatoni alla pajata* (pasta with calves' intestines), along with good non-offal pasta dishes, eaten outside in summer by the ruins of the Portico d'Ottavia.

Grappolo d'Oro

Piazza della Cancelleria 80 ☎06.686.4118. Curiously

untouched by the hordes in nearby Campo de' Fiori, this restaurant serves imaginative Roman cuisine in a traditional trattoria atmosphere.

Al Pompiere

Via Santa Maria dei Calderari 38 ☎06.686.8377. Housed in a frescoed old palace in the heart of the Ghetto, this fusty old restaurant serves up some of the best Roman-Jewish food you'll find. Prices are moderate, and its warren of high-ceilinged rooms is usually crowded, especially late on.

Roscioli

Via dei Giubbonari 21–23 ☎06.687.5287. Closed Sun. Is it a deli, a wine bar, or fully fledged restaurant? Actually it's all three, and you can either just have a glass of wine and some cheese or go for the full menu, which has great pasta dishes and *secondi* at lunchtime and in the evening. It's pricey, and the service can be on the snooty side, but the food is terrific.

Da Sergio

Vicolo delle Grotte 27 ☎06.686.4293. Mon–Sat 11.30am–3.30pm & 7pm–midnight. Towards the river from Campo de' Fiori, this is an out-of-the-way, cosy trattoria with a traditional, limited menu and the deeply authentic feel of old Rome. Inexpensive, and with outdoor seating in summer.

Bars

L'Angolo Divino

Via dei Balestrari 12. Tues–Sun 11am–2.30pm & 5.30pm–2am. Quite a peaceful haven after the furore of Campo de' Fiori, this wine bar has a large selection of wine, and simple, typical wine-bar food fare – bread, cheese, cold cuts and the like.

Bartaruga

Piazza Mattei 7. This very theatrical bar attracts members of the city's entertainment demi-monde, in a wonderfully camp setting, eclectically furnished with all sorts of eighteenth-century bits and pieces.

La Curia di Bacco

Via del Biscione 79. Daily 4pm–2am. This long, thin, bustling wine bar was hollowed out of the ruins of the ancient Teatro di Pompeii, near Campo de' Fiori. A young crowd, some good wines, pricey beer and

▼ ROSCIOLI

interesting snacks, including crostini, bruschette and cheese plates.

Il Goccetto

Via dei Banchi Vecchi 14. Family-run wine bar and shop, patronized by devoted regulars. There is an extensive menu of wines by the glass and a selection of light appetizers, deli meats and cheeses.

Mad Jack's

Via Arenula 20. One of the city's many Irish pubs, but one of the nicest and most authentic. The Guinness is pretty good, and there are light snacks available too, to go with the warm welcome. Frequented by Italians as well as tourists and expats.

Vineria

Campo de' Fiori 15. Long-established bar/wine shop right on the Campo, patronized by devoted regulars. Has recently made some concessions to comfort and started offering light meals.

Clubs and venues

Rialto Sant'Ambrogio

Via Sant'Ambrogio 4 ⓣ06.6813.3640. Daily 10.30pm–3am, closed mid-June to Sept. Known to locals simply as "Rialto", this *centro sociale* in the Jewish Ghetto is a venue for art exhibitions and theatrical performances but is best known for its music scene and electronica DJs.

▲ MAD JACK'S

Rock Castle Café

Via B. Cenci 8 ⓣ06.6880.7999. In the Jewish Ghetto, this student hangout consists of six medieval-style rooms, all for dancing and mingling.

The Tridente

The northern part of Rome's city centre is sometimes known as the Tridente due to the shape of the roads leading down from the apex of Piazza del Popolo – Via del Corso in the centre, Via di Ripetta on the left and Via del Babuino on the right. If anywhere can be considered the district's centre, it's Piazza di Spagna. This, and the area around, is travellers' Rome, historically the artistic quarter of the capital, for which eighteenth- and nineteenth-century Grand Tourists would make in search of the colourful, exotic city. It has always had an artistic feel: Keats and Giorgio de Chirico used to live on Piazza di Spagna, Goethe had lodgings along Via del Corso, and places like Caffè Greco and Babington's Tea Rooms were the meeting-places of a local artistic and expat community for almost two centuries. Today these institutions have given ground to more modern-day traps for the tourist dollar, while Via Condotti and around is now strictly international designer territory, with some of Rome's fanciest stores. But the air of a Rome being discovered, even colonized, by foreigners persists – even if most of them are flying-visit teenagers.

Piazza di Spagna

Piazza di Spagna underlines the area's international credentials, taking its name from the Spanish Embassy that has stood here since the seventeenth century. It's a long, thin straggle of a square, almost entirely enclosed by buildings and centring on the distinctive boat-shaped Fontana della Barcaccia, the last work of Bernini's father, which apparently remembers the great flood of Christmas Day 1598, when a barge from the Tiber was washed up on the slopes of Pincio Hill close by. The square itself is fringed by high-end clothes and jewellery shops and is normally thronged with tourists, but for all that it is one of the city's most appealing open spaces.

Via Condotti

Running west from Piazza di Spagna to Via del Corso, Via Condotti and the parallel Via Borgognona are home to the biggest names in fashion: Armani, Christian Dior, Gucci, Prada, Salvatore Ferragamo and Valentino all have shops here, as well as jewellery from Cartier and Bulgari.

Keats-Shelley Memorial House

Piazza di Spagna 26. Mon–Fri 9am–1pm & 3–6pm, Sat 11am–2pm & 3–6pm, closed Sun; €3.50; Ⓦwww.keats-shelley-house.org. The house where the poet John Keats died in 1821 now serves as the Keats-Shelley Memorial House, an archive of English-language literary and historical works and a museum of manuscripts and

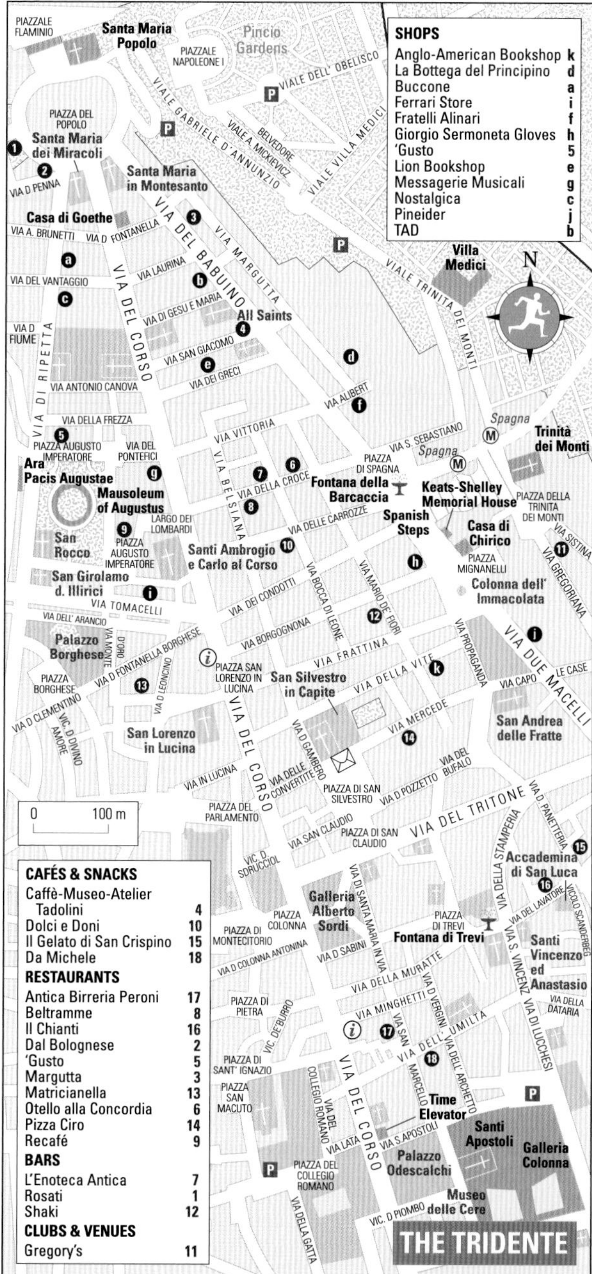
SHOPS
Anglo-American Bookshop k
La Bottega del Principino d
Buccone a
Ferrari Store i
Fratelli Alinari f
Giorgio Sermoneta Gloves h
'Gusto 5
Lion Bookshop e
Messagerie Musicali g
Nostalgica c
Pineider j
TAD b
CAFÉS & SNACKS
Caffè-Museo-Atelier Tadolini 4
Dolci e Doni 10
Il Gelato di San Crispino 15
Da Michele 18
RESTAURANTS
Antica Birreria Peroni 17
Beltramme 8
Il Chianti 16
Dal Bolognese 2
'Gusto 5
Margutta 3
Matricianella 13
Otello alla Concordia 6
Pizza Ciro 14
Recafé 9
BARS
L'Enoteca Antica 7
Rosati 1
Shaki 12
CLUBS & VENUES
Gregory's 11
THE TRIDENTE
Piazzale Flaminio
Santa Maria Popolo
Pincio Gardens
Piazzale Napoleone I
Viale dell' Obelisco
Viale Gabriele d'Annunzio
Viale A. Mickiewicz
Belvedore
Viale Villa Medici
Piazza del Popolo
Santa Maria dei Miracoli
Santa Maria in Montesanto
Via d Penna
Casa di Goethe
Via del Babuino
Via Margutta
Via A. Brunetti
Via d Fontanella
Via del Vantaggio
Via del Corso
Via Laurina
Via di Gesu e Maria
All Saints
Via San Giacomo
Via dei Greci
Via d Fiume
Via di Ripetta
Via Antonio Canova
Via della Frezza
Via Alibert
Villa Medici
Viale Trinità dei Monti
N
Spagna
Trinità dei Monti
Via S. Sebastiano
Via Vittoria
Piazza Augusto Imperatore
Via del Ponteflci
Ara Pacis Augustae
Mausoleum of Augustus
Via Belsiana
Via della Croce
Piazza di Spagna
Fontana della Barcaccia
Keats-Shelley Memorial House
Piazza della Trinità dei Monti
Spanish Steps
Largo dei Lombardi
Via delle Carrozze
Casa di Chirico
Via Sistina
San Rocco
Santi Ambrogio e Carlo al Corso
Piazza Mignanelli
Via Gregoriana
San Girolamo d. Illirici
Via Bocca di Leone
Via Mario de' Fiori
Colonna dell' Immacolata
Via dei Condotti
Via Tomacelli
Via dell' Arancio
Palazzo Borghese
Via Monte d'Oro
Via Borgognona
Via Propaganda
Via Due Macelli
Via Fontanella Borghese
Piazza San Lorenzo in Lucina
Via Frattina
Piazza Borghese
Via d Leoncino
San Silvestro in Capite
Via della Vite
Via Capo le Case
Via d Clementino
Vic. d Divino Amore
San Andrea delle Fratte
San Lorenzo in Lucina
Via Mercede
Via d Gambero
Via in Lucina
Via delle Convertite
Via del Bufalo
Piazza di San Silvestro
Via d Pozzetto
0 100 m
Piazza del Parlamento
Via del Tritone
Via d. Panetteria
Via San Claudio
Piazza di San Claudio
Via della Stamperia
Accademia di San Luca
Vic. d. Sdrucciol
Galleria Alberto Sordi
Piazza Colonna
Piazza di Montecitorio
Via di Santa Maria in Via
Piazza di Trevi
Fontana di Trevi
Via del Lavatore
Vicolo Scanderbeg
Santi Vincenzo ed Anastasio
Via d Colonna Antonina
Via d Sabini
Via della Muratte
Via S. Vincenzo
Via della Dataria
Piazza di Pietra
Via Minghetti
Via d Vergini
Vic. de' Burro
Via San Marcello
Via dell' Umiltà
Via dell' Archetto
Via di Lucchesi
Piazza di Sant' Ignazio
Piazza San Macuto
Via del Collegio Romano
Time Elevator
Santi Apostoli
Galleria Colonna
Via Lata
Via S. Apostoli
Palazzo Odescalchi
Piazza del Collegio Romano
Via della Gatta
Vic. d Piombo
Museo delle Cere

▲ KEATS-SHELLEY MEMORIAL HOUSE

mementos relating to the Keats circle of the early nineteenth century – namely Keats himself, Shelley and Mary Shelley, and Byron (who at one time lived across the square). Keats didn't really enjoy his time in Rome, referring to it as his posthumous life": he only came to the city under pressure from doctors and friends when it was arguably already too late to save his failing health. He spent months in pain here before he finally died, at the age of just 25, confined to the house with his artist friend Joseph Severn. Among many bits of manuscript, letters and the like, you can see the poet's death mask, stored in the room where he died, and capturing a resigned grimace.

Casa di Chirico

Open first Sun of every month 10am–1pm, tours every 45min, or by appointment Tues–Sat 10am–5pm; €5; ☎06.679.6546. Almost next door to the Keats-Shelley House, the fourth-floor **Casa di Chirico** was the home of the Greek-Italian metaphysical artist Giorgio de Chirico for thirty years until his death in 1978. It's now a small museum that gives a fantastic glimpse into how De Chirico lived, as well as having a great many of his paintings on display: there are works from his classic, proto-surrealist period in the entrance hall and first living area, including portraits of himself, often dressed up, and others of his wife, who modelled for him until he died. Upstairs, in keeping with the untouched nature of the house, De Chirico's cell-like bedroom is left with his books and rather uncomfortable-looking single bed, while down the hall, the artist's studio, lit by a skylight in the terrace above, has his brushes and canvases.

The Spanish Steps

The Spanish Steps sweep down in a cascade of balustrades and balconies, the hangout of young hopefuls waiting to be chosen as artists' models during the nineteenth century, and nowadays not much changed in their role as a venue for international posing and flirting late into the summer nights. The Steps, like the square, could in fact just as easily be known as the "French Steps" because of the French church of Trinitá dei Monti they lead up to, and because it was largely a French initiative to build them. After a few decades of haggling over the plans, they were finally laid in 1725, to a design by Francisco de Sanctis; now forming one of the city's most distinctive and deliberately showy attractions, they are perfect for strollers to glide up and down.

Trinità dei Monti

Daily 10am–noon & 4–6pm. Crowning the Spanish Steps, Trinità dei Monti is a largely sixteenth-century church designed by Carlo Maderno and paid for by the French king. Its rose-coloured Baroque facade overlooks the rest of Rome from its hilltop site, and it's worth clambering up just for the views. While here you may as well pop your head around the door for a couple of impressive works by Daniele da Volterra, notably a soft beautifully composed fresco of *The Assumption* in the third chapel on the right, which includes a portrait of his teacher Michelangelo, and a *Deposition* across the nave, which is similarly ingeniously arranged. The French Baroque painter, Poussin, considered the latter –which was probably painted from a series of cartoons by Michelangelo – as the world's third greatest painting (Raphael's *Transfiguration* was, he thought, the best).

The Pincio Gardens

The terrace and gardens of the Pincio, a short walk from the top of the Spanish Steps, were laid out by Valadier in the early nineteenth century. Fringed with dilapidated busts of classical and Italian heroes, they give fine views over the roofs, domes and TV antennae of central Rome, right across to St Peter's and the Janiculum Hill. The view is the main event here, but there are also plenty of shady benches if you fancy a break, and the quirky nineteenth-century water clock at the back is worth a look. You can also hire bikes, rollerblades and odd little four-wheel carriages for getting around the gardens and the adjacent Villa Borghese (see p.147).

Via del Babuino

Leading south from Piazza del Popolo to the Piazza di Spagna, Via del Babuino and the narrow Via Margutta – where the film maker Federico Fellini once lived – was, in the 1960s, the core of a thriving art community and home to the city's best galleries and a fair number of its artists. High rents forced out all but the most successful, and the neighbourhood now supports a prosperous trade in antiques and designer fashions. Via del Babuino – literally "Street of the Baboon" – derives its name from the statue of Silenus that reclines outside the Tadolini studio about halfway down on the right. In ancient times the wall behind was a focus for satirical graffiti, although it is now coated with graffiti-proof paint. Inside the studio, the **Museo-Atelier Canova-Tadolini** (see p.100) is a café-restaurant, but a highly original one, littered with the sculptural work of four generations of the Tadolini family.

Piazza del Popolo

The oval-shaped expanse of Piazza del Popolo is a dignified meeting of roads laid out in 1538 by Pope Paul III to make an impressive entrance to the city; it owes its present symmetry to Valadier, who added the central fountain in 1814. The monumental Porta del Popolo

▼ VIEW ACROSS PIAZZA DEL POPOLO

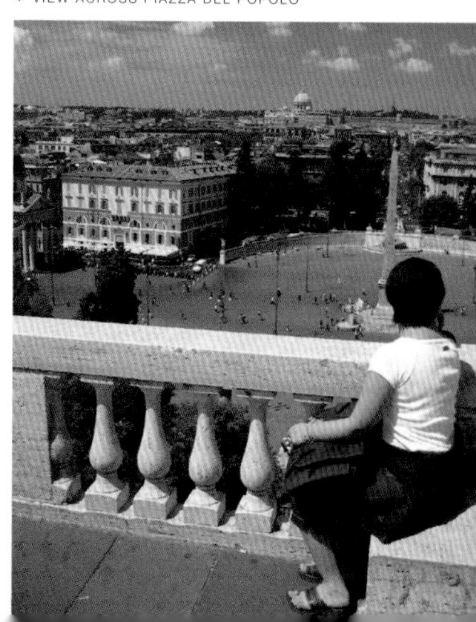

La Notte Bianca

The Piazza del Popolo is one venue among many for the wonderful "La Notte Bianca" – one night in September that sees all sorts of musical performances and arts events taking place all over the city, in various, mainly outdoor venues and locations. It's a marvellous time to be here if you can, public transport runs all night, and you can plan your tour of the city by visiting the website – ⓦwww.lanottebianca.it.

went up in 1655 and was the work of Bernini; the Chigi family symbol of his patron, Alexander VII – a heap of hills surmounted by a star – can clearly be seen above the main gateway. During summer, the steps around the obelisk and fountain, and the cafés on either side of the square, are popular hangouts. But the square's real attraction is the unbroken view it gives all the way back down Via del Corso to the central columns of the Vittorio Emanuele Monument. If you get to choose your first view of the centre of Rome, make it this one.

Santa Maria del Popolo

Mon–Sat 7am–noon & 4–7pm, Sun 8am–1.30pm & 4.30–7.30pm. Santa Maria del Popolo holds some of the best Renaissance art of any Roman church, with frescoes by Pintoricchio in the first chapel of the south aisle, and fine sculpture and mosaics in the Raphael-designed Chigi chapel (second from the entrance in the northern aisle). Designed for the banker Agostino Chigi in 1516, the chapel was not finished until the seventeenth century and most of the work was undertaken by other artists: Michelangelo's protégé, Sebastiano del Piombo, was responsible for the altarpiece, and two of the sculptures in the corner niches, of Daniel and Habakkuk, are by Bernini. The church's star attractions are perhaps the two pictures by Caravaggio in the left-hand chapel of the north transept: the *Conversion of St Paul* and the *Crucifixion of St Peter*, whose realism was considered extremely risqué in their time.

Casa di Goethe

Tues–Sun 10am–6pm; €3; ⓦwww.casadigoethe.it. A short way down Via del Corso from Piazza del Popolo, on the left at no. 18, the **Casa di Goethe** is a small and genuinely engaging museum. Goethe had long dreamed of travelling to Italy, inspired by a journey his father made years earlier, and he came here – incognito, as Filippo Miller – in 1786, after touring the north of the country. Goethe appeared to have stayed in houses all over Italy, but he did spend over two years in this one, and wrote much of his classic travelogue *Italian Journey* here – indeed, each room is decorated with a quote from the book. The house has been restored as a modern exhibition space and holds books, letters, prints and drawings, plus a reconstruction of his study in Vienna. Among the objects on display are Piranesi prints of public spaces in Rome, watercolours by Goethe himself and drawings by the German artist **Tischbein**, with whom he shared the house.

Mausoleum of Augustus

Forming the central core of the largely modern square of Piazza del Augusta Imperatore, the massive Mausoleum of Augustus is the burial place of the emperor and his family, though these days it's not much more than a peaceful ring of cypresses, circled by paths, flowering shrubs and the debris of tramps. Augustus died in 14 AD, and his passing effectively signalled the end of the Augustan age – and the order, prosperity and expansion that defined it. As Augustus himself had it, according to Suetonius: "I found Rome built simply out of bricks: I left her clad in marble." The mausoleum has been transformed into many buildings over the years, and is now open to the public. Inside, the passageways and central crypt, where the ashes of the members of the Augustan dynasty were kept, don't add much to the picture you get from the outside, and in any case tours are sporadic and these days almost non-existent.

Ara Pacis Augustae

Daily 9am–7pm; €6.50, audio guide €3.50. On the far side of the square, the **Ara Pacis Augustae** or "Altar of Augustan Peace" is now enclosed in a purpose-built structure designed by the New York-based architect Richard Meier. A marble block enclosed by sculpted walls, the altar was built in 13 BC, probably to celebrate Augustus's victory over Spain and Gaul and the peace it heralded. Much of it had been dug up piecemeal over the years, but the bulk was uncovered in the middle of the last century, a few hundred yards south, where it had originally stood. It is a superb example of imperial Roman sculpture, with a frieze on one side depicting the imperial family at the height of its power. It shows Augustus, his great general Marcus Agrippa and Augustus's wife Livia, followed by a victory procession containing her son (and Augustus's eventual successor) Tiberius and niece Antonia and her husband, Drusus, among others, while on the opposite side, the veiled figure is believed to be Julia, Augustus's daughter.

Fontana di Trevi

Piazza dei Trevi. One of Rome's more surprising sights, easy to stumble upon by accident, the Fontana di Trevi is a huge, very Baroque gush of water over statues and rocks built onto the backside of a Renaissance palace. There was a Trevi fountain, designed by Alberti, around the

▲ ARA PACIS AUGUSTAE

▲ FONTANA DI TREVI

corner in Via dei Crociferi, a smaller, more modest affair by all accounts, but Urban VIII decided to upgrade it in line with his other grandiose schemes of the time and employed Bernini, among others, to design an alternative nearby. Work didn't begin until 1732, when Niccolò Salvi won a competition held by Clement XII to design the fountain, and even then it took thirty years to finish the project. It's now, of course, the place you come to chuck in a coin if you want to guarantee your return to Rome, though you might remember Anita Ekberg throwing herself into it in *La Dolce Vita* (there are police here to discourage you from doing the same).

Time Elevator

Via dei Santissimi Apostoli 20 ⓣ06.977.46243, ⓦwww.time-elevator.it. Daily 10.30am–7.30pm; €11, 5–12 years €8. Flight-simulator seats and headphones (English audio available) set the stage for a 45min virtual tour of three thousand years of Roman history; an excellent way to prime the kids for the sights they will be seeing, not to mention their parents – though it probably wouldn't suit toddlers. Shows every 30min.

Galleria Colonna

Via della Pilotta 17 ⓦwww.galleriacolonna.it. Sat 9am–1pm, closed Aug; €7. The Galleria Colonna is somewhat outranked by many of the other Roman palatial collections but is worth forty minutes or so if you happen to be near when it's open, if only for the chandelier-decked Great Hall, which glorifies the achievements of the nobleman Marcantonio Colonna, notably his great victory against the Turks at the Battle of Lepanto in 1589. Of the paintings, the highlight is a collection of landscapes by Dughet (Poussin's brother-in-law), but other works that stand out are Carracci's early – and unusually spontaneous – *Bean Eater*, a *Narcissus* by Tintoretto and a *Portrait of a Venetian Gentleman* caught in supremely confident pose by Veronese.

Shops

Anglo-American Bookshop

Via della Vite 102. Mon 3.30–7.30pm, Tues–Sat 9am–1pm & 3.30–7.30pm. One of the best selections of new English books in Rome, especially good on history and academic books.

La Bottega del Principino

Via Margutta 59b. Mon–Sat 9.30am–7.30pm. An interesting little shop, quite different from the fancy antiques stores that surround it, offering quite an eclectic array of bric-à-brac – everything from eighteenth-century farm equipment to crystal chandeliers from the 1940s.

Buccone
Via di Ripetta 19. Mon–Thurs 9am–8.30pm, Fri & Sat 9am–midnight, Sun 10am–5pm. Every alcoholic beverage you could dream of, with a large selection of wines from all over the world – they even stock ten-litre bottles of grappa.

Ferrari Store
Via Tomacelli 147/152. Daily 10am–7.30pm. What better souvenir to take back than an accessory from this Italian motor racing icon? It's not a cheap store by any means, but there's a range of things to buy whatever your budget – from a €30 remote-control car to pricey Ferrari-themed jewellery.

Fratelli Alinari
Via Alibert 16a. Mon–Sat 3.30–7.30pm. If you want to know what Rome's piazzas looked like before McDonald's came to town, come here for a fine selection of black-and-white photographs of Rome. There are branches in Milan and Florence, too.

Galleria Alberto Sordi
Via del Corso. Daily 10am–10pm. This Y-shaped nineteenth-century shopping arcade has reopened after years of neglect, renamed after an Italian actor due to the fact that actors used to hang around inside seeking work. Now it's a sleek and stylish home to some great shops and provides a welcomingly cool escape from the Via del Corso crowds on hot days.

Giorgio Sermoneta Gloves
Piazza di Spagna 61. Mon–Sat 9am–8pm, Sun 10am–7pm. A glove specialist, with a large collection of Italian gloves in every price range, that has for the past 35 years catered to celebrities, politicians and tourists.

'Gusto
Piazza Augusto Imperatore 7. Everything for the aspirant gourmet: wines, decanters, glasses, and all the top-of-the-line kitchen gadgets and what-nots you could ever hope to find. Also has a large selection of cookbooks in English.

Lion Bookshop
Via dei Greci 33. Veteran English bookshop with a comfortable lounge area where you can take a break from browsing and enjoy a coffee or tea – a great store.

Messagerie Musicali
Via del Corso 472. One of the city's best mainstream collections of CDs, plus a wide array of foreign magazines and books.

▲ 'GUSTO

Nostalgica

Via di Ripetta. Old-fashioned Italian football shirts from around €70 – ironically enough, made in England.

Pineider

Via Due Macelli 68. This exclusive store has been selling beautiful handmade paper, invitations and writing materials for Roman society since 1774.

TAD

Via del Babuino 155a. Mon noon–8pm, Tues–Sat 10am–8pm. This stylish store looks tiny from the outside, but in fact houses departments selling clothes, perfume and cosmetics, flowers and home furnishings, as well as a hairdressing salon and ultra-cool café. Like most of the other shops on the street, it's as sleek and expensive as it gets for the most part, but it does have some clothes and accessories at prices most people can afford.

Cafés and snacks

Museo-Atelier Canova-Tadolini

Via del Babuino 150a. It's a bit odd eating here amongst the grand sculptures of this café-cum-museum, and certainly not cheap. But this is one of the few places to sit down along this busy street, serving decent sandwiches, salads, and simple pasta dishes. There are a few outside tables, too, to watch the designer bags bustle by.

Dolci e Doni

Via delle Carrozze 85. Daily 8am–8pm. A truly sumptuous array of pastries and cakes right in the heart of the Tridente. Don't miss the lemon cheesecake. Tea and other snacks too.

Il Gelato di San Crispino

Via della Panetteria 42. Considered by many to be the best ice cream in Rome. Wonderful flavours – all natural – will make the other *gelato* you've known pale by comparison.

Da Michele

Via dell' Umilta 31. Sun & Mon–Thurs 9am–7.30pm, Fri 9am–2pm, closed Sat. This classic Roman snack joint used to be in the Jewish Ghetto (when it was known as *Zi Fenizia*) but was replaced by a burger bar, and the Ghetto's loss is very much the Trevi area's gain. Under its changed name it still does kosher pizza to go – the house speciality is pizza with fresh anchovies and *indivia* (endives) – roast chicken and *supplì* (fried rice balls).

Restaurants

Antica Birreria Peroni

Via San Marcello 19 ☎06.679.5310. Mon–Sat noon–midnight. Big bustling *birreria* with an excellent menu of simple food that's meant to soak up lots of beer. There are the usual starters and pasta dishes, plus a good selection of meat dishes, *scamorza* cheese and *wurstel* specialities – all served in a lovely old wood-panelled turn-of-the-century restaurant full of photos of old Rome.

Beltramme

Via della Croce 39. No phone. Daily noon–3pm & 7–11pm. Originally this place sold only wine, by the *fiasco* or flask. Now, a few blocks from the Spanish Steps, it is a full-blown restaurant and just about always packed. But if you want authentic Roman food and atmosphere at affordable prices – €10 for a *primo*, €15 for a *secondo* – then this is the place. Service can be a bit slow. No credit cards.

Il Chianti

Via del Lavatore 81/82a ⓣ06.678.7550. Closed Sun. In the heart of tourist Rome, just metres from the Trevi Fountain, this Tuscan specialist is a find in a part of town not generally known for its good-value food and drink. There are good spreads of Tuscan cheese and cold meats, a selection of meat dishes, and the usual pasta dishes and pizzas. You can sit outside in summer if you can bear the travelling musicians who congregate to entertain the tourists.

Dal Bolognese

Piazza del Popolo 1 ⓣ06.361.1426. Tues–Sun 12.45–3pm & 8.15–11pm. One of Rome's premier restaurants for Emilian cuisine, and in an undeniably great location. Expensive, but delicious.

'Gusto

Piazza Augusto Imperatore 9 ⓣ06.322.6273. Daily 12.30–3pm & 7.30pm–2am. A slick but moderately priced establishment that has grown to be Rome's most successful culinary empire. The food is unique and often wonderful, and the atmosphere very chic. There's a reasonably priced and popular Mediterranean buffet lunch every day, plus unusual, well-executed desserts and a very complete wine list.

Margutta

Via Margutta 118 ⓣ06.3265.0577. Daily 12.30–3pm & 7.30–11.30pm. An upmarket, vegetarian restaurant that serves generous helpings – albeit at rather high prices. They also have another branch near the Pantheon – *Margutta Vegetariano alle Cornacchie*, Piazza Rondanini 53, ⓣ06.6813.4544.

Matricianella

Via del Leone 4 ⓣ06.683.2100. Closed Sun. Very handily placed just off Via del Corso, this old favourite is perhaps the best place to try real Roman food in the city centre, with classic deep-fried dishes like *baccala* and various vegetable *fritti*, classic Roman pasta such as *cacio e pepe*, and a great wine list – all of which you can consume in the bustling main dining room or on the outside terrace.

Otello alla Concordia

Via della Croce 81 ⓣ06.678.1454. Mon–Sat 11.30am–3pm & 7.30–11pm. This place used to be one of Fellini's favourites – he lived just a few blocks away on Via Margutta – and remains an elegant yet affordable restaurant. There's a good range of Roman and Italian dishes, but ask for "spaghetti Otello" (never on the menu) for a taste of pure tradition – fresh tomatoes and basil with garlic.

Pizza Ciro

Via della Mercede 43/45 ⓣ06.678.6015. Daily noon–3pm & 7pm–midnight. A big, friendly pizzeria that

▲ OTELLO ALLA CONCORDIA

also does first courses, main courses and desserts. A basic and unpretentious choice right in the heart of the city.

Recafé

Piazza Augusto Imperatore 9 ☎06.6813.4730. Daily 12.45pm–1am. The entrance on Via del Corso is a Neapolitan café, while on the Piazza Augusta Imperatore side you can enjoy proper Neapolitan pizzas, good pasta and salad dishes and excellent grilled *secondi* for moderate prices – €9 or so for a *primo*, €12–18 for a *secondo*. There are Neapolitan sweets and *fritti* too. The ambience is deliberately chic and the large outside terrace always has a buzz about it.

Bars

L'Enoteca Antica

Via della Croce 76b. Daily 11am–1am. An old Spanish Steps-area wine bar with a selection of hot and cold dishes, including soups and attractive desserts. Intriguing trompe l'oeil decorations inside, majolica-topped tables outside.

Rosati

Piazza del Popolo 5. Daily 8am–midnight. This was the bar that hosted left-wingers, bohemians and writers in years gone by, though now it's cocktails and food that draw the crowds to the outside terrace.

Shaki

Via Maria de' Fiori 29. Daily 11am–11pm. Wine bar of the nearby gourmet store, serving salads, soups, light lunches and snacks at outside tables, a few short steps from Piazza di Spagna. Good wine, and very handy, if a little too self-consciously chic.

Clubs and venues

Gregory's

Via Gregoriana 54d ☎06.679.6386. Tues–Sun 8pm–3am. Just up the Spanish Steps and to the right, this elegant nightspot pulls in the crowds with its live jazz, improvised by Roman and international musicians. Tues–Sun 5.30pm–3am.

▼ L'ENOTECA ANTICA

The Forum, Colosseum and around

There are remnants of ancient Rome all over the city, but the most famous and concentrated collection of sights – the Forum and Colosseum together with the Palatine and Celian hills – stretches southeast from the Capitoline Hill. This area is reasonably traffic-free and self-contained and you can spend a good half-day, perhaps longer, picking your way through the rubble of what was once the core of the ancient world. The most obvious place to start is the original, Republican-period Forum, the political and commercial heart of the ancient city. You can then visit the later Imperial Forums that lie across Via dei Fori Imperiali before heading up the legendary Palatine Hill, once home to the city's most powerful citizens. Just beyond the Forum, the Colosseum is perhaps the most iconic image of Rome, a beautiful construction seemingly at odds with its violent past, while nearby, the Celian Hill is a lovely place to wander, with a peaceful park and diverting churches.

The Imperial Forums

The original Roman Forum was the centre of the Rome of the Republican era but the rise of the empire, and Rome's increased importance as a world power, led to the extensions of the Imperial Forums nearby. Julius Caesar began the expansion in around 50 BC, and work was continued after his assassination by his nephew and successor Augustus, and later by the Flavian emperors –Vespasian, Nerva and finally

Visiting the Forum, Palatine and Colosseum

The **Forum**, **Palatine** and **Colosseum** are open daily (summer 8.30am–6.15pm; winter 9am–4.30pm). Entry to the Forum is free, while entry to the Palatine and Colosseum costs €11 for a combined ticket. **Queues**, to the Colosseum especially, can be a problem: while they do move quickly, they're rarely less than 100m long and often stretch through the arcade on the metro station side of the stadium and into the scrum of touts outside. To avoid them, turn up before the Colosseum opens, or buy an **Archeocard** or **Romapass** (see p.206), which allow you to use a different queue. A **visitor centre**, opposite the church of Santi Cosma e Damiano (daily 9.30am–6.30pm), has more information should you need it, and a café to relieve your aching feet.

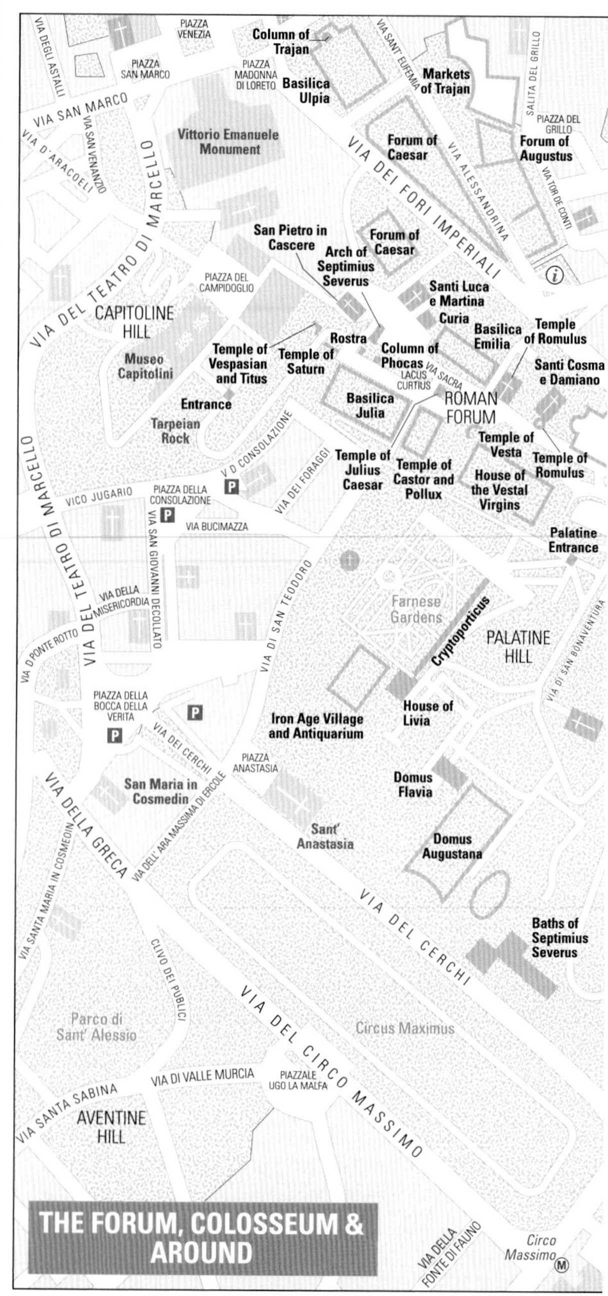
THE FORUM, COLOSSEUM & AROUND
Column of Trajan
Basilica Ulpia
Markets of Trajan
Forum of Caesar
Forum of Augustus
Vittorio Emanuele Monument
San Pietro in Cascere
Arch of Septimius Severus
Forum of Caesar
Santi Luca e Martina
Curia
Basilica Emilia
Temple of Romulus
Santi Cosma e Damiano
Rostra
Column of Phocas
LACUS CURTIUS
Temple of Vespasian and Titus
Temple of Saturn
Basilica Julia
ROMAN FORUM
Temple of Vesta
Temple of Romulus
House of the Vestal Virgins
Temple of Julius Caesar
Temple of Castor and Pollux
CAPITOLINE HILL
Museo Capitolini
Entrance
Tarpeian Rock
Palatine Entrance
Farnese Gardens
Cryptoporticus
PALATINE HILL
House of Livia
Iron Age Village and Antiquarium
Domus Flavia
Domus Augustana
Baths of Septimius Severus
San Maria in Cosmedin
Sant' Anastasia
Circus Maximus
Parco di Sant' Alessio
AVENTINE HILL
Circo Massimo
PIAZZA VENEZIA
PIAZZA SAN MARCO
PIAZZA MADONNA DI LORETO
PIAZZA DEL GRILLO
PIAZZA DEL CAMPIDOGLIO
PIAZZA DELLA CONSOLAZIONE
PIAZZA DELLA BOCCA DELLA VERITA
PIAZZA ANASTASIA
PIAZZALE UGO LA MALFA
VIA DEGLI ASTALLI
VIA SAN MARCO
VIA SAN VENANZIO
VIA D'ARACOELI
VIA SANT' EUFEMIA
SALITA DEL GRILLO
VIA DEI FORI IMPERIALI
VIA ALESSANDRINA
VIA TOR DE CONTI
VIA DEL TEATRO DI MARCELLO
VIA SACRA
V. D. CONSOLAZIONE
VIA DEI FORAGGI
VICO JUGARIO
VIA BUCIMAZZA
VIA SAN GIOVANNI DECOLLATO
VIA DELLA MISERICORDIA
VIA D. PONTE ROTTO
VIA DI SAN TEODORO
VIA DI SAN BONAVENTURA
VIA DEI CERCHI
VIA DELL' ARA MASSIMA DI ERCOLE
VIA DELLA GRECA
VIA SANTA MARIA IN COSMEDIN
CLIVO DEI PUBLICI
VIA DEL CERCHI
VIA DEL CIRCO MASSIMO
VIA DI VALLE MURCIA
VIA SANTA SABINA
VIA DELLA FONTE DI FAUNO

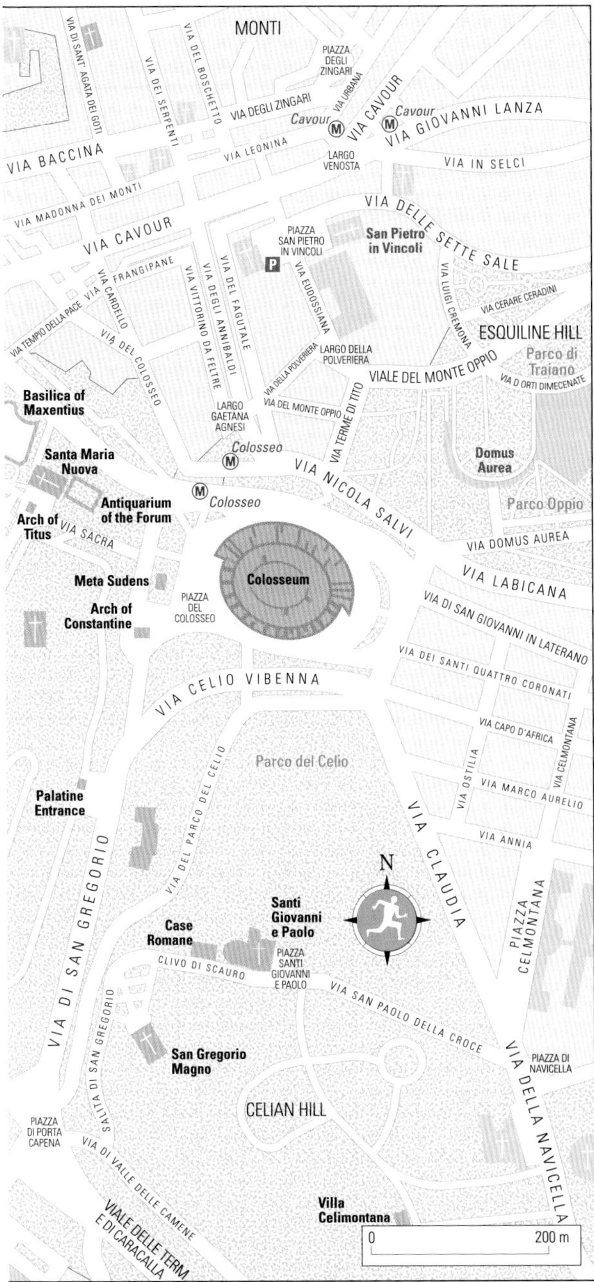
MONTI
PIAZZA DEGLI ZINGARI
VIA DI SANT' AGATA DEI GOTI
VIA DEL BOSCHETTO
VIA DEI SERPENTI
VIA DEGLI ZINGARI
VIA URBANA
VIA CAVOUR
Cavour
VIA GIOVANNI LANZA
VIA BACCINA
VIA LEONINA
LARGO VENOSTA
VIA IN SELCI
VIA MADONNA DEI MONTI
VIA DELLE SETTE SALE
PIAZZA SAN PIETRO IN VINCOLI
San Pietro in Vincoli
P
VIA FRANGIPANE
VIA CARDELLO
VIA TEMPIO DELLA PACE
VIA VITTORINO DA FELTRE
VIA DEGLI ANNIBALDI
VIA DEL FAGUTALE
VIA EUDOSSIANA
VIA LUIGI CREMONA
VIA CERARE CERADINI
ESQUILINE HILL
VIA DEL COLOSSEO
VIA DELLA POLVERIERA
LARGO DELLA POLVERIERA
VIALE DEL MONTE OPPIO
Parco di Traiano
VIA D ORTI DIMECENATE
Basilica of Maxentius
LARGO GAETANA AGNESI
VIA DEL MONTE OPPIO
VIA TERME DI TITO
Colosseo
Santa Maria Nuova
VIA NICOLA SALVI
Domus Aurea
Antiquarium of the Forum
Parco Oppio
Arch of Titus
VIA SACRA
VIA DOMUS AUREA
Meta Sudens
Colosseum
VIA LABICANA
Arch of Constantine
PIAZZA DEL COLOSSEO
VIA DI SAN GIOVANNI IN LATERANO
VIA DEI SANTI QUATTRO CORONATI
VIA CELIO VIBENNA
VIA CAPO D'AFRICA
VIA CELMONTANA
Parco del Celio
VIA OSTILIA
VIA MARCO AURELIO
Palatine Entrance
VIA DEL PARCO DEL CELIO
VIA CLAUDIA
VIA ANNIA
VIA DI SAN GREGORIO
N
PIAZZA CELMONTANA
Santi Giovanni e Paolo
Case Romane
PIAZZA SANTI GIOVANNI E PAOLO
CLIVO DI SCAURO
VIA SAN PAOLO DELLA CROCE
SALITA DI SAN GREGORIO
San Gregorio Magno
VIA DELLA NAVICELLA
PIAZZA DI NAVICELLA
CELIAN HILL
PIAZZA DI PORTA CAPENA
VIA DI VALLE DELLE CAMENE
VIALE DELLE TERM E DI CARACALLA
Villa Celimontana
0
200 m

Trajan. The recently excavated remains litter the sides of Via dei Fori Imperiali, and are now in large part open to the public. On the north side, the **Forum of Trajan** is of most interest, particularly the semicircular **Markets of Trajan** (Tues–Sun 9am–6pm; €3) and the **Column of Trajan**, erected to celebrate the emperor's victories in Dacia, and covered top to bottom with reliefs commemorating the highlights of the campaign. The forums to Augustus (further along) and Caesar (on the south side) might also detain you for a while.

Santi Cosma e Damiano

Daily 8am–1pm & 3–7pm. Across the road from the Forum of Augustus, the vestibule of the church of **Santi Cosma e Damiano** was originally created from the Temple of Romulus in the Forum, which you can look down into from the nave of the church. Turn around, and you'll see the mosaics in the apse, showing the naturalistic figures of the two saints being presented to Christ by St Peter and St Paul, flanked by St Felix on the left and St Theodore on the right. Outside, the cloister is wonderfully peaceful compared to the busy roads around. For a €1 donation you can also visit the massive Neapolitan **presepio** or Christmas crib, displayed in a room in the corner here, a huge piece of work with literally hundreds of figures spread amongst the ruins of ancient Rome.

The Roman Forum

The two or so hectares that make up the Forum were once the heart of the Mediterranean world, and although the glories of ancient Rome are hard to glimpse here now, there's a symbolic allure to the place and a desolate drama, especially early in the morning or at dusk, that makes it one of the world's most compelling (not to mention most ruined) sets of ruins anywhere in the world. You need an imagination and a little history to fully appreciate the place, but the public spaces are easy enough to discern, especially the spinal **Via Sacra**, the best-known street of ancient Rome, along which victorious emperors and generals would ride in procession to give thanks at the Capitoline's Temple of Juno. A little way beyond, the large cube-shaped building is the **Curia**, built on the orders

▼ THE ROMAN FORUM

▲ ARCH OF SEPTIMIUS SEVERUS

of Julius Caesar as part of his programme for expanding the Forum, although what you see now is a third-century AD reconstruction. The Senate met here, and inside three wide stairs rise to the left and right, on which about 300 senators could be accommodated with their folding chairs. In the centre is the speaker's platform, with a porphyry statue of a togaed figure. Nearby, the **Arch of Septimius Severus** was constructed in the early third century AD by his sons Caracalla and Geta to mark their father's victories in what is now Iran. The friezes on it recall Severus and in particular Caracalla, who ruled Rome with undisciplined terror for seven years. To the left of the arch, the low brown wall is the **Rostra**, from which important speeches were made (it was from here that Mark Anthony most likely spoke about Caesar after his death). Left of the Rostra are the long stairs of the **Basilica Julia**, built by Julius Caesar in the 50s BC after he returned from the Gallic wars, and, a bit further along, rails mark the site of the **Lacus Curtius** – the spot where, according to legend, a chasm opened during the earliest days and the soothsayers determined that it would only be closed once Rome had sacrificed its most valuable possession into it. Marcus Curtius, a Roman soldier who declared that Rome's most valuable possession was a loyal citizen, hurled himself and his horse into the void and it duly closed. Further on, to the right, the enormous pile of rubble topped by three graceful Corinthian columns is the **Temple of Castor and Pollux**, dedicated in 484 BC to the divine twins, or Dioscuri, who appeared miraculously to ensure victory for the Romans in a key battle. Beyond here, the **House of the Vestal Virgins** is a second-century AD reconstruction of a building originally built by Nero: four floors of rooms around a central courtyard, still with its pool in the centre and fringed by the statues or inscribed pedestals of the women themselves, with the round Temple of Vesta at the near end. Almost opposite, a shady walkway to the left leads up to the **Basilica of Maxentius**, sometimes called the Basilica of Constantine – in terms of size and ingenuity, probably the Forum's most impressive remains. Begun by Maxentius, it was continued by his co-emperor and rival, Constantine, after he had defeated Maxentius at the Battle of the Milvian Bridge in 312 AD. Back on the Via Sacra, the hill climbs more steeply to the **Arch of Titus**, built by Titus's brother, Domitian, after the emperor's death in 81 AD to commemorate his triumphant return after victories in Judea in 70 AD. It's a long-standing tradition that Jews don't pass under this arch.

The Palatine Hill

Daily 8.30am–7pm; €11, includes the Colosseum (including exhibitions, otherwise €9); you can make a reservation on ☎06.3996.7700 (Mon–Sat 9am–1.30pm & 2.30–5pm; €1.50 and avoid the queues); guided tours in English at noon €3.50. Entrance and ticket booths by the Arch of Titus (Roman Forum) and on Via di San Gregorio. Rising above the Roman Forum, the Palatine is supposedly where the city of Rome was founded, and is home to some of its most ancient remnants. In a way it's a more pleasant site to tour than the Forum, a good place to have a picnic and relax after the rigours of the ruins below. In the days of the Republic, the Palatine was the most desirable address in Rome (the word "palace" is derived from Palatine), and the big names continued to colonize it during the Imperial era, trying to outdo each other with ever larger and more magnificent dwellings.

Following the main path up from the Forum, the **Domus Flavia** was one of the most splendid residences, although it's now almost completely ruined. To the left, the top level of the gargantuan **Domus Augustana** spreads to the far brink of the hill – not the home of Augustus as its name suggests, but the private house of any emperor (or "Augustus"). You can look down from here on its vast central courtyard with fountains and wander to the brink of the deep trench of the Stadium, on the far side of which the ruins of the **Baths of Septimius Severus** cling to the side of the hill. Walking in the opposite direction from the Domus Flavia, steps lead down to the **Cryptoporticus**, a long passage built by Nero to link his Domus Aurea with the Palatine, and decorated along part of its length with well-preserved Roman stucco-work. You can go either way along the passage. A left turn leads to the **House of Livia**, originally believed to have been the residence of Livia. A right down the passage and up some steps takes you to the **Farnese Gardens**, among the first botanical gardens in Europe, laid out in the mid-sixteenth century and now a tidily planted, shady retreat from the exposed heat of the ruins. The terrace at the opposite end looks down on the excavations of an **Iron Age village** that perhaps marks the real centre of Rome's ancient beginnings. The large grey building here houses the **Museo Palatino**, which

▼ THE PALATINE HILL FROM THE FORUM

▲ ARCH OF CONSTANTINE

contains a vast assortment of statuary, pottery, terracotta antefixes and architectural fragments.

The Arch of Constantine

Leaving the Roman Forum by way of the Via Sacra, the huge Arch of Constantine on your right was placed here in the early decades of the fourth century AD after Constantine had consolidated his power as sole emperor. The arch demonstrates the deterioration of the arts during the late stages of the Roman Empire – most of the sculptural decoration here had to be removed from other monuments, and the builders were probably quite ignorant of the significance of the pieces they borrowed: the round medallions are taken from a temple dedicated to the Emperor Hadrian's lover, Antinous, and show Antinous and Hadrian engaged in a hunt. The other pieces, removed from the Forum of Trajan, show Dacian prisoners captured in Trajan's war there.

The Colosseum

Daily 8.30am–5.30pm; €11, includes the Palatine Hill. The Colosseum is perhaps Rome's most awe-inspiring ancient monument: an enormous ampitheatre that, despite the depredations of nearly 2000 years of earthquakes, fires, riots, wars and, not least, plundering for its seemingly inexhaustible supply of ready-cut travertine blocks, still stands relatively intact. You'll not be alone in appreciating it, and during summer the combination of people and scaffolding can make a visit more like touring a contemporary building site than an ancient monument. But visit late in the evening or in early morning before the tour buses arrive, and the arena can seem more like the marvel it really is. Originally known as the Flavian Amphitheatre (the name Colosseum is a much later invention), it was begun around 72 AD by the Emperor Vespasian, who was anxious to extinguish the memory of Nero, and so chose the site

▲ INSIDE THE COLOSSEUM

of Nero's outrageous Domus Aurea for the stadium. Inside, there was room for a total of around 60,000 people seated and 10,000 or so standing, and the system of exits (vomitoria) for each section has served as a model for stadiums around the world. The seating was allocated on a strict basis, with the emperor and his attendants occupying the best seats in the house, and the social class of the spectators diminishing nearer the top. There was a labyrinth below that was covered with a wooden floor and punctuated at various places with trap doors and lifts to raise and lower the animals that were to take part in the games. The floor was covered with canvas to make it waterproof and the canvas was covered with several centimetres of sand to absorb blood; in fact, our word "arena" is derived from the Latin word for sand. Once inside, you can wander around most of the lower level, and all the way round the upper level, though even here you are still only about halfway up the original structure; all the higher parts of the stadium are closed these days. You can gaze down into the innards of the arena, but there's been no original arena floor since its excavation in the nineteenth century and as such it too is out of bounds to visitors. The upper floor on the northern side contains a decent bookshop and a space for regular temporary exhibitions; an area by the lifts is given over to a display of fragments of masonry from the Colosseum.

The Celian and Aventine Hills and south of the centre

The leafy Celian and Aventine hills make up one of the city's most pleasant corners. Some of the animals that were to die in the Colosseum were kept in a zoo up on the Celian Hill, just behind the arena, while the Aventine was once the heart of plebeian Rome and is now an upscale residential area with fine views across the river. Between the two stand the ruins of the Circus Maximus stadium and the Baths of Caracalla, popular places to relax for the ancient citizens. South and west from the hill are two distinct neighbourhoods: Testaccio, a working-class enclave that has become increasingly hip and gentrified (and home to much of the city's nightlife), and the more up-and-coming Ostiense, worth a visit for the Centrale Montemartini branch of the Capitoline Museums. Between these districts is Rome's Protestant Cemetery, where the poets Keats and Shelley are buried. Further south, beyond the ancient city wall, lie the magnificent, rebuilt basilica of San Paolo fuori le Mura and the Via Appia Antica with its atmospheric Christian catacombs. It's also worth taking a trip down to EUR, Rome's futuristic 1930s experiment in town planning.

Santi Giovanni e Paolo

Daily 8.30am–noon & 3.30–6.30pm. Recognised by its colourful campanile, this church is dedicated to Giovanni and Paolo, two dignitaries in the court of Constantine who were beheaded here in 361 AD after refusing military service. A railed-off tablet in mid-nave marks the shrine where the saints were martyred and buried, although the church is best-known these days as a popular venue for weddings.

Case Romane

Clivio di Scauro. Daily 10am–1pm & 3–6pm, except Tues & Wed; €6. The relics of what is believed to be the residence of Giovanni and Paolo (see above) – around twenty rooms in all, patchily frescoed with pagan and Christian subjects, which demand some imagination to realize them as the palatial living quarters they were. However, there are standouts, such as the Casa dei Genii, frescoed with winged youths and cupids, and the courtyard or nymphaeum,

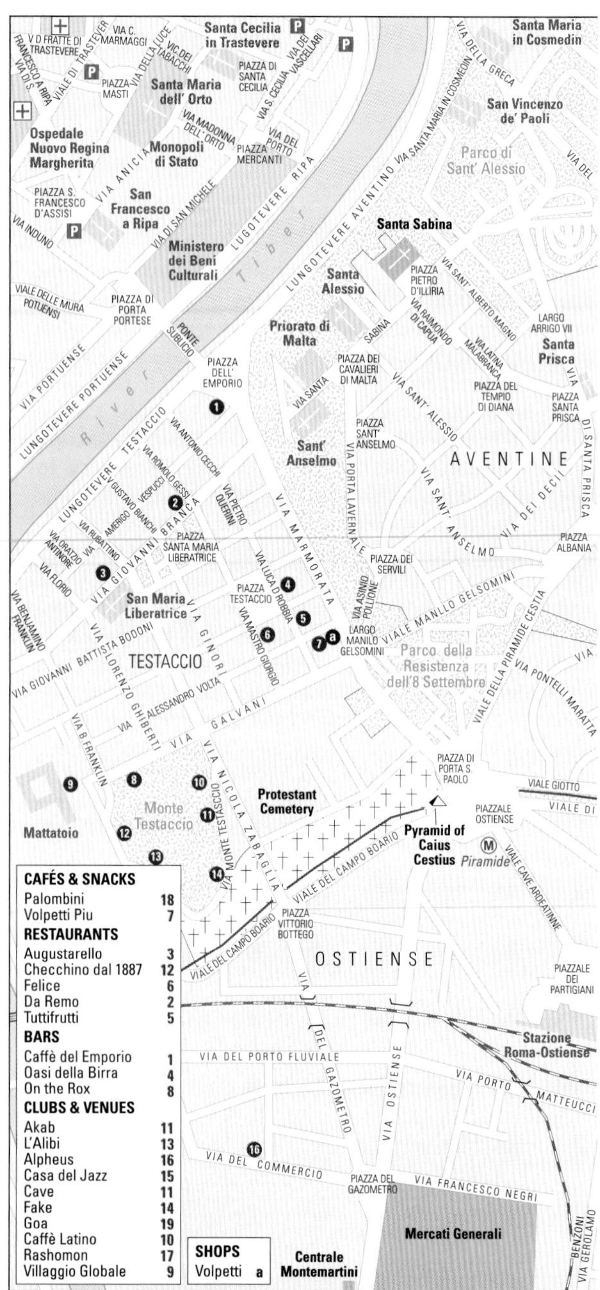

Santa Cecilia in Trastevere
Santa Maria in Cosmedin
Santa Maria dell' Orto
San Vincenzo de' Paoli
Parco di Sant' Alessio
Ospedale Nuovo Regina Margherita
Monopoli di Stato
San Francesco a Ripa
Ministero dei Beni Culturali
Santa Sabina
Santa Alessio
Priorato di Malta
Santa Prisca
Sant' Anselmo
AVENTINE
TESTACCIO
San Maria Liberatrice
Parco della Resistenza dell'8 Settembre
Protestant Cemetery
Pyramid of Caius Cestius
Piramide
Monte Testaccio
Mattatoio
OSTIENSE
Stazione Roma-Ostiense
Mercati Generali
Centrale Montemartini
River Tiber
CAFÉS & SNACKS
Palombini 18
Volpetti Piu 7
RESTAURANTS
Augustarello 3
Checchino dal 1887 12
Felice 6
Da Remo 2
Tuttifrutti 5
BARS
Caffè del Emporio 1
Oasi della Birra 4
On the Rox 8
CLUBS & VENUES
Akab 11
L'Alibi 13
Alpheus 16
Casa del Jazz 15
Cave 11
Fake 14
Goa 19
Caffè Latino 10
Rashomon 17
Villaggio Globale 9
SHOPS
Volpetti a
San Paolo fuori le Mura (1km), Eur (2km) & 17 18 & 19 (400m)

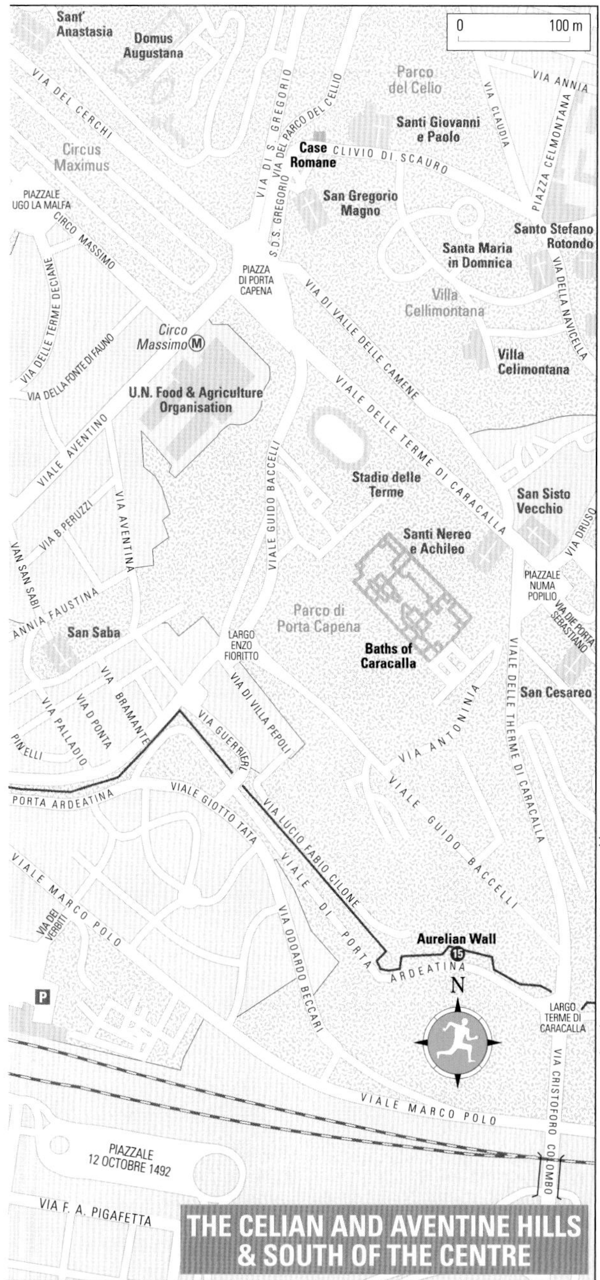
Sant' Anastasia
Domus Augustana
Parco del Celio
Santi Giovanni e Paolo
Case Romane
Circus Maximus
San Gregorio Magno
Santo Stefano Rotondo
Santa Maria in Domnica
Villa Cellimontana
Villa Celimontana
Circo Massimo
U.N. Food & Agriculture Organisation
Stadio delle Terme
San Sisto Vecchio
Santi Nereo e Achileo
Parco di Porta Capena
Baths of Caracalla
San Saba
San Cesareo
Aurelian Wall
VIA DEL CERCHI
VIA DI S. GREGORIO
VIA DEL PARCO DEL CELLIO
CLIVIO DI SCAURO
VIA CLAUDIA
VIA ANNIA
PIAZZA CELMONTANA
PIAZZALE UGO LA MALFA
CIRCO MASSIMO
S.D.S. GREGORIO
PIAZZA DI PORTA CAPENA
VIA DI VALLE DELLE CAMENE
VIA DELLA NAVICELLA
VIA DELLE TERME DECIANE
VIA DELLA FONTE DI FAUNO
VIALE DELLE TERME DI CARACALLA
VIALE AVENTINO
VIALE GUIDO BACCELLI
VIA B. PERUZZI
VIA AVENTINA
VIA DRUSO
PIAZZALE NUMA POPILIO
VIA DIE PORTA SEBASTIANO
ANNIA FAUSTINA
LARGO ENZO FIORITTO
VIA DI VILLA PEPOLI
VIA BRAMANTE
VIA D PONTA
VIA PALLADIO
PINELLI
VIA GUERRIERI
VIA ANTONINIA
VIALE DELLE THERME DI CARACALLA
PORTA ARDEATINA
VIALE GIOTTO TATA
VIA LUCIO FABIO CILONE
VIALE DI PORTA ARDEATINA
VIALE MARCO POLO
VIA DEI VERBITI
VIA ODOARDO BECCARI
LARGO TERME DI CARACALLA
VIA CRISTOFORO COLOMBO
PIAZZALE 12 OCTOBRE 1492
VIA F. A. PIGAFETTA
0 100 m
N
P
15
Museo delle Mura & Via Appia Antica (1km) & Catacombs (2km)

THE CELIAN AND AVENTINE HILLS & SOUTH OF THE CENTRE

which has a marvellous fresco of a goddess, perhaps Prosperine preparing for her marriage to Pluto, being attended on and poured a drink, sandwiched between cupids in boats, fishing and loading supplies. There's also an interesting antiquarium, with a good haul of finds from the site.

San Gregorio Magno

Daily 8.30am–12.30pm & 3–6.30pm; ring the bell marked "portinare" to gain admission. Just a little further down the hill from Casa Romane (see p.111), this church occupies a commanding position looking across to the lollipop pines of the Palatine Hill opposite. Saint Gregory founded the monastery that's still here, and was a monk here before becoming pope in 590 AD. The interior is fairly ordinary, but the lovely Cosmati floor remains intact, and the chapel of the saint at the end of the south aisle has a beautifully carved bath showing scenes from St Gregory's life along with his marble throne, a beaten-up specimen that actually predates the saint by 500 years. The chapels to the left of the entrance are also worth a look but are often closed.

The Circus Maximus

The Circus Maximus was once the ancient city's main venue for chariot races. It fills a long, green expanse between the Palatine and Aventine hills, but is now bordered by heavily trafficked roads. The arena had a capacity of some 300,000 spectators, and if it were still intact would no doubt match the Colosseum for grandeur. As it is, a litter of stones at the Viale Aventino end is all that remains, together with – at the southern end – a little medieval tower, and, behind a chain-link fence traced out in marble blocks at the base of the Palatine, the outline of the Septizodium, an imperial structure designed to show off the glories of the city and its empire to those arriving on the Via Appia.

Santa Sabina

Piazza Pietro d'Illiria. Daily 6.30am–12.45pm & 4–7pm.
Crowning the Aventine Hill, the delightful church of Santa Sabina is a strong contender for Rome's most beautiful basilica – its nave and portico were restored back to their fifth-century appearance in the 1930s. Look especially at the main doors, which are contemporary with the church and boast eighteen panels carved with Christian scenes, forming a complete illustrated Bible (including one of the oldest representations of the Crucifixion). Santa Sabina is also the principal church of the Dominicans, and inside, just near the doors, a smooth piece of black marble, pitted with holes, was apparently thrown by the devil at St Dominic himself while at prayer, shattering the marble pavement but miraculously not harming the saint. It's also claimed that the orange trees in the garden behind, which you can glimpse on your way to a room once occupied by St Dominic himself, are descendants of those planted by the saint. Wherever the truth lies, the views from the gardens are splendid – right across the Tiber to the centre of Rome and St Peter's.

The Baths of Caracalla

Viale Terme di Caracalla 52. Mon 9am–1pm, Tues–Sun 9am–sunset; €6.

The remains of this ancient Roman leisure centre give a far better sense of the monumental scale of Roman architecture than most of the extant ruins in the city – so much so that Shelley was moved to write *Prometheus Unbound* here in 1819. The walls still rise to very nearly their original height and there are many fragments of mosaics – none spectacular, but quite a few bright and well preserved. The complex included gymnasiums, gardens and an open-air swimming pool as well as the hot, tepid and cold series of baths. As for Caracalla, he was one of Rome's worst and shortest-lived rulers, so it's no wonder there's nothing else in the city built by him. The baths were for many years used for occasional opera performances during the summer (one of Mussolini's better ideas); these have recently re-started, and are a thrilling and inexpensive way to see the baths at their most atmospheric.

▲ THE BATHS OF CARACALLA

Testaccio

The working-class neighbourhood of Testaccio groups around a couple of main squares. A tight-knit community with a market and a number of bars and small trattorias, it was for many years synonymous with the slaughterhouse, or **mattatoio**. In the past couple of decades the area has become a trendy place to live, and the slaughterhouse, once the area's main employer, is now home to the Centro Sociale and "Villaggio Globale", a space used for concerts, raves and the like. For years there has been talk of sprucing it up, but so far nothing has happened, and it's likely to remain as it is for some time to come. It also houses a branch of the **Museum of Contemporary Art of Rome** (MACRO; Tues–Sun 4pm–midnight), which stages temporary exhibitions of an adventurous nature.

Monte Testaccio

Monte Testaccio, which gives the area its name, is a 35-metre-high mound created out of the shards of Roman amphorae that were dumped here over several centuries. It's an odd sight, the ceramic curls clearly visible through the tufts of grass that crown its higher reaches, the bottom layers hollowed out by the workshops of car and bike mechanics – and, now, clubs and bars (see p.122).

The Protestant Cemetery

Entrance on Via Caio Cestio 5. Mon–Sat 9am–5pm; donation expected. Bus 23 to Piazzale Ostiense. The Protestant Cemetery isn't in fact a Protestant cemetery at all, but is reserved for non-Roman Catholics of all nationalities. It is nonetheless one of the shrines to the English in Rome, and a fitting conclusion to a visit to the Keats-Shelley Memorial

▲ THE PROTESTANT CEMETERY

House on Piazza di Spagna, since it is here that both poets are buried, along with a handful of other well-known names. Most visitors come to see the grave of Keats, who lies next to his friend, the painter Joseph Severn, in a corner of the old part of the cemetery, his stone inscribed as he wished with the words "Here lies one whose name was writ in water". Shelley's ashes were brought here at his wife's request and interred, after much obstruction by the papal authorities, in the newer part of the cemetery at the top – the Shelleys had visited several years earlier, the poet praising it as "the most beautiful and solemn cemetery I ever beheld".

▼ THE PYRAMID OF CAIUS CESTIUS AND PORTA SAN PAOLO

The Pyramid of Caius Cestius

Piazzale Ostiense. The most distinctive landmark in this part of town is the mossy pyramidal tomb of one Caius Cestius, who died in 12 BC. Cestius had spent some time in Egypt, and part of his will decreed that all his slaves should be freed – the white pyramid you see today was thrown up by them in only 330 days of what must have been joyful building. It's occasionally open to the public, but you can visit the cats who live here, and the volunteers who care for them, any afternoon between 2.30pm and 4.30pm.

Centrale Montemartini

Via Ostiense 106. Tues–Sun 9am–7pm; €4.50, €8.50 for Capitoline Museums as well, valid 7 days. This former electricity generating station was requisitioned to display the cream of the Capitoline Museums' sculpture while the main buildings were being renovated and became so popular that it's now a permanent outpost, attracting visitors south to the formerly industrial area of Ostiense. The huge rooms of the power station are ideally suited to showing ancient sculpture, although checking out the massive turbines and furnaces has a fascination of its own, and more than competes for your attention. Among many compelling objects are the head, feet and an arm from a colossal statue, once 8m high, found in Largo Argentina, a large Roman copy of Athena, a fragmented mosaic of hunting scenes, and a lovely naturalistic statue of a girl seated on a stool with her legs crossed, from the third century BC. There's also a figure of Hercules and next to it a soft *Muse Polymnia*, the former braced for activity, the latter leaning on a rock and staring thoughtfully into the distance.

San Paolo fuori le Mura

Daily 7am–6.30pm, winter until 6pm. Metro line #B or bus #271 from Piazza Venezia (bus doesn't run at weekends). A kilometre or so further south from the Centrale Montemartini, the basilica of San Paolo fuori le Mura (St Paul's Outside-the-Walls) is one of the five patriarchal basilicas of Rome, occupying the supposed site of St Paul's tomb. Of the five, this basilica has probably fared the least well over the years, the victim of a devastating fire in 1823 that almost entirely destroyed the church - what you see now is largely a nineteenth-century reconstruction. It's very successful, and the huge barn-like structure, with its clerestory windows and roof beams supported by enormous columns, has a powerful and authentic sense of occasion and history: evidenced by the medallions of all the popes fringing the nave and transepts above, starting with St Peter to the right of the apse and ending with Benedict XVI at the top of the south aisle. In the south transept, the paschal candlestick is a remarkable piece of Romanesque carving, supported by half-human beasts and showing scenes from Christ's life; the bronze aisle doors were also rescued from the old basilica and date from 1070,

▼ SAN PAOLO FUORI LE MURA

▲ THE AURELIAN WALL

as was the thirteenth-century tabernacle by Arnolfo di Cambio; and the arch across the apse is embellished with mosaics donated by the Byzantine queen Galla Placidia in the sixth century. There's also the cloister, just behind here – probably Rome's finest piece of Cosmatesque work, its spiralling, mosaic-encrusted columns enclosing a peaceful rose garden.

The Aurelian Wall

Built by the Emperor Aurelian in 275 AD to enclose Rome's hills and protect the city from invasion, the Aurelian Wall still surrounds much of the city, but its best-preserved stretch runs 2km between Porta San Paolo and Porta San Sebastiano (which lies a few hundred metres of Largo Terme di Caracalla). Here, the **Museo delle Mura** (Tues–Sat

Visiting Via Appia Antica and the catacombs

Buses run south along Via Appia Antica and conveniently stop at, or near to, most of the main attractions, starting with Porta San Sebastiano. You can walk it, but bear in mind that much of the Via Appia Antica isn't particularly picturesque, at least until you get down to the Catacombs of San Sebastiano, and the best thing to do is take a bus to San Sebastian and double back or walk on further for the attractions you want to see. Bus #118 runs from Piazzale Ostiense almost as far as the San Sebastiano catacombs; you can also take bus #218, which goes down Via Ardeatina, or bus #660, which goes from beyond the Tomb of Cecilia Metella to Colli Albani metro station. However, the easiest option is to take the **Archeobus**, which runs from Termini and Piazza Venezia, among other city centre locations, roughly every hour; tickets cost €8 for a return trip that lasts all day and you can hop on and off as you wish. Or you could walk from Porta San Sebastiano and take everything in on foot, which allows you to stop off at the Parco Regionale dell'Appia Antica **information office** for the area – it's actually classified as a national park – at Via Appia Antica 58, on the right just before you get to Domine Quo Vadis (summer daily 9.30am–5.30pm, winter daily 9.30am–4.30pm; ⓣ06.512.6314; ⓦwww.parcoappiaantica.org). You can hire **bikes** from here for €3 an hour or €10 a day; pick up a good map and other information on the various Appia Antica sights. Finally, there are a couple of handy – and decent – **restaurants** down by San Sebastiano: *L'Archeologica*, just past the church, and the *Cecilia Metella*, right opposite; neither is especially cheap but both have pleasant gardens for al fresco eating.

9am–2pm; €2.60) occupies two floors of the city gate and has displays showing Aurelian's original plans and lots of photos of the walls past and present. You can climb up to the top of the gate for great views over the Roman campagna beyond, and walk a few hundred metres along the wall itself.

Via Appia Antica

The Via Appia Antica, which starts at the Porta San Sebastiano, is the most famous of the consular roads that used to strike out in each direction from ancient Rome. It was built by one Appio Claudio in 312 BC, and is the only Roman landmark mentioned in the Bible. During classical times the "Appian Way" was the most important of all the Roman trade routes, carrying supplies right down through Campania to the port of Brindisi. It's no longer the main route south out of the city – that's Via Appia Nuova from nearby Porta San Giovanni – but it remains an important part of early Christian Rome, its verges lined with numerous pagan and Christian sites, including, most famously, the underground burial cemeteries or catacombs of the first Christians.

Domine Quo Vadis

Via Appia Antica 51. About 500m from Porta San Sebastiano, where the road forks, the church of Domine Quo Vadis is the first and most obvious sight on Via Appia. Legend has this as the place where St Peter saw Christ while fleeing from certain death in Rome and asked "Where goest thou, Lord?", to which Christ replied that he was going to be crucified once more, leading Peter to turn around and accept his fate. The small church is ordinary enough inside, except for its replica of a piece of marble that's said to be marked with the footprints of Christ – the original is in the church of San Sebastiano (see p.120).

Catacombs of San Callisto

Via Appia Antica 126. Daily except Wed 9am–noon & 2–5pm; €5. The largest of Rome's catacombs, the Catacombs of San Callisto were founded in the second century AD and many of the early popes (of whom San Callisto was one) are buried here. There are regular tours in English, and the site also features some well-preserved seventh- and eighth-century frescoes, and the crypt of Santa Cecilia, who was buried here after her martyrdom, before being shifted to the church dedicated to her in Trastevere – a copy of Carlo Maderno's famous statue marks the spot.

Mausoleo delle Fosse Ardeatine

Mon–Fri 8.15am–3.30pm, Sat & Sun 8.15am–5pm; free. This is a catacomb of a different kind, ten minutes' walk from San Callisto, close by the #218 bus stop, where a site remembers the massacre of over 300 civilians during the Nazi occupation of Rome, after the Resistance had ambushed and killed 32 soldiers in the centre of the city. The Nazis exacted a harsh vengeance, killing ten civilians for every dead German, burying the bodies here and then exploding mines to cover up their crime. The bodies were dug up after the war and reinterred in the mausoleum here.

Catacombs of San Sebastiano

Via Appia Antica 136. Mon–Sat 9am–noon & 2.30–5pm. €5. These catacombs are situated under a much-renovated basilica that was originally built by Constantine on the spot where the bodies of the apostles Peter and Paul are said to have been laid for a time. Half-hour tours take in paintings of doves and fish, a contemporary carved oil lamp and inscriptions dating the tombs themselves. The most striking features, however, are not Christian at all, but three pagan tombs (one painted, two stuccoed) discovered when archeologists were burrowing beneath the floor of the basilica upstairs. Just above here, Constantine is said to have raised his chapel to Peter and Paul, and although St Peter was later removed to the Vatican and St Paul to San Paolo fuori le Mura, the graffiti above records the fact that this was indeed, albeit temporarily, where the two Apostles' remains rested.

The Circus of Maxentius

Daily 9am–1pm; €2.60. A couple of hundred metres further on from the San Sebastiano catacombs, the group of brick ruins trailing off into the fields to the left are the remains of the Villa and Circus of Maxentius, a large complex built by the emperor in the early fourth century AD before his defeat by Constantine. It's a clear, long oval of grass, similar to the Circus Maximus (see p.114), but slightly better preserved and in a more bucolic location – making it a fantastic place to eat a picnic, lolling around in the grass or perching on the ruins.

▲ PALAZZO DELLA CIVILITA, EUR

The Tomb of Cecilia Metella and beyond

Tues–Sun 9am–4.30pm; €2, €6 including Terme di Caracalla and Villa dei Quintilli. Further along the Via Appia, this circular tomb dates from the Augustan period, and converted into a castle in the fourteenth century. Known as "Capo di Bove" for the bulls on the frieze around it, the tomb itself, a huge brick-built drum, is little more than a large pigeon coop these days; various fragments and finds are littered around the adjacent, later courtyards, and down below you can see what's left of an ancient lava flow from thousands of years earlier.

EUR

Main piazzas at south end of Via Cristoforo Colombo. Take bus #714 from Termini or metro line B. The EUR district (pronounced "eh-oor") was planned by Mussolini for the 1942 Esposizione Universale Roma, but not finished until well after the war. It's not so much a neighbourhood as a statement in stone: its monumental fascist architecture and grand processional boulevards recall Imperial Rome (especially the Palazzo della Civilità or "Square Colosseum"). But overall it's a pretty strange and soulless place, something of a white elephant despite the busy offices and shops. Apart from the architecture, EUR's main attraction is its museums, the most interesting of which is the **Museo della Civiltà Romana**, Piazza Agnelli 10 (Tues–Sat 9am–2pm, Sun 9am–1.30pm; €6.50, €8.50 including planetarium). Among numerous ancient Roman finds, this has a large model of the fourth-century city that's perfect for setting the rest of the city in context. The museum now incorporates the city's new **Planetario e Museo Astronomico** – though this is no great shakes, especially if you don't speak Italian.

Shops

Volpetti

Via Marmorata 47. It's worth seeking out this Testaccio deli, truly one of Rome's very best, with a fantastic selection of cold meats, cheeses and, well, just about everything.

Cafés and snacks

Palombini

Piazzale Adenauer 12. Great EUR café whose outside terrace and large interior are a haven amidst EUR's brutal boulevards. Appropriately housed on the ground floor of EUR's official "restaurant building", it's a café, *tabacchi* and wine shop all rolled into one, and serves excellent cakes and sandwiches.

Volpetti Piu

Via A. Volta 8. Mon–Sat 11am–9pm. *Tavola calda* that's attached to the famous deli a few doors down. Great pizza, *supplì*, chicken, deep-fried veg and much more.

Restaurants

Augustarello

Via G. Branca 98 ☎06.574.6585. Mon–Sat noon–3.30pm & 7.30–11.30pm. Moderately priced Testaccio establishment serving genuine Roman cuisine in an old-fashioned atmosphere. A good place to come if you appreciate oxtail and sweetbreads, although even strict vegetarians can find good choices.

Checchino dal 1887

Via Monte Testaccio 30 ☎06.574.6318. Tues–Sat noon–3pm & 8–11.30pm. A historic symbol of Testaccio cookery, with an excellent wine cellar, too. Expensive, but worth it for its rustic atmosphere and excellent menu of authentic Roman meat and offal dishes.

Felice

Via Mastro Giorgio 29 ☎06.574.6800. Mon–Sat 12.30–2.45pm & 8–10.30pm. Don't be put off by the "riservato" signs on the tables – the owner likes to "select" his customers. Smile and make Felice understand that you're hungry and fond of Roman cooking. Try *bucatini cacio e pepe* or lamb, and, in winter, artichokes.

Da Remo

Piazza Santa Maria Liberatrice 44 ☎06.574.6270. Mon–Sat 7.30pm–1am. *Remo* is the best kind of pizzeria: usually

▼ VOLPETTI

▲ DA REMO

crowded with locals, very basic, and serving the thinnest, crispiest Roman pizza you'll find. It's also worth trying the heavenly bruschette and other snacks like *supplì* and *fior di zucca*. Perfect pre-clubbing food – and very cheap.

Tuttifrutti

Via Luca della Robbia 3a ⓣ06.575.7902. Tues–Sun 7.30–11.55pm. This Testaccio favourite is pretty much the perfect restaurant – family-run, with good food, decent prices and lots of customers. The menu changes daily, and offers interesting variations on traditional Roman dishes. Recommended.

Bars

Caffè Emporio

Piazza dell'Emporio 2, ⓦwww.caffemporio.com. Daily 4pm-2am. Just steps from the Tiber, this revamped lounge-bar draws an ultra-hip crowd. Plenty of beers on tap and lots of distilled liquors.

Oasi della Birra

Piazza Testaccio 41. Mon–Sat 7.30pm–1am. Unassumingly situated under a Piazza Testaccio wine bar, the cosy basement rooms here house an international selection of beers that rivals anywhere in the world – 500 in all, and with a ton of wine to choose from as well. You can eat generously assembled plates of cheese and salami, and a great selection of bruschette and polenta dishes.

On the Rox

Via Galvani 54. Tues–Sat 8pm–4am, Sun 7pm–2am. Around the corner from the nightspots of Via di Monte Testaccio, and bang in the heart of the Via Galvani strip of night-time joints, this is as convivial a bar as you could imagine, run by a couple of Danes.

Clubs and venues

Akab/Cave

Via Monte Testaccio 69 ⓣ06.5740.4485. Metro B Piramide or bus #23, 30, 75, 95, 280, 716, 719 or Tram #3. Thurs–Sun 11pm–4.30am.

Danceclub built into an old carpenter's shop on two levels, one on ground level, the other a cavelike room below. *Akab's* biggest night is Tuesday's "L-Ektrica" party.

L'Alibi

Via Monte Testaccio 44 ⓣ06.574.3448. Free admission Tues–Thurs, Fri €10, Sat €15, including drink. Predominantly – but by no means exclusively – male venue that's one of Rome's oldest and best gay clubs. Downstairs there's a multi-room cellar disco and upstairs an open-air bar. The big terrace is perfect during the warm months.

Alpheus

Via del Commercio 36 ⓣ06.574.7826, ⓦwww.alpheus.it. Metro B Piramide or bus #23, 769, 770. Tues–Sun 10pm–4.30am. Housed in an ex-factory off Via Ostiense, a little way beyond Testaccio, the Alpheus has space for three simultaneous events – usually a disco, concert and exhibition or piece of theatre. Saturday is Gorgeous, a gay night.

Casa del Jazz

Viale di Porta Ardeatina 55 ⓣ06.704.731, ⓦwww.casajazz.it. Metro #B to Piramide or bus #714. Sponsored by the city, and very much the project of jazz-loving mayor Walter Veltroni, this converted villa in leafy surroundings is the ultimate jazz-lovers' complex, with a book and CD store and restaurant, recording studios and a 150-seat auditorium that hosts gigs most nights of the week. Admission €5–10.

Fake

Via di Monte Testaccio 64 ⓣ06.4544.7627. Wed–Sun 11.30pm–4am. International DJs spin R&B, hip-hop and electronica in this stark club built under a mountain of ancient terracotta amphorae.

Goa

Via Libetta 13 ⓣ06.574.8277. Metro B Garbatella or Bus #29, 769, 770. Tues & Thurs–Sat 11pm–5am. Long-running Ostiense club near the Basilica San Paolo that was opened by famous local DJ Giancarlino, and plays techno, house and drum & bass. *Goa* has an ethnic feel, with incense and a shop selling handmade items. There are sofas to help you recover after high-energy dancing.

Rashomon

Via degli Argonauti 16 ⓣ347.340.5710, ⓦwww.myspace.com/rashomonclub. Wed–Sun 11pm–5am. Minimalist decor meets industrial design in this live music and electronica venue. The best night is their Saturday "Loaded" party, blending house, disco and techno.

Villaggio Globale

Lungotevere Testaccio 22 ⓣ06.575.7233. Bus #95, 170, 719, 781. Winter months only; opening hours depend on events. Situated in the old slaughterhouse along the river, the "global village" has something on almost every night, whether it's world music, indie rock or avant-garde performance art, in its *Spazio Boario*. Closed Aug.

The Quirinale, Termini and around

Of the hills that rise up on the eastern side of the centre of Rome, the Quirinale is perhaps the most appealing. It was the first to be properly developed, when, in the late sixteenth century, the papacy relocated to the Palazzo del Quirinale (now the residence of the Italian president) and those who could afford it moved up to the higher ground from the malarial city centre. The district holds some of the city's most compelling sights, including the enormous Palazzo Barberini, home of some of the best of Rome's art and, just beyond, the Palazzo Massimo, where a good deal of the city's ancient treasure is on display. This area, around Stazione Termini, is also where you might end up staying, as it is home to a good portion of the city's hotels. Beyond here, just outside the city centre, Via Nomentana holds a couple of churches – Sant'Agnese fuori le Mura and Santa Costanza – that are well worth making the trip out to; and the district of San Lorenzo forms a hub for the city's students and a handful of clubs and restaurants.

Piazza Barberini

At the top end of the busy shopping street of Via del Tritone, Piazza Barberini is centred around Bernini's **Fontana del Tritone**, whose god of the sea gushes a high jet of water from a conch shell. Traditionally, this was the Barberini family's quarter of the city, and works by Bernini in their honour – they were the sculptor's greatest patrons – are thick on the ground around here. He finished the Tritone fountain in 1644, going on shortly after to design the **Fontana delle Api** (Fountain of the Bees) across the road at the bottom end of Via Veneto – a smaller, quirkier work, with a broad scallop shell studded with bees, the symbol of the Barberinis.

Santa Maria della Concezione

Via Veneto 27. Daily 9am–noon & 3–6pm; donation expected for the cemetery. The church of Santa Maria della Concezione was

▲ FONTANA DEL TRITONE

another Barberini-sponsored project, and although not a particularly distinguished building, it is worth a visit for its ghoulish Capuchin cemetery, erected in 1793 and home to the bones of 4000 monks, set into the walls of a series of chapels – a monument to "Our Sister of Bodily Death", in the words of St Francis. The bones appear in abstract or Christian patterns or as fully clothed skeletons, their faces peering out of their cowls in various twisted expressions of agony – one of the more macabre and bizarre sights of Rome.

Via Veneto

The pricey bars and restaurants lining Via Veneto were once the haunt of Rome's beautiful people, made famous by Fellini's 1960 film *La Dolce Vita*. But they left a long time ago, and the street, despite being home to some of the city's fanciest hotels, has never quite recovered the cachet it had in the sixties and seventies. Nonetheless, its pretty tree-lined aspect, pavement cafés, swanky stores and uniformed hotel bellmen lend it an upmarket European air that is quite unlike anywhere else in the city.

Palazzo Barberini

Via delle Quattro Fontane 13. Tues–Sun 8.30am–7.30pm; €6; apartment tours every 45min. The Palazzo Barberini is home to the **Galleria Nazionale d'Arte Antica** – a rich patchwork of mainly Italian art from the early Renaissance to the late Baroque period. It's a splendid collection, highlighted by works by Titian, El Greco and Caravaggio. But perhaps the most impressive feature of the gallery is the building itself, worked on at

▲ PALAZZO BARBERINI

different times by the most favoured architects of the day – Bernini, Borromini and Maderno. The first floor Gran Salone is dominated by Pietro da Cortona's manic fresco of *The Triumph of Divine Providence*, one of the best examples anywhere of exuberant Baroque trompe l'oeil work – it almost crawls down the walls to meet you. Of the paintings, be sure to see Caravaggio's *Judith Beheading Holofernes*; Fra' Filippo Lippi's warmly maternal *Madonna and Child*, painted in 1437 and introducing background details, notably architecture, into Italian religious painting for the first time; Raphael's beguiling *Fornarina* – a painting of the daughter of a Traveteran baker thought to have been his mistress (Raphael's name appears clearly on the woman's bracelet); Bronzino's rendering of the marvellously erect *Stefano Colonna*; and a portrait of *Henry VIII* by Hans Holbein. Finally you can visit the Barberini apartments on regular guided tours, and it's just about worth it for the glimpse you get of Borromini's staircase – a spiral riposte to the main Bernini staircase on the other side of the building. However, the

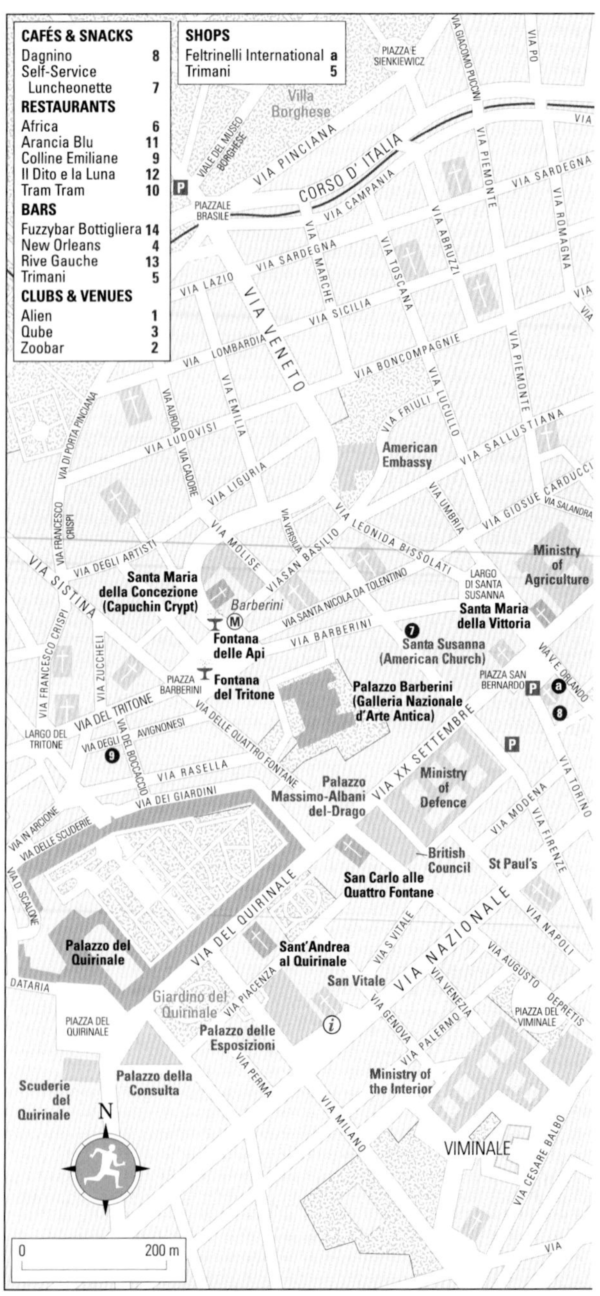

CAFÉS & SNACKS
Dagnino 8
Self-Service Luncheonette 7
RESTAURANTS
Africa 6
Arancia Blu 11
Colline Emiliane 9
Il Dito e la Luna 12
Tram Tram 10
BARS
Fuzzybar Bottigliera 14
New Orleans 4
Rive Gauche 13
Trimani 5
CLUBS & VENUES
Alien 1
Qube 3
Zoobar 2
SHOPS
Feltrinelli International a
Trimani 5
Villa Borghese
Via Pinciana
Corso d'Italia
Via Veneto
American Embassy
Santa Maria della Concezione (Capuchin Crypt)
Barberini
Fontana delle Api
Fontana del Tritone
Piazza Barberini
Palazzo Barberini (Galleria Nazionale d'Arte Antica)
Santa Susanna (American Church)
Santa Maria della Vittoria
Ministry of Agriculture
Palazzo Massimo-Albani del-Drago
Ministry of Defence
British Council
St Paul's
San Carlo alle Quattro Fontane
Sant'Andrea al Quirinale
San Vitale
Palazzo del Quirinale
Giardino del Quirinale
Palazzo delle Esposizioni
Ministry of the Interior
Palazzo della Consulta
Scuderie del Quirinale
Piazza del Quirinale
Via Nazionale
Via del Quirinale
Via XX Settembre
Via Sistina
Via del Tritone
Viminale
0 200 m

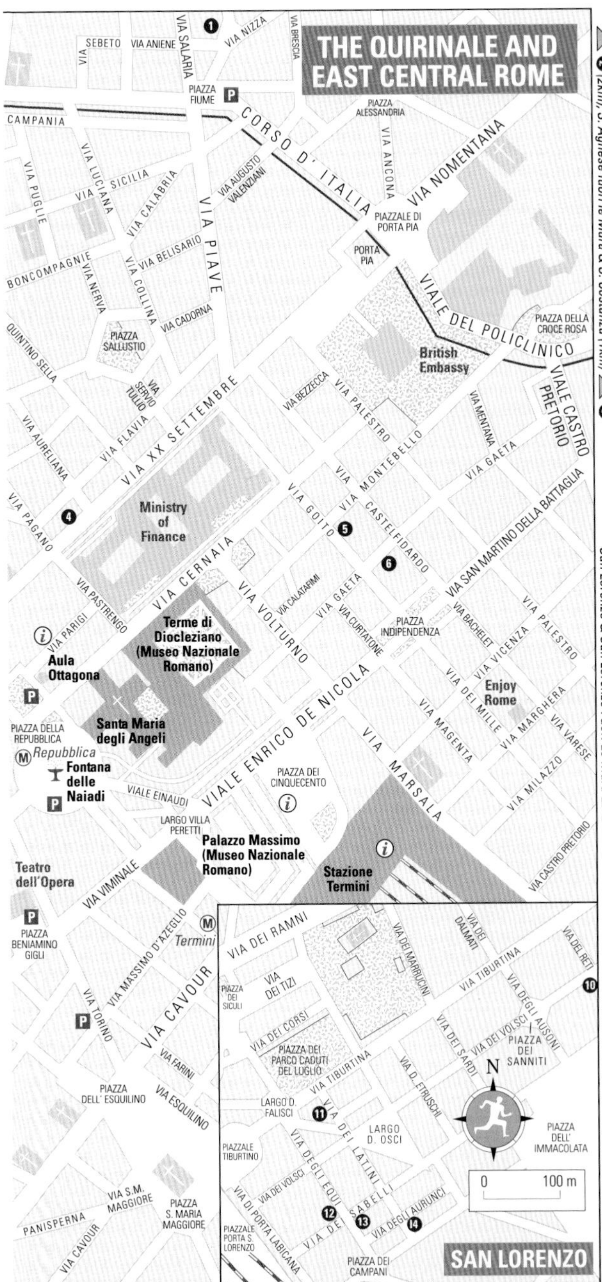

❷ (2km), S. Agnese fuori le Mura & S. Costanza (1km) ❸
San Lorenzo & San Lorenzo Fuori Le Mura

apartments are not spectacularly interesting, so don't bother hanging around if there isn't a tour about to leave.

San Carlo alle Quattro Fontane

Via del Quirinale 23. Mon–Sat 10am–1pm & 3–6pm, Sat noon–1pm. The church of San Carlo alle Quattro Fontane – next door to the four fountains that give it its name – was Borromini's first real design commission. In it he displays all the ingenuity he later became known for, cramming the church elegantly into a tiny and awkwardly shaped site that apparently covers roughly the same surface area as one of the main piers of St Peter's. Tucked in beside the church, the cloister is also squeezed into a tight but elegant oblong, topped with a charming balustrade.

Sant'Andrea al Quirinale

Via del Quirinale. Closed Tues 8am–noon & 4–7pm. A flamboyant building that Bernini planned as a kind of flat oval shape to fit into its wide but shallow site. Like San Carlo up the road, it's unusual and ingenious inside, and was apparently the church that Bernini himself was most proud of, its wide, elliptical nave cleverly made into a grand space despite its relatively small size. Once you've taken this in, for a €1 fee you can visit the sacristy, whose frescoes are similarly artful, with cherubs pulling aside painted drapery to let in light from mock windows, and the upstairs rooms of St Stanislaus Kostka, where the Polish saint lived (and died) in 1568. The rooms have changed quite a lot since then, with paintings by the Jesuit artist Andrea Pozzo illustrating the life of the saint and culminating in a chapel that focuses on a disturbingly lifelike painted statue of Stanislaus lying on his deathbed.

▼ ONE OF THE QUATTRO FONTANE

Palazzo del Quirinale

Piazza del Quirinale. Sun 8.30am–noon; €5; www.quirinale.it. Opposite the church is the featureless wall of the Palazzo del Quirinale, a sixteenth-century structure that was the official summer residence of the popes until Unification, when it became the royal palace. It's now the home of Italy's president (a largely ceremonial role) and its views stretch right across the centre of Rome. The main feature of the piazza outside is the huge statue of the Dioscuri, or Castor and Pollux: massive five-metre-tall Roman copies of classical Greek statues, brought here by Pope Sixtus V in the early sixteenth century to embellish the square – part of the pope's attempts to dignify and beautify the city with many large, vista-laden squares and long, straight avenues. Inside, the palace is well worth a visit if you're in town on a

Sunday, with some spectacular rooms glorifying Pope Paul V among others, worked on by seventeenth-century luminaries like Carlo Maderno and Pietro da Cortona, and a fragment of Melozzo da Forlì's fifteenth-century fresco of Christ, painted for the apse of Santi Apostoli – the rest is in the Vatican (see p.175).

Via XX Settembre

Via XX Settembre spears out to the Aurelian Wall from Via del Quirinale and was the route by which troops entered the city on September 20, 1870 – the place where they breached the wall is marked with a column. It's not Rome's most appealing thoroughfare by any means, flanked by the deliberately faceless bureaucracies of the national government, erected after Unification. However, halfway down the Fontana dell'Acqua Felice is worth a look: it focuses on a massive, bearded figure of Moses playfully fronted by four basking lions, and marks the end of the Acqua Felice aqueduct, part of Pope Sixtus V's late-sixteenth-century attempts to spruce up the city centre with large-scale public works.

Santa Maria della Vittoria

Via XX Settembre 17. Daily 7am–noon & 3.30–7pm. While its interior is one of the most elaborate examples of Baroque decoration in Rome, Santa Maria della Vittoria's best-known feature is Bernini's carving of the *Ecstasy of St Theresa of Avila*, the centrepiece of the sepulchral chapel of Cardinal Cornaro. St Theresa is one of the Catholic Church's most enduring mystics, and Bernini's sculpture records the moment when, in 1537, she had a vision of an angel piercing her heart with a dart. It's a very Baroque piece of work in the most populist sense – not only is the event quite literally staged, but St Theresa's ecstasy verges on the worldly as she lies back in groaning submission beneath a mass of dishevelled garments and drapery. The Cornaro cardinals are depicted murmuring and nudging each other as they watch the spectacle from theatre boxes.

Via Nazionale

A couple of minutes' walk downhill from the Quirinale Palace, Via Nazionale connects Piazza Venezia and the centre of town with the area around Stazione Termini and the eastern districts beyond. A focus for much development after Unification, its heavy, overbearing buildings were constructed to give Rome some semblance of modern sophistication when it became capital of the new country, but most are now occupied by hotels and relatively bland shops and boutiques.

Piazza della Repubblica

Typical of Rome's nineteenth-century regeneration, Piazza della Repubblica (formerly Piazza Esedra) is a stern and dignified semicircle of buildings that used to be rather dilapidated but is now – with the help of a new and very stylish hotel – once again resurgent. The piazza's arcades make a fine place to stroll, despite the hum of traffic, which roars ceaselessly around the centrepiece of Fontana delle Naiadi, with its languishing nymphs and sea monsters. The piazza's semi-circular shape follows the outline of the Baths of Diocletian, the

▲ PIAZZA DELLA REPUBBLICA

remains of which lie across the piazza (see below).

Santa Maria degli Angeli

Piazza della Repubblica. Mon–Sat 7am–6.30pm, Sun 7am–7.30pm. The church of Santa Maria degli Angeli was built on the ruins of the Baths of Diocletian after a Sicilian priest had a vision of angels here in 1541. It was commissioned by Pope Pius IV and designed by Michelangelo in 1563, a year before his death. Although not Rome's most welcoming church by any means, it gives the best impression of the size and grandeur of the baths complex: the crescent shape of the facade remains from the original caldarium, or hot room, (it had previously been hidden by a newer facing), the large transept was once the tepidarium, or luke-warm room, and eight of its huge pink-granite pillars are originals from the baths. After a couple of centuries of piecemeal adaptation, Luigi Vanvitelli rearranged the interior in 1749, by and large imitating Michelangelo's designs. The monumental entrance to the chapel of St Bruno and the choir stalls and decorations are just some of his modifications. The meridian that strikes diagonally across the floor in the south transept, flanked by representations of the twelve signs of the zodiac, was until 1846 the regulator of time for Romans (now a cannon shot fires daily at noon from the Janiculum Hill).

The Aula Ottagona

Mon–Sat 9am–2pm, Sun 9am–1pm; same ticket as the Museo delle Terme di Diocleaziano – see below. The exit from the church leaves you behind another remnant of the baths, the Aula Ottagona, which contains marble statues taken from the baths of Caracalla and Diocletian, and two remarkable statues of a boxer and athlete from the Quirinale Hill. Excavations underground – accessible by stairs – show the furnaces for heating water for the baths and the foundations of another building from the time of Diocletian. However, at time of writing it was closed.

Museo delle Terme di Diocleziano

Piazza della Repubblica. Tues–Sun 9am–7pm. €7, includes Palazzo Altemps, Palazzo Massimo, Crypta Balbi, valid 3 days. Behind the church of Santa Maria degli Angeli, the huge halls and courtyards of Diocletian's baths have been renovated and they (plus an attached Carthusian monastery) now hold what is probably the least interesting part of the Museo Nazionale Romano – the Museo delle Terme di Diocleziano. The museum's most evocative part is the large cloister of the church whose sides are crammed with statuary, funerary monuments and fragments from all over Rome. The galleries that wrap around the cloister hold a reasonable, if rather academically presented collection of pre-Roman and Roman finds: busts, terracotta statues, armour and weapons found in Roman tombs.

▲ PALAZZO MASSIMO

Palazzo Massimo

Largo di Villa Perretti 1. Tues–Sun 9am–7pm; €7, includes Palazzo Altemps, Terme di Diocleziano, Crypta Balbi, valid 3 days, €4 for the audio guide. The snazzily restored Palazzo Massimo is home to one of the two principal parts of the **Museo Nazionale Romano** (the other is in the Palazzo Altemps) – a superb collection of Greek and Roman antiquities, second only to the Vatican's. As one of the great museums of Rome, there are too many highlights to do it justice here, and there is something worth seeing on every floor. Start at the basement, which has displays of exquisite gold jewellery from the second century AD, and – startlingly – the mummified remains of an 8-year-old girl, along with a fantastic coin collection. The ground floor of the museum is devoted to statuary of the early Empire, including a gallery with an unparalleled selection of unidentified busts found all over Rome – amazing pieces of portraiture, and as vivid a representation of patrician Roman life as you'll find. There are also identifiable faces from the so-called Imperial family – a bronze of Germanicus, a marvellous small bust of Caligula, several representations of Livia, Antonia and Drusus, and a hooded statue of Augustus. On the far side of the courtyard is Greek sculpture, including bronzes of a Hellenistic prince holding a spear and a wounded pugilist at rest. The first-floor gallery has groupings of later Imperial dynasties in roughly chronological order, starting with the Flavian emperors – Vespasian et al – and leading on to Trajan in the next room, who appears with his wife Plotina as Hercules, next to a bust of his cousin Hadrian. The collection continues with the Antonine emperors – Antoninus Pius in a heroic nude pose and, in several busts, flanked by likenesses of his daughter Faustina Minor. Faustina married Antoninus's successor, Marcus Aurelius, who appears in the next room. Further on are the Severans, with the fierce-looking Caracalla looking across past his father Septimus Severus to his brother Geta, whom he later murdered. Finally there's the second floor, which you can only visit on an organised tour, which takes in some of the finest Roman frescoes and mosaics ever found. There is a stunning set of frescoes from the Villa di Livia, depicting an orchard dense with fruit and flowers and patrolled by partridges and doves, wall paintings rescued from what was perhaps the riverside villa of Julia and Agrippa, and mosaics showing naturalistic scenes – sea creatures, people boating – from the so-called Villa di Baccano on Via Cassia, and including four chariot drivers and their horses, so finely crafted that from a distance they look as if they've been painted.

Stazione Termini

Stazione Termini was named after the nearby Baths (Terme) of Diocletian: it's nothing to do with it being the terminus of Rome's rail lines. The building is an ambitious piece of modern architecture that was completed in 1950 and still entirely dominates the streets around with its low-slung, self-consciously futuristic lines. It received a huge and sleek renovation that has converted part of its cavernous ticket hall to retail and restaurant space and upgraded the building in general – making it a nice spot for a browse and a wander, and a marvellous place to catch a train. In front of the station, Piazza dei Cinquecento is a good place to find buses and taxis, but otherwise it and the areas around are pretty much low-life territory, and although not especially dangerous, not a great place to hang around for long either.

Sant'Agnese fuori le Mura

Via Nomentana 364 (main entrance at Via S Agnese 315); take tram #3. Mon 9am–noon, Tues–Sat 9am–noon & 4–6pm, Sun 4–6pm; €5 for the catacombs. At the north end of Via XX Settembre, Via Nomentana leads to the church of Sant'Agnese fuori le Mura, dedicated to the 13-year-old saint who was martyred in Domitian's Stadium (now Piazza Navona) in 303 AD. It was built by Constantine, although, apart from the inevitable Baroque updating, much of the building standing over Agnes' grave was reworked by Pope Honorius I in the seventh century. The apse mosaic is contemporary to Honorius's building, showing Agnes next to the pope, who holds a model of his church, in typical Byzantine fashion. Downstairs, the catacombs that sprawl below the church are among the best preserved and most crowd-free in all of Rome. Indeed, if you only have time for one set of catacombs during your stay (and they really are all very much alike), these are among the best. The custodian also sells little terracotta lamps in the shape of fish, or conventional Roman-style lamps with the "Chi-Rho" sign on – probably the most ancient symbol of Christianity.

Santa Constanza

349 Via Nomentana. Usually open the same hours as Sant'Agnese; free. Right next door to Sant'Agnese, the church of Santa Constanza illustrates the transition from the pagan to the Christian city better than perhaps any other building in Rome. Built in 350 AD as a mausoleum for Constantia and Helena, the daughters of the Emperor Constantine, it's a

round structure which follows the traditional shape of the great pagan tombs, and the mosaics on the vaulting of its circular ambulatory – fourth-century depictions of vines, leaves and birds – would have been as at home on the floor of a Roman domus as in a Christian church. Unfortunately, the porphyry sarcophagus of Santa Constanza herself has been moved to the Vatican, and what you see in the church is a plaster copy.

San Lorenzo fuori le Mura

Piazzale del Verano. Daily: summer 7am–noon & 4–7.30pm; winter closes 5.30pm. The student neighbourhood of San Lorenzo, behind Termini, is home to the church of San Lorenzo fuori le Mura, one of the seven great pilgrimage churches of Rome, and a typical Roman basilica, fronted by a columned portico and with a lovely twelfth-century cloister to its side. The original church here was built by Constantine over the site of St Lawrence's martyrdom – the saint was reputedly burned to death on a gridiron, halfway through his ordeal apparently uttering the immortal words, "Turn me, I am done on this side." Because of its proximity to Rome's railyards, the church was bombed heavily during World War II, but it has been rebuilt with sensitivity, and remains much as it was originally. Inside there are features from all periods: a Cosmati floor, thirteenth-century pulpits and a paschal candlestick. The mosaic on the inside of the triumphal arch is a sixth-century depiction of the founder offering his church to Christ. The catacombs below (currently closed for restoration) are where St Lawrence was apparently buried – when open, a dank path leads to the pillars of Constantine's original structure. There's also a Romanesque cloister with a well-tended garden.

Shops

Feltrinelli International

Via Emanuele Orlando 84 ☎06.482.7878. Mon–Sat 9am–8pm,

▼ SAN LORENZO FUORI LE MURA

Sun 10.30am–1.30pm & 4–8pm. This international branch of the nationwide chain has an excellent stock of books in English, as well as in French, German, Spanish and Portuguese.

Trimani

Via Goito 20 ☎06.446.9661. One of the city's best wine shops, and handily close to Termini if you want to stock up before heading off to the airport. Also has a wine bar around the corner serving decent food (see opposite).

Cafés and snacks

Dagnino

Galleria Esedra, Via E. Orlando 75. Daily 7.30am–10.30pm. Good for a coffee, snack or light lunch, this long-established Sicilian bakery is a peaceful retreat in the Termini area, with tables outside in this small shopping arcade.

Self-Service Luncheonette

Salita di San Nicola da Tolentino 19/21. Mon–Sat 8am–3pm. Great food served cafeteria-style – a lunchtime hit with local office-workers and hungry tourist alike.

Restaurants

Africa

Via Gaeta 26 ☎06.494.1077. Tues–Sun noon–3.30pm & 7.30–11pm. Arguably the city's most interesting ethnic food – Eritrean – and a culinary sign of the city's recently arrived populations from the horn of Africa.

Arancia Blu

Via dei Latini 57 ☎06.445.4105. Daily 8.30pm–midnight. This ultra-trendy San Lorenzo vegetarian restaurant reckons itself a cut above. But in a city with very few vegetarians it doesn't have to try too hard. Good food using fresh ingredients in an imaginative fashion: specialities include various stuffed veggie pasta dishes – ravioli, cannelloni and the like – and decent salads.

Colline Emiliane

Via degli Avignonesi 22 ☎06.481.7538. Tues–Sat 12.45–2.45pm & 7.30–10.45pm, Sun 12.45–2.45pm only, closed Mon. Many Italians consider the cuisine of the Emilia Romagna region to be the country's best. Try it for yourself, lovingly prepared by a family, ironically, from Marche. Located just down from Piazza Barberini, on a quiet backstreet parallel to Via del Tritone. Moderate prices.

Il Dito e la Luna

Via dei Sabelli 49/51 ☎06.494.0726. Creative Sicilian cuisine in a bistro-like San Lorenzo restaurant popular with thirty-something Romans. Go early, as they tend to run out of dishes.

Tram Tram

Via dei Reti 44–46 ☎06.490.416. Tues–Sun noon–3pm & 7.30pm–midnight. Despite the grungy location, this trendy, animated San Lorenzo restaurant is a cosy spot, and serves good Pugliese pasta dishes, seafood and unusual salads. Reservations are recommended. There's also a bar if you want to carry on drinking after dinner.

Bars

Fuzzybar Bottigliera

Via degli Aurunci 6/8. Mon 12.30–3pm, Tue–Fri 12.30–3pm & 6.30pm–2am, Sat 6.30pm–2am. The best of

▲ TRAM TRAM

San Lorenzo's many new wine bars, and a thoroughly unpretentious place to sample Italian wines. Happy hour is heavily frequented by the neighbourhood's university students.

Rive Gauche

Via dei Sabelli 43. Daily 7pm–3am. The San Lorenzo district's smoky, noisy, cavernous evocation of intellectual Left Bank Paris – more or less. Lots of Irish beer choices and snacks to sustain your night of drinking. Happy Hour till 9pm.

Trimani

Via Cernaia. Classy wine bar that's good for a lunchtime tipple or some gastronomic indulgence. You'll spend around €15 to sample a range of good-quality cheeses and cured pork, or soup and salad, with a glass of wine.

Clubs and venues

Alien

Via Velletri 13/19 ⓣ06.841.2212, ⓦwww.aliendisco.it. Bus #63. Tues–Sun 11pm–4am. The two halls here have starkly contrasting decor, one redolent of maharaja plushness, the other done up in modernistic black and white, and the music is a mixture of house and techno. It also has a summer venue, *Alien 2 Mare*, at the nearby seaside resort of Fregene, at Piazzale Fregene 5 (ⓣ06.6656.4761).

Qube

Via Portonaccio 212 ⓣ06.4358.7454. Metro B Tiburtina or Bus #409. Thurs–Sat 10.30pm–4am. Big Tiburtina club hosting a variety of different nights each week, including live music. Not the most original for music but its Friday gay and drag night – *Mucca Assassina* ("Killer Cow") – draws a big crowd.

Zoobar

Via Bencivenga 1 ⓣ339.272.7995 Bus #23, 30, 75, 95, 170, 280, 716, 781 or Tram #3. Thurs–Sat 11pm–3.30am. This club is now in a new location out near Nomentana station but still plays a wide range of music – oldies, ska, funk, R&B and much more.

▼ TRIMANI

Monti and San Giovanni

The Monti quarter is named after the two hills it encompasses: the Esquiline, the city's highest and largest, once the most fashionable residential quarter of ancient Rome; and the Viminale, the smallest – home to the Interior Ministry and not much else. Overall it's an appealing district, with cobbled streets and cosy bars and restaurants mixed in with the busy avenues and ponderous nineteenth-century buildings of the Via Cavour and Via Merulana – the main spines of the area. Most visitors encounter this part of town at some point – it's home to key sights like Nero's Domus Aurea and the basilica of Santa Maria Maggiore, and near to the many hotels around Termini station. Also, just to the south and east, are three of Rome's most interesting churches: triple-layered San Clemente, the complex of San Giovanni in Laterano – which gives its name to the surrounding San Giovanni district – and Santa Croce in Gerusalemme.

San Pietro in Vincoli

Daily 8am–12.30pm & 3–7pm. San Pietro in Vincoli is one of Rome's most delightfully plain churches. It was built to house an important relic, the two sets of chains (*vincoli*) that bound St Peter when imprisoned in Jerusalem and held him in the Mammertime Prison, which miraculously fused together when they were brought in contact with each other. The chains can still be seen in the *confessio* beneath the high altar, but most people come for the tomb of Pope Julius II at the far end of the southern aisle. The aisle occupied Michelangelo on and off for much of his career and was the cause of many a dispute with Julius and his successors. He reluctantly gave it up to paint the Sistine Chapel – the only statues that he managed to complete are the *Moses*, *Leah and Rachel*, which remain here, and two *Dying Slaves*, which are now in the Louvre. The figures are among the artist's most captivating works, especially Moses: because of a medieval mistranslation of scripture, he is depicted with satyr's horns

▲ THE CHAINS OF ST PETER, SAN PIETRO IN VINCOLI

instead of the "radiance of the Lord" that Exodus tells us shone around his head. Nonetheless this powerful statue is so lifelike that Michelangelo is alleged to have struck its knee with his hammer and shouted "Speak, damn you!"

Santa Pudenziana

Daily 8am–noon & 4–6pm. Dedicated to St Prassede's supposed sister, this church was for many years believed to have been built on the site where St Peter lived and worshipped and once housed two relics: the chair that St Peter used as his throne and the table at which he said Mass, though both have long gone – to the Vatican and the Lateran Palace respectively. However, it still has one feature of ancient origin – its superb fifth-century apse mosaics, fluid and beautiful works centring on a golden enthroned Christ surrounded by the apostles.

Santa Maria Maggiore

Daily 7am–7pm. Museum daily 9.30am–6.30pm; €4. One of the city's four patriarchal basilicas (the others are San Giovanni in Laterano, San Paolo fuori le Mura and St Peter's), Santa Maria Maggiore is a blend of different architectural eras and includes one of Rome's best-preserved Byzantine interiors – a fact belied by its dull eighteenth-century exterior. It was originally built during the fifth century after the Virgin Mary appeared to Pope Liberius in a dream on the night of August 4, 352 AD. She told him to erect a church in her honour on the Esquiline Hill – the exact spot would be marked the next morning by newly fallen snow outlining the plan of the church. Despite it being the height of summer, Liberius duly found the miraculous blueprint and the event is commemorated every year on August 5, when at midday mass white rose petals are showered on the congregation from the ceiling, and at night the fire department operates an artificial snow machine in the piazza in front of the church.

Inside, the **basilica** is fringed on both sides with strikingly well-kept mosaics, most of which date from the time of Pope Sixtus III and recount incidents from the Old Testament. The chapel in the right transept holds the elaborate tomb of Sixtus V – another, less famous Sistine Chapel, decorated with frescoes and stucco reliefs showing events from his reign. Outside is the tomb of the Bernini family; opposite, the Pauline Chapel is home to the tombs of the Borghese pope, Paul V, and his immediate predecessor Clement VIII. Between the two chapels, the *confessio* contains a kneeling statue of Pope Pius IX, and, beneath it, a reliquary that is said to contain fragments of the crib of Christ. The high altar, above, contains the relics of St Matthew, among other Christian martyrs, but it's the mosaics of the arch that really dazzle, a vivid representation of scenes from the life of Christ. There's a **museum** underneath the basilica (daily 9am–6.30pm; €4), which sports what, even by Roman standards, is a wide variety of relics, and a **loggia** above the main entrance (tours daily at 9am & 1pm, bookable in advance; €3), which has some magnificent mosaics showing Christ among various saints, sitting above four scenes that tell the story of the miracle of the snow.

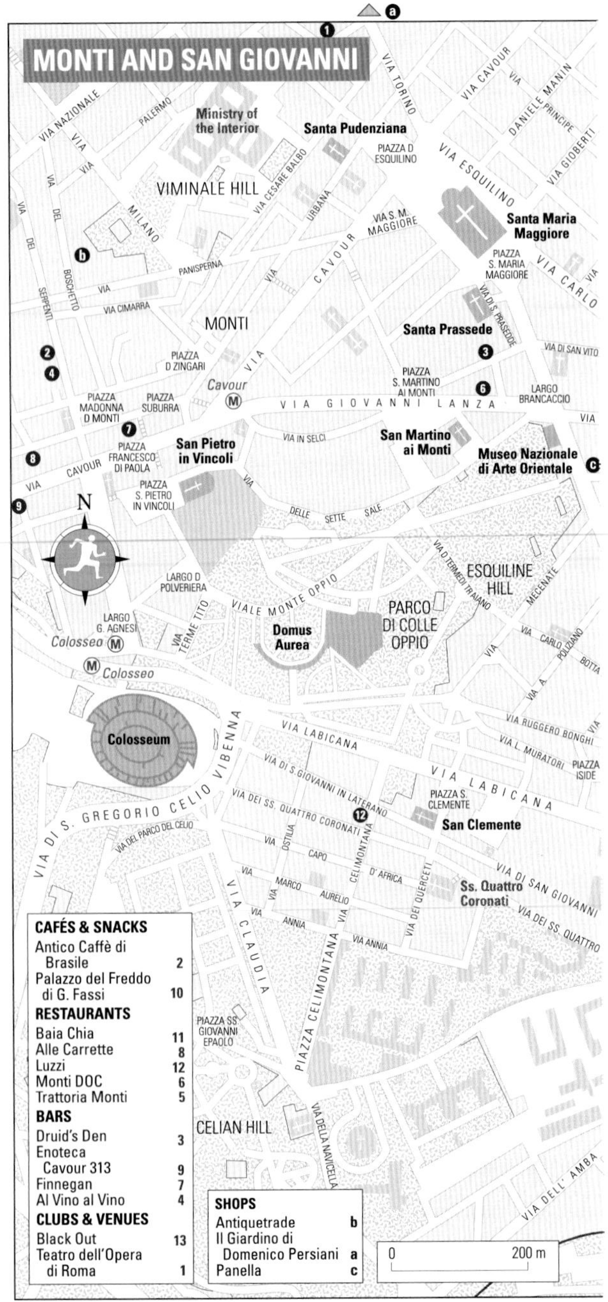
MONTI AND SAN GIOVANNI
Ministry of the Interior
Santa Pudenziana
PIAZZA D ESQUILINO
VIMINALE HILL
Santa Maria Maggiore
PIAZZA S. MARIA MAGGIORE
MONTI
Santa Prassede
PIAZZA D ZINGARI
Cavour
PIAZZA S. MARTINO AI MONTI
LARGO BRANCACCIO
PIAZZA MADONNA D MONTI
PIAZZA SUBURRA
VIA GIOVANNI LANZA
PIAZZA FRANCESCO DI PAOLA
San Pietro in Vincoli
San Martino ai Monti
Museo Nazionale di Arte Orientale
PIAZZA S. PIETRO IN VINCOLI
VIA DELLE SETTE SALE
N
LARGO D POLVERIERA
ESQUILINE HILL
VIALE MONTE OPPIO
PARCO DI COLLE OPPIO
LARGO G. AGNESI
Colosseo
Domus Aurea
Colosseum
VIA LABICANA
VIA DI S. GREGORIO
CELIO VIBENNA
VIA DI S.GIOVANNI IN LATERANO
VIA DEI SS. QUATTRO CORONATI
PIAZZA S. CLEMENTE
San Clemente
VIA CAPO D' AFRICA
VIA MARCO AURELIO
VIA CLAUDIA
Ss. Quattro Coronati
VIA DI SAN GIOVANNI
VIA ANNIA
PIAZZA SS GIOVANNI EPAOLO
PIAZZA CELIMONTANA
CELIAN HILL
VIA DELLA NAVICELLA
VIA DELL' AMBA
VIA NAZIONALE
VIA TORINO
VIA CAVOUR
VIA PRINCIPE
VIA DANIELE MANIN
VIA GIOBERTI
VIA ESQUILINO
VIA S. M. MAGGIORE
VIA CARLO
VIA DI SAN VITO
VIA URBANA
VIA CESARE BALBO
VIA PALERMO
VIA MILANO
VIA PANISPERNA
VIA CIMARRA
VIA DEI SERPENTI
VIA DEL BOSCHETTO
VIA IN SELCI
VIA D TERME DI TRAIANO
VIA MECENATE
VIA TERME TITO
VIA CARLO BOTTA
VIA POLIZIANO
VIA A.
VIA RUGGERO BONGHI
VIA L. MURATORI
PIAZZA ISIDE
VIA DEL PARCO DEL CELIO
VIA OSTILIA
VIA CELIMONTANA
VIA DEI QUERCETI
VIA DEI SS. QUATTRO
CAFÉS & SNACKS
Antico Caffè di Brasile 2
Palazzo del Freddo di G. Fassi 10
RESTAURANTS
Baia Chia 11
Alle Carrette 8
Luzzi 12
Monti DOC 6
Trattoria Monti 5
BARS
Druid's Den 3
Enoteca Cavour 313 9
Finnegan 7
Al Vino al Vino 4
CLUBS & VENUES
Black Out 13
Teatro dell'Opera di Roma 1
SHOPS
Antiquetrade b
Il Giardino di Domenico Persiani a
Panella c
0
200 m

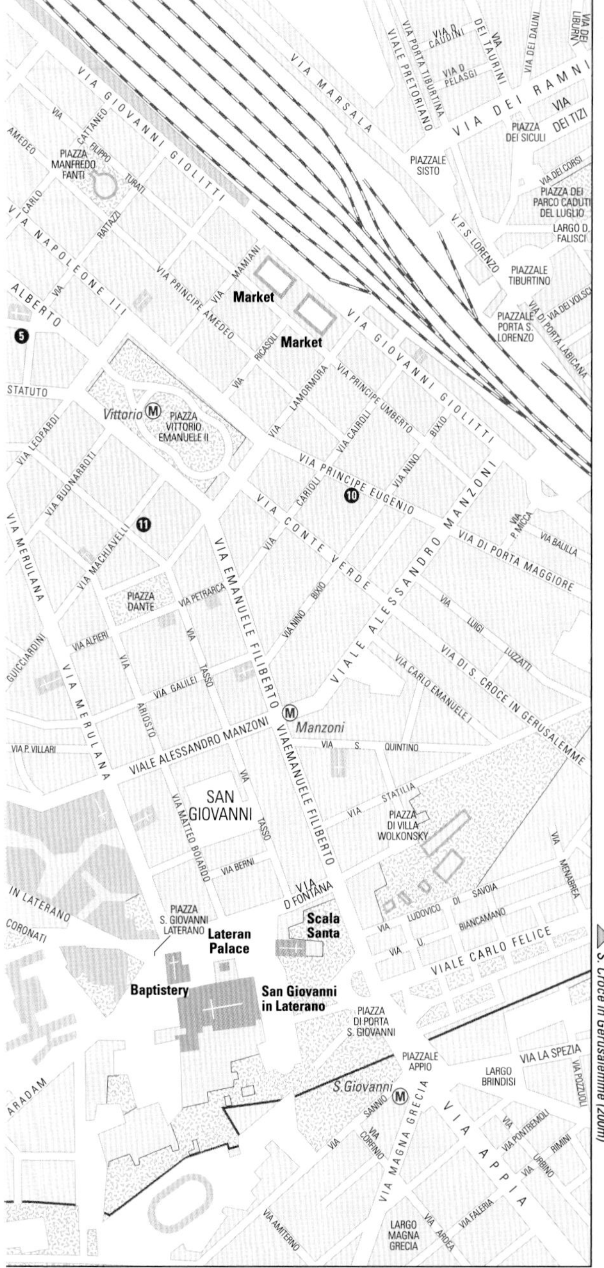
VIA GIOVANNI GIOLITTI
VIA MARSALA
VIALE PRETORIANO
VIA PORTA TIBURTINA
VIA D. CAUDINI
VIA D. PELASGI
VIA DEI TAURINI
VIA DEI DAUNI
VIA DEI LIBURNI
VIA DEI RAMNI
VIA DEI TIZI
PIAZZA DEI SICULI
PIAZZALE SISTO
VIA DEI CORSI
PIAZZA DEI PARCO CADUTI DEL LUGLIO
LARGO D. FALISCI
V. P. S. LORENZO
PIAZZALE TIBURTINO
PIAZZALE PORTA S. LORENZO
VIA DEI VOLSCI
VIA DI PORTA LABICANA
PIAZZA MANFREDO FANTI
VIA CATTANEO
FILIPPO TURATI
VIA AMEDEO
CARLO ALBERTO
VIA NAPOLEONE III
RATTAZZI
VIA PRINCIPE AMEDEO
VIA MAMIANI
Market
Market
VIA RICASOLI
VIA LAMORMORA
VIA PRINCIPE UMBERTO
VIA CAIROLI
BIXIO
STATUTO
Vittorio
PIAZZA VITTORIO EMANUELE II
VIA LEOPARDI
VIA BUONARROTI
VIA PRINCIPE EUGENIO
VIA NINO
CAIROLI
VIA CONTE VERDE
VIA MERULANA
VIA MACHIAVELLI
VIA EMANUELE FILIBERTO
VIALE ALESSANDRO MANZONI
VIA P. MICCA
VIA BALILLA
VIA DI PORTA MAGGIORE
PIAZZA DANTE
VIA PETRARCA
VIA NINO BIXIO
VIA LUIGI LUZZATTI
VIA DI S. CROCE IN GERUSALEMME
VIA CARLO EMANUELE I
GUICCIARDINI
VIA ALFIERI
VIA TASSO
VIA GALILEI
ARIOSTO
Manzoni
VIA P. VILLARI
VIA S. QUINTINO
VIALE ALESSANDRO MANZONI
SAN GIOVANNI
VIA MATTEO BOIARDO
VIA TASSO
VIA BERNI
VIA STATILIA
PIAZZA DI VILLA WOLKONSKY
VIA MENABREA
VIA D. FONTANA
VIA LUDOVICO DI SAVOIA
BIANCAMANO
VIA U.
VIALE CARLO FELICE
IN LATERANO
CORONATI
PIAZZA S. GIOVANNI LATERANO
Lateran Palace
Scala Santa
Baptistery
San Giovanni in Laterano
PIAZZA DI PORTA S. GIOVANNI
PIAZZALE APPIO
LARGO BRINDISI
VIA LA SPEZIA
VIA POZZUOLI
S.Giovanni
VIA SANNIO
VIA CORFINIO
VIA MAGNA GRECIA
VIA APPIA
VIA PONTREMOLI
VIA URBINO
RIMINI
VIA FALERIA
VIA ARDEA
LARGO MAGNA GRECIA
VIA AMITERNO
ARADAM
S. Croce in Gerusalemme (200m)
(200m)

▲ APSE MOSAIC, SANTA PRASSEDE

Santa Prassede

Daily 7am–noon & 4–6.30pm. The ninth-century church of Santa Prassede occupies an ancient site where it's claimed St Prassede harboured Christians on the run from the Roman persecutions. She apparently collected the blood and remains of the martyrs and placed them in a well where she herself was later buried; a red marble disc in the floor of the nave marks the spot. The apse mosaics are the most striking features, particularly those in the Chapel of Saint Zeno, which make it glitter like a jewel-encrusted box.

Museo Nazionale di Arte Orientale

Via Merulana 248. Mon, Wed, Fri & Sat 8.30am–2pm, Tues, Thurs & Sun 8.30am–7.30pm, closed 1st & 3rd Mon of every month; €4. Housed in the imposing Palazzo Brancaccio, the Museo Nazionale di Arte Orientale is a first-rate collection of oriental art. Italy's connection with the Far East goes back to Marco Polo in the thirteenth century, and the quality of this collection of Islamic, Chinese, Indian and Southeast Asian art reflects this long relationship. There are finds dating back to 1500 BC from a necropolis in Pakistan; architectural fragments, art works and jewellery from Tibet, Nepal and Pakistan; a solid collection from China, with predictable Buddhas and vases alongside curiosities such as Han dynasty figures and a large Wei dynasty Buddha with two boddhisatvas; and coins from twelfth century Iran and northwest India.

Piazza Vittorio Emanuele II

Piazza Vittorio Emanuele II lies at the centre of a district which became known as the "quartiere piemontese" when the government located many of its major ministries here after Unification. The arcades of the square, certainly, recall central Turin, as do the solid palatial buildings that surround, but it's more recently become the immigrant quarter of Rome, with a heavy concentration of African, Asian and Middle Eastern shops and restaurants. You'll easily hear a dozen different languages spoken as you pass through, although the open-air **market** that used to surround the piazza has moved a few blocks east to Via Giolitti, between Via Ricasoli and Via Lamarmora, where there are two covered halls, one selling clothes, the other food.

The Domus Aurea

Currently closed for renovation, but occasionally open to the public. Once covering a vast area between the Palatine and Esquiline, Nero's Domus Aurea or "Golden House" was not intended to be a residence at all; rather it was a series of banqueting rooms, small baths, terraces and gardens, facing what at the time was a lake. Rome was used to Nero's excesses, but it had never seen anything like the Golden House before; the vaults were supposed to have been coated in gold leaf, there was hot and cold running water in the baths, and the grounds – which covered a full square mile – held vineyards and game. Nero didn't get to enjoy it for long – he died a couple of years after it was finished – and later emperors were determined to erase it from Rome's cityscape; Vespasian built the Colosseum over the lake and Trajan built his baths on top of the rest of the complex. It was pretty much forgotten until its wall paintings were discovered by Renaissance artists, including Raphael. Inside, the temperature always hovers at around 10°C and this and the almost 100 percent humidity makes it necessary to wear a sweater or jacket even in the middle of summer. Tours can at first be confusing, as you become aware of just how much Trajan set out to obliterate the place – his baths' foundations merge into parts of the palace, and vice versa – but the guide helps you imagine how it once looked. Most spectacular is the domed Octagonal Room, with a hole in the middle, which is supposed to have rotated as the day progressed to emulate the passage of the sun. Elsewhere there are paintings depicting people looking back through windows at the viewer, garlands of flowers and foliage, interspersed with mythical animals and, best of all, a room illustrating Homer's story of Achilles being sent to the island of Skyros disguised as a woman to prevent him being drawn into the Trojan wars.

San Giovanni in Laterano

Daily 7am–6.30pm. Cloisters daily 9am–6pm; €2. The area immediately south and east of the Esquiline Hill is known as San Giovanni, after the great basilica that lies at its heart – the city's cathedral, and the headquarters of the Catholic Church before the creation of the separate Vatican state. There has been a church on this site since the fourth century, and the present building evokes Rome's staggering wealth of history, with a host of features from different periods. The doors to the church were taken from the Roman Curia or Senate House, while the obelisk that stands outside was brought here from Thebes by Constantine and dates from the fifteenth century BC. Inside, the first pillar on the left of the right-hand aisle shows a fragment of Giotto's fresco of Boniface VIII proclaiming the first Holy Year in 1300, a gentle piece with gorgeous colours that's oddly overshadowed by the grandeur of the rest of the building. On the next pillar

▲ SAN GIOVANNI IN LATERANO

along, a more recent monument commemorates Sylvester I, Bishop of Rome during much of Constantine's reign, and incorporates part of his original tomb, said to sweat and rattle its bones when a pope is about to die. The nave itself is lined with eighteenth-century statues of the apostles in flashy Rococo style, each one of which gives a clue as to their identity or manner of death: St Matthew, the tax collector, is shown with coins falling out of a sack; St Bartholomew holds a knife and his own skin (he was flayed alive). At the head of the nave, the heads of St Peter and St Paul, the church's prize relics, are kept secure behind the papal altar, while the baldachino just in front is a splash of Gothic grandeur made by the Tuscan sculptor Giovanni di Stefano in the fourteenth century: it shelters the glassed-over bronze tomb of Martin V – the Colonna pope who was responsible for returning the papacy to Rome from Avignon in 1419.

Outside the church, the cloisters are one of the most pleasing parts of the complex, decorated with early thirteenth-century Cosmati work, while next door is the Lateran Palace, home of the popes in the Middle Ages.

The Baptistry

San Giovanni in Laterano. Daily 7am–12.30pm & 4–7.30pm; free. San Giovanni's baptistry is the oldest surviving in the Christian world – the octagonal structure was built during the fifth century and has been the model for many such buildings since. Oddly, it doesn't really feel its age, although the mosaics in the side chapels and the bronze doors to the chapel on the right, brought here from the Baths of Caracalla, quickly remind you where you are.

The Scala Santa and Sancta Sanctorum

Piazza di San Giovanni in Laterano 14. April–Sept daily 6.15am–noon & 3.30–6.45pm; Oct–March daily 6.15am–noon & 3–6.15pm. The Scala Santa is claimed to be the staircase from Pontius Pilate's house down which Christ walked after his trial. It was said to have been brought to Rome by St Helena and was placed here by Pope Sixtus V. The 28 steps are protected by boards, and the only way you're allowed to climb them is on your knees, which pilgrims do regularly – although there are other staircases either side for the less penitent. At the top, the Sancta Sanctorum holds an ancient (sixth- or seventh-century) painting of Christ said to be the work of an angel, hence its name – acheiropoeton, or "not done by human hands". You can't enter the chapel, and, fittingly perhaps, you can only really get a view of it by kneeling and peering through the grilles.

▲ CLIMBING THE SCALA SANTA

Santi Quattro Coronati

Daily 6.15am–8pm; cloister and San Silvestro chapel Mon–Sat 9.30am–noon & 4.30–6pm, Sun 9–10.40am & 4–5.45pm. Between San Giovanni in Laterano and the Colosseum, the church of Santi Quattro Coronati is dedicated to four soldier martyrs who died because they refused to worship a statue of Aesculapius during the persecutions of Diocletian. Originally built in 1110, its interior feels quiet and ancient, a world away from the crowds around the Colosseum – an atmosphere that is intensified by the pretty cloister, accessed through a door in the north aisle. A convent of Augustinian nuns lives here now, and it's them you sometimes have to ask for the key to get into the chapel of St Sylvester, which contains the oldest extant frescoes in Rome – painted in 1248 and relating the story of how the fourth-century pope cured the emperor Constantine of leprosy and then baptized him. Constantine is shown giving his crown to the pope in a symbolic transfer of power.

San Clemente

Mon–Sat 9am–12.30pm & 3–6pm, Sun 10am–12.30pm & 3–6pm; €5 for the lower church and temple. The church of San Clemente perhaps encapsulates better than any other the continuity of history in Rome – being in fact a conglomeration of three places of worship from three very different eras. The ground-floor church is a superb example of a medieval basilica: its facade and courtyard face east in the archaic fashion, and there are some fine mosaics in the apse and – perhaps the highlight of the main church – some beautiful and vivid fifteenth-century frescoes in the chapel of St Catherine by Masolino. The choir is partitioned off with beautiful white marble slabs bearing the earliest papal insignia in the city, the monogram of Pope John II, who reigned from 533 to 535. Downstairs there's the nave of an earlier church, dating back to 392 AD, and the tomb of Pope St Clement I, to whom the church is dedicated (the third pope after St Peter and said to have been ordained by him). At the eastern end of the fourth-century church, steps lead down to a third level, the remains of a Roman house – a labyrinthine set of rooms that includes a dank Mithraic temple of the late second century. In the temple is a statue of Mithras slaying a bull and the seats upon which the worshippers sat during their ceremonies.

Santa Croce in Gerusalemme

Follow Viale Carlo Felice from San Giovanni in Laterano to Piazza Santa Croce in Gerusalemme (5min walk). Daily 6.45am–7.30pm. Despite its later Renaissance and Baroque adornments, the church of Santa Croce in Gerusalemme feels very ancient, and is supposed to stand on the site of the palace of Constantine's mother St Helena. It houses the relics of the true cross she brought back from Jerusalem, stored in a surreal Mussolini-era chapel up some steps at the end of the left aisle. The church's Renaissance apse frescoes show the discovery of the fragments of the cross and are very fine indeed – a beautiful, naturalistic scene depicting trees and mountains and St Helena at the centre.

▲ COFFEE BEANS, ANTICO CAFFÈ DI BRASILE

Steps behind lead down to the original level of Helena's house – now a chapel dedicated to the saint and decorated with Renaissance mosaics.

Shops

Antiquetrade

Via del Boschetto 4 ☎06.4782.5539. Antiques of all kinds and eras can turn up here, although the speciality is fine old prints. Not especially cheap, but a satisfying place to browse through Rome's history firsthand.

Il Giardino di Domenico Persiani

Via Torino 92 ☎06.488.3886. A quiet garden filled to the brim with all sorts of ceramic creations. Everything from glazed tiles to full-sized copies of famous statuary. Pieces are made to order.

Panella

Via Merulana 54 ☎06.487.2435, Mon–Fri 8am–1.30pm & 5–8pm, Sat 8am–1.30pm & 4.30–8pm, Sun 8.30am–1.30pm. Fantastic bakery that is a shrine to the art of bread-making; makes it own pasta too.

Cafés and snacks

Antico Caffè di Brasile

Via dei Serpenti 23. Mon–Sat 6am–8.30pm, Sun 7am–2pm. Reliable old Monti stand-by that has been selling great coffee, snacks and cakes for around a century, with a handful of seats and tables at the back should you want to take the weight off.

Palazzo del Freddo di Giovanni Fassi

Via Principe Eugenio 65. Tues–Sun noon–midnight. A wonderful, airy 1920s ice cream parlour. Brilliant fruit ice creams and great *frullati* too.

Restaurants

Baia Chia

Via Machiavelli 5 ☎06.679.2770. Daily 8pm–midnight. Moderately priced Sardinian restaurant that does great fish dishes – try the fish baked in salt. Excellent desserts too.

Alle Carrette

Via Madonna dei Monti 95 ☎06.679.2770. Daily 8pm–midnight. Inexpensive large pizzeria just up Via Cavour that normally has long queues for the exceptional pizza and phenomenal desserts they serve here.

Luzzi

Via San Giovanni in Laterano 88 ☎06.709.6332. Noon–3pm & 7pm–midnight. Closed Wed. Midway between San Giovanni in Laterano and the Colosseum, this bustling restaurant is a good choice amid the tourist joints of the neighbourhood. The food is hearty and simple, if unspectacular, there's outside seating and it's extremely cheap – *secondi* go for €6–9. There are pizzas too, but only in the evening.

Monti DOC

Via G. Lanza 93 ☎06.487.2696. Tues–Fri 1–3.30pm & 7pm–1am, Sat & Sun 7pm–1am. Comfortable Santa Maria Maggiore neighbourhood wine bar, with a comprehensive wine list and nice food: cold cuts and cheese, soups, quiches, salads and pastas, including some good veggie dishes, chalked on the blackboard daily.

Trattoria Monti

Via di San Vito 13a ☎06.446.6573. Tues–Sun noon–3pm & 7–11pm. Small family-run restaurant that specialises in the cuisine of the Marche region, which means hearty food from a short menu. As homely and friendly a restaurant as you could want – something places in this neighbourhood often aren't.

Bars

Druid's Den

Via San Martino ai Monti 28. Mon–Thurs & Sun 6pm–1.30am, Fri & Sat 6pm–3am. Appealing Irish pub near Santa Maria Maggiore with a genuine Celtic feel (and owners). It has a mixed expat/Italian clientele, and is not just for the homesick. Cheap and lively, with occasional impromptu music.

Enoteca Cavour 313

Via Cavour 313. Mon–Sat 12.30–2.30pm & 7.30pm–12.30am. A lovely old wine bar that makes a handy retreat after seeing the ancient sites. Lots of wines and delicious (though not cheap) snacks and salads.

Finnegan

Via Leonina 66. Decent Irish pub with live football on TV, pool, and a friendly ex-pat crowd. Seating outside, too, on this bustling Monti street.

Al Vino al Vino

Via dei Serpenti 19. Daily 11.30am–1.30pm & 5pm–12.30am. The Monti district's most happening street is home to this seriously good wine bar with a choice of over 500 labels, many by the glass. Snacks are generally Sicilian specialities.

▼ ENOTECA CAVOUR 313

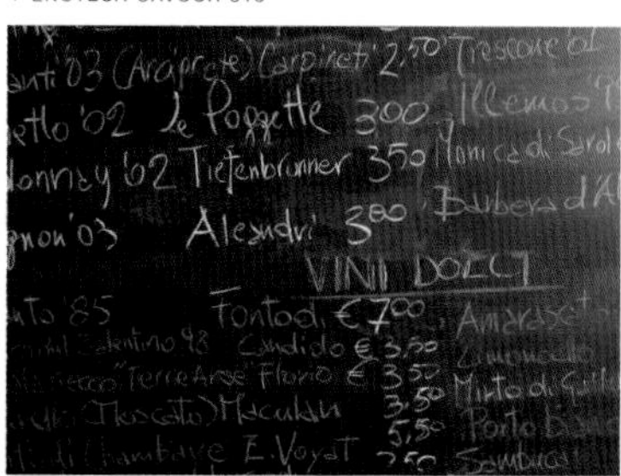

Clubs and venues

Black Out

Via Saturnia 18 ⓣ06.7049.6791. Metro A San Giovanni or Re di Roma or Bus #85. Thurs–Sat 11pm–4am. Murky, industrial San Giovanni club that plays punk, heavy metal and Goth music, with occasional gigs by US and UK bands. Closed in summer.

Teatro dell'Opera di Roma

Piazza Beniamino Gigli 1 ⓣ06.481.601, ⓦwww.operaroma.it. Box office Mon–Sat 9am–5pm, Sun 9am–1.30pm. Nobody compares it to La Scala, but cheap tickets are a lot easier to come by at Rome's opera and ballet venue – they start at around €20 for opera, less for ballet – and important artists sometimes perform here. If you buy the very cheapest tickets, bring some high-powered binoculars: you'll need them in order to see anything at all.

The Villa Borghese and north of the centre

During the Renaissance, the market gardens and olive groves north of the city walls were appropriated as summer estates by Rome's wealthy elite, particularly those affiliated to the papal court. One of the most notable of these estates, the Villa Borghese, was the summer playground of the Borghese family and is now a public park and home to two of Rome's best museums: the unmissable Galleria Borghese, housing a resplendent art collection, and the Villa Giulia, built by Pope Julius III for his summer repose and now the National Etruscan Museum. North of Villa Borghese stretch Rome's nineteenth- and early twentieth-century residential districts – not of much interest in themselves except perhaps for the Mussolini-era Foro Italico, which is worth visiting either to see Roma or Lazio play at its Olympic Stadium, or simply to wander around the grandiose statues, avenues and mosaics.

Villa Borghese

The vast green expanse of the Villa Borghese – accessible by way of the Pincio Gardens, or from entrances at the top of Via Veneto or Via Pinciana – is about as near as you can get to peace in the city centre. The beautiful landscaped grounds and palace were designed for Cardinal Scipione Borghese in 1605 and bought by the city at the turn of the nineteenth century. There are plenty of attractions for those who want to do more than just stroll or sunbathe: a tiny boating lake, a zoo and some of the city's finest museums (see p.148). Bike rental is available from the corner of Viale Obelisco and Viale Orologio and other places in the Pincio Gardens (€4.50/hr, €8/2hrs, €11/3hrs), as well as go-karts (€2.50/30min, €4/hr) and rollerblades (€4/hr).

▼ STATUE IN THE VILLA BORGHESE

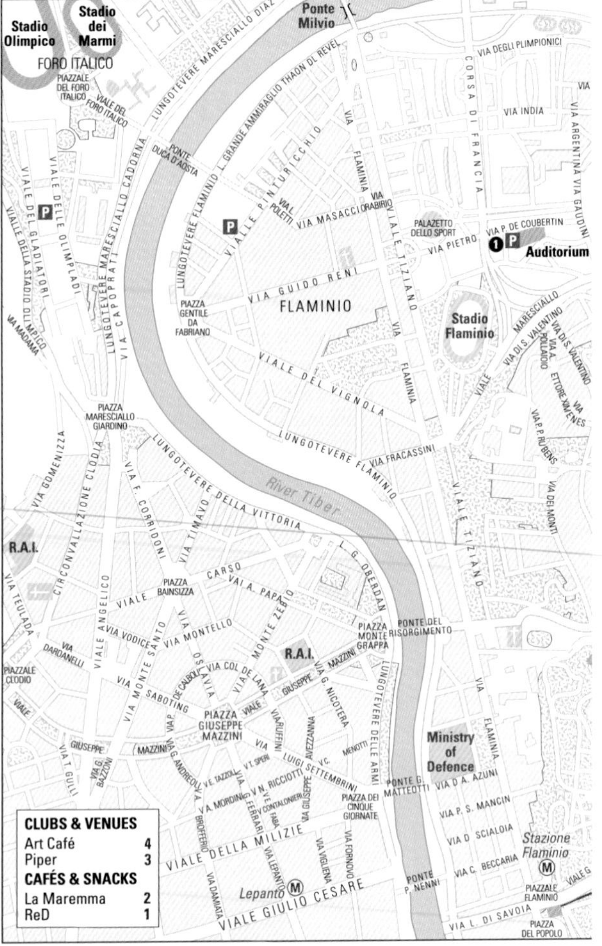

Museo e Galleria Borghese

Piazza le Scipione Borghese. Tues–Sun 9am–7pm; €8.50; pre-booked visits are obligatory, as a limited number of people are allowed in every 2hr; ⓣ06.32.810, ⓦwww.galleriaborghese.it. Cardinal Scipione Borghese was a shrewd and prodigious patron of the arts and his superb collection is open to the public in the Museo e Galleria Borghese. The **ground floor** contains sculpture, a mixture of ancient Roman items and seventeenth-century works, roughly linked together with late eighteenth-century ceiling paintings showing scenes from classical literature. Apart from the first room, which has as its centrepiece Canova's famous statue of Pauline Borghese posed as Venus, with flimsy drapery that leaves little to

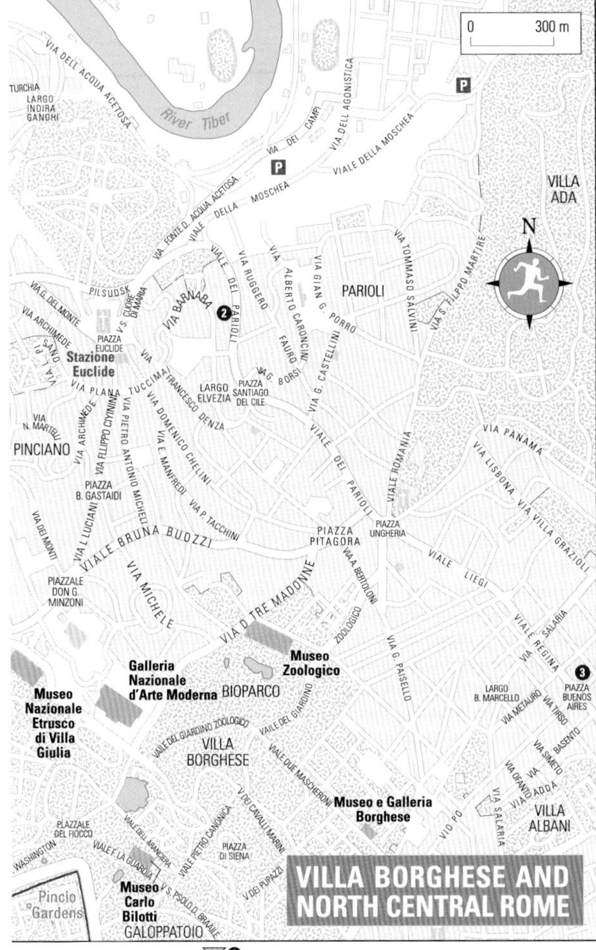

the imagination, the focus is on Bernini, whose sculptures are the highlight of almost every room. The face of his marvellous statue of David is a self-portrait, said to have been carved with the help of a mirror held by Scipione Borghese himself. Other highlights include his dramatic, poised *Apollo and Daphne*; *The Rape of Proserpine* dating from 1622, a coolly virtuosic work that shows in melodramatic form the abduction of the beautiful nymph Proserpine; as well as a larger-than-life statue of Aeneas, carrying his father, Anchises, out of the burning city of Troy, sculpted by both Bernini and his then 15-year-old son in 1613. There are paintings, too, including notable works such as Caravaggio's

▲ BERNINI'S DAVID

works by Bellini and the other Venetians of the early 1500s, including Titian's *Sacred and Profane Love*, painted in 1514 to celebrate the marriage of the Venetian noble Nicolo Aurelio. Check out also the **Gallery of Lanfranco**, at the back of the building, where there are a series of self-portraits done by Bernini at various stages of his long life and a lifelike bust of Cardinal Scipione executed by Bernini in 1632, portraying him as the worldly connoisseur of fine art and fine living that he was, as well as a bust of Paul V, and a sculpture of a *Young Man and Faun*, the sculptor's earliest known work.

David Holding the Head of Goliath, and a self-portrait as *Bacchus*, among others.

The bulk of the paintings, however, reside upstairs, in the first-floor **Pinacoteca**, one of the richest collections of paintings in the world, although unfortunately you're only allowed half an hour up here. Among many, there are canvases by Raphael, his teacher Perugino and other masters of the Umbrian school from the late fifteenth and early sixteenth centuries, not least Raphael's *Deposition*. Look for the *Lady with a Unicorn*, and *Portrait of a Man*, both also by Raphael, and, over the door, a copy of the artist's portrait of a tired-out Julius II, painted in 1513, the last year of the pope's life. There's also a delicate *Venus and Cupid with a Honeycomb* by Cranach, Lorenzo Lotto's touching *Portrait of a Man*, a painting of Diana by Domenichino showing the goddess and her attendants celebrating and doing a bit of target practice, and finally

Museo Carlo Bilotti

Tues–Sun 9am–7pm; €6. Recently opened in the orangery of the Villa Borghese, this is, like the Galleria Borghese, made up of a family bequest, this time of Carlo Bilotti – a perfume and cosmetics baron who, until his death in 2006, collected art and hobnobbed with the brightest and best in the international art world. Good portraits of him by Larry Rivers, and of his wife and daughter by Andy Warhol, open the exhibition and add to the slightly self-congratulatory air of the place, but the real reason for coming is to enjoy the small collection of high quality works by the great modern Greek-Italian painter, Giorgio De Chirico.

Bioparco

Via del Giardino Zoologico, Villa Borghese ⓣ06.360.8211, ⓦwww.bioparco.it; daily: Jan–March & Nov–Dec 9.30am–5pm;

April–Oct 9.30am–6pm, open till 7pm Sat & Sun April–Sept; €8.50 adults, €6.50 3- to 12-year-olds. Large, typical city-centre zoo, much improved and reinvented as the "Bioparco", focusing on conservation and education yet still providing the usual animals kids are after – tigers, apes, giraffes, elephants, hippos and much more – though the separate Rettilario (Reptile house) for some reason costs an extra €2.50, a bit of a rip-off. The zoological museum next door is less engaging but still worth a visit.

Galleria Nazionale d'Arte Moderna

Via delle Belle Arti 131 Ⓦwww.gnam.arti.beniculturali.it. Tues–Sun 8.30am–7.30pm. €6.50. Rome's museum of modern art is maybe the least enticing of the Villa Borghese's museums – a lumbering, Neoclassical building housing a collection of nineteenth- and twentieth-century Italian (and a few foreign) names. However, it can make a refreshing change after several days of having the senses bombarded with Etruscan, Roman and Renaissance art. The nineteenth-century collection contains a splendid range of paintings by the Tuscan Impressionists (the Macchiaoli school), as well as works by Courbet, Van Gogh and Cezanne. The twentieth-century collection features work by Modigliani, de Chirico, Giacomo Balla, Boccioni and other Futurists, along with the odd Mondrian and Klimt, plus some postwar canvases by the likes of Rothko, Pollock and Cy Twombly, Rome's own American artist, who lived in the city for most of his life.

Museo Nazionale Etrusco di Villa Giulia

Piazzale Villa Giulia 9. Tues–Sun 8.30am–7.30pm. €4. The Villa Giulia is a harmonious collection of courtyards, loggias, gardens and temples put together in a playful Mannerist style for Pope Julius III in the mid-sixteenth century. It now houses the Museo Nazionale Etrusco di Villa Giulia, the world's primary collection of Etruscan treasures, along with the Etruscan collection in the Vatican (see p.172). Not much is known about the Etruscans, but the Roman's predecessors were a creative and civilized people, evidenced here by a wealth of sensual sculpture, jewellery and art. They were also deeply religious and much of the collection focuses on preparing for the afterlife. The most famous exhibit is the remarkable *Sarcophagus of the Married Couple* (in the octagonal room in the east wing) – a touchingly lifelike portrayal of a husband and wife lying on a couch. It dates from the sixth century BC and was discovered in the tombs of Cerveteri. Look also at

▼ ETRUSCAN VOTIVE STATUE, VILLA GIULIA

the delicate and beautiful cistae – drum-like objects, engraved and adorned with figures, that were supposed to hold all the things needed for the care of the body after death – and, in the same room, marvellously intricate pieces of gold jewellery, delicately worked into tiny horses, birds, camels and other animals, as well as mirrors, candelabra and religious statues – votive offerings designed to appease the gods. Further on you'll find a drinking horn in the shape of a dog's head that is so lifelike you almost expect it to bark; a holmos, or small table, to which the maker attached 24 little pendants around the edge; and a bronze disc breastplate from the seventh century BC decorated with a weird, almost modern abstract pattern of galloping creatures.

Foro Italico

Bus #32 (Ple. M. Giardino), 271 (Ple. M. Diaz), 280 (P. Mancini), Tram #2 (P. Mancini). The Foro Italico sports complex is one of the few parts of Rome to survive intact pretty much the way Mussolini planned it. The centrepiece is the Ponte Duca d' Aosta, which connects Foro Italico to the town side of the river, and is headed by a white marble obelisk capped with a gold pyramid, engraved MUSSOLINI DUX in beautiful 1930s calligraphy. Beyond the bridge, an avenue patched with mosaics revering the Duce leads up to a fountain surrounded by more mosaics of muscle-bound figures revelling in healthful sporting activities. Either side of the fountain are the two main stadiums: the larger of the two, the Stadio Olimpico on the left, was used for the Olympic Games in 1960 and is

▲ STADIO DEI MARMI

still the venue for Rome's two soccer teams (see opposite); the smaller, the **Stadio dei Marmi** ("stadium of marbles"), is ringed by sixty great male statues, groins modestly hidden by fig leafs, in a variety of elegantly macho poses – each representing both a sport and a province of Italy.

The Auditorium

Tours Sat & Sun 10.30am–4.30pm, weekdays groups only; book in advance on ⓣ06.8024.1281, ⓦwww.auditorium.com; €9. Ten minutes' walk from the western end of Viale dei Parioli, Rome's new Auditorium is in fact three auditoriums built into one complex, their large bulbous shapes making them look like three giant, lead-skinned armadillos crouched together. Designed by the favourite Italian architect, Renzo Piano, and opened in spring 2006, it's an ingenious building: the foyers all join up and, above, the three buildings make a large amphitheatre, used for outdoor performances given in the piazza. It's clever, too, in the way it has incorporated the remains of a Republican-era

Seeing a Football Match

Rome's two big football teams, AS Roma and SS Lazio, play on alternate Sundays between September and May at the Stadio Olimpico, northwest of the city centre. Unsurprisingly, feelings run extremely high between the two teams, and derbies are big – and sometimes violent – occasions. The Stadio Olimpico is enormous, with a capacity of 100,000, and at most games, except perhaps Roma-Lazio clashes, you should be able to get a ticket for all but the cheapest seats on the night. Take your passport with you to buy a ticket as they always want some sort of ID. The diehard fans traditionally occupy the Curva areas at each end of the ground (Lazio in the Curva Nord, Roma in Curva Sud), and tickets in these areas cost €15–25. It's usually easier to pick up seats in the corner stands, or distinti, for €25–35; seats in the side stands, or tribuna, cost €60–100. See ⓦwww.romantickets.com for tickets, but prices are around fifty percent higher than what you'll pay if you buy direct. To do this, try Lazio Point, Via Farini 34 (Mon–Sat 9am–7pm; ⓣ06.482.6768); the Lazio ticket office (ⓣ06.323.7333), up to 48 hours before the game; or the Lazio shop, Via Calderini 66, close to Piazza Mancini, or the stadium itself. The As Roma Store sells tickets, as well as fan supplies (Piazza Colonna 360 ⓣ06.6920.0642; Piazza Indipendiente 8 ⓣ06.4470.2689; both daily 10am–6pm), again up to 48 hours before a game; or go to Orbis at Piazza Esquilino 37 (Mon–Sat 9.30am–1pm & 4–7.30pm; ⓣ06.482.7403, no credit cards).

Getting there by public transport: you can reach the Olympic Stadium by taking tram #2 from Piazzale Flaminio to Piazza Mancini or bus #910 from Termini and then walking acros s the river to the stadium. Or take bus #32 from Piazza Risorgimento or #271 from Piazza Venezia direct to the stadium.

villa between two of the concert halls, which was discovered when building began, and halted the project for two years while it was excavated. You can walk right around the building outside, exploring the Parco della Musica, as it's known. The main entrance is on Via Pietro de Coubertin, where there's a great book and CD shop and a decent café, or you can cut through to the park from Viale Maresciallo Pilsudksi, where a children's playground is joined – in winter – by a skating rink. For information on attending concerts, see p.154.

Restaurants

La Maremma

Viale Parioli 93 ⓣ06.808.6002.

There are quite a few restaurants along the sweeping boulevard of Viale Parioli, but this is probably the most unpretentious – an all-day pizzeria serving thin Roman or thicker Neapolitan pizzas, *fritti*, *crostini* and a few simple grilled dishes.

Cinema – Festa Internazionale di Roma

Now in its third year, this film festival takes place during nine days in mid-October at the Auditorium and at other venues – some outdoors – around town. Previous visitors have included Sean Connery and Nicole Kidman, but the atmosphere is relaxed compared to its more venerable rivals on the circuit. Tickets cost around €10 and can be purchased from the Auditorium direct. See ⓦwww.romacinemafest.org for more details.

ReD

Via Pietro de Coubertin 30 ☎06.8069.1630. Part of the Auditorium complex, this self-consciously sleek designer bar-restaurant is good for a drink or something to eat before or after a performance. During the day you might like to stop by for its €15 buffet lunch.

Clubs and venues

Art Café

Via del Galoppatoio 33 ☎06.3600.6578. Housed in the underground car park in Villa Borghese, this is one of Rome's trendiest clubs. Expect to queue, and dress up.

Auditorium/Parco della Musica

Via Pietro de Coubertin 15 ☎199.109.783. Ⓦwww.auditorium.com. Bus #53, 280, 910 or Tram #2, 19. Box office Daily 11am–6pm. Concert tickets typically €20–30. This new landmark musical complex is Rome's most prestigious venue, home to its premier orchestra, the Accademia Nazionale di Santa Cecilia, who are resident part of the year in its largest hall. Two smaller venues host smaller chamber, choral, recital and experimental works. The complex also hosts major rock and jazz names when they come to town.

Piper

Via Tagliamento 9 ☎06.855.5398. Established in the Seventies by cult singer Patty Pravo, Piper has different nightly events (fashion shows, screenings, parties, gigs and the like) and a smart-but-casual mixed-aged crowd. Music varies hugely, as do entrance prices, depending on the night. Its summer venue, from the end of May to the beginning of September, is by the sea at the *AcquaPiper di Guidonia*, Via Maremmana, before the 23.9km marker (☎0774.326.538).

Trastevere and the Janiculum Hill

Across the river from the centre of town, the district of Trastevere (the name means literally "across the Tiber") was the artisan area of the city in classical times, neatly placed for the trade that came upriver from Ostia. Outside the city walls, it was for centuries heavily populated by immigrants, and this uniqueness and separation lent the neighbourhood a strong identity that lasted well into this century. Nowadays the area is a long way from its working-class roots, and the many bars and restaurants can be thronged with tourists, lured by the charm of its narrow streets and closeted squares. It's among the more pleasant places to stroll in Rome, peaceful in the morning, lively come the evening – with dozens of trattorias setting tables out along the cobbled streets – and still buzzing late at night, when its bars and clubs provide a focus for one of Rome's most dynamic nocturnal scenes. Even if the local Festa de' Noantri ("celebration of we others"), held every July, seems to symbolize the slow decline of local spirit rather than celebrate its existence, there is still good reason to come to Trastevere.

Porta Portese market

On a Sunday it's worth approaching Trastevere from the south, walking over the Ponte Sublicio to Porta Portese; from here the Porta Portese flea market stretches down Via Portuense to Trastevere train station in a congested medley of antiques, old motor spares, cheap clothing, trendy clothing, cheap and trendy clothing, and assorted junk. Haggling is the rule, and keep a good hold of your wallet or purse. Come early if you want to buy, or even move – most of the bargains have gone by 10am, by which time the crush of people can be intense.

San Francesco a Ripa

Piazza San Francesco d'Assisi. Mon–Sat 7am–1pm & 4–7.30pm, Sun 7am–noon & 4–7pm. The church of San Francesco a Ripa is best known for two things: the fact that St Francis himself once stayed here – you can see the actual room he stayed in if you're lucky enough to find it open – and the writhing, orgasmic statue of a minor saint, the Blessed Ludovica Albertoni, sculpted by Bernini towards the end of his career. As a work of Baroque sauciness, it bears comparison with his more famous *Ecstasy of St Theresa* in the church of Santa Maria in Vittoria (see p.129); indeed it's perhaps even more shameless in its depiction of an

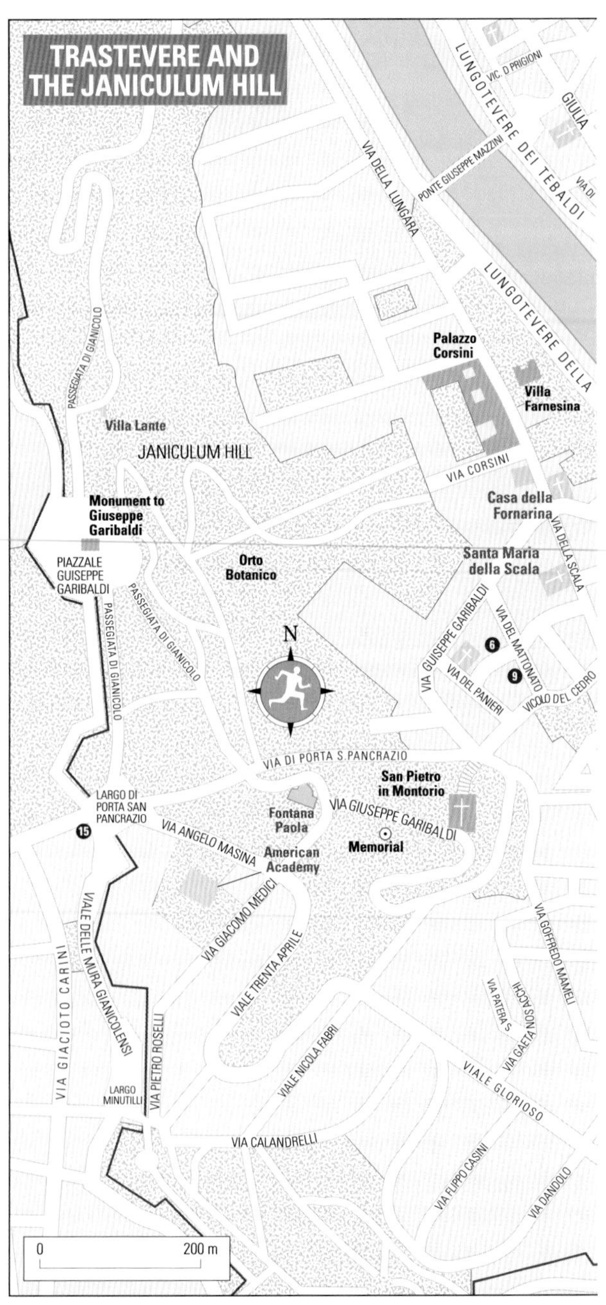

TRASTEVERE AND THE JANICULUM HILL
LUNGOTEVERE DEI TEBALDI
VIC. D PRIGIONI
GIULIA
VIA DI
PONTE GIUSEPPE MAZZINI
VIA DELLA LUNGARA
LUNGOTEVERE DELLA
Palazzo Corsini
Villa Farnesina
VIA CORSINI
Casa della Fornarina
VIA DELLA SCALA
Santa Maria della Scala
PASSEGIATA DI GIANICOLO
Villa Lante
JANICULUM HILL
Monument to Giuseppe Garibaldi
PIAZZALE GUISEPPE GARIBALDI
Orto Botanico
PASSEGIATA DI GIANICOLO
PASSEGIATA DI GIANICOLO
N
VIA GUISEPPE GARIBALDI
VIA DEL MATTONATO
VIA DEL PANIERI
VICOLO DEL CEDRO
6
9
VIA DI PORTA S.PANCRAZIO
San Pietro in Montorio
LARGO DI PORTA SAN PANCRAZIO
15
Fontana Paola
VIA GIUSEPPE GARIBALDI
Memorial
VIA ANGELO MASINA
American Academy
VIA GIACOMO MEDICI
VIALE DELLE MURA GIANICOLENSI
VIA GIACIOTO CARINI
VIALE TRENTA APRILE
VIA GOFFREDO MAMELI
VIA PATERA S
VIA GAETA NOS ACCHI
VIA PIETRO ROSELLI
VIALE NICOLA FABRI
VIALE GLORIOSO
LARGO MINUTILLI
VIA CALANDRELLI
VIA FLIPPO CASINI
VIA DANDOLO
0
200 m

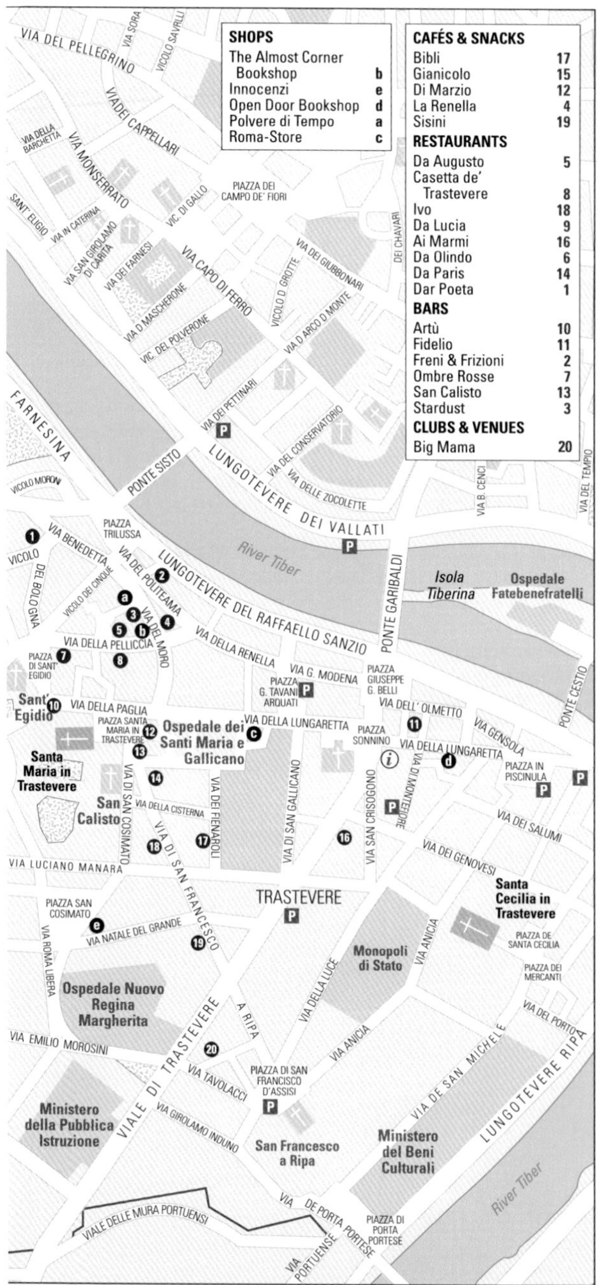

Porta Portese market

earthily realised divine ecstasy – the woman is actually kneading her breasts.

Santa Cecilia in Trastevere

Daily 9.30am–12.30pm & 4–6.30pm. Crypt excavations €2.50. Cavellini fresco Mon–Sat 10.15am–12.15pm, Sun 11.15am–12.15pm; €2.50. In its own quiet piazza off Via Anicia, the church of Santa Cecilia in Trastevere was originally built over the site of the second-century home of St Cecilia, who was – along with her husband – persecuted for her Christian beliefs. The story has it that Cecilia was locked in the caldarium of her own baths for several days but refused to die, singing her way through the ordeal (Cecilia is patron saint of music). Her head was finally half hacked off with an axe, though it took several blows before she died. Below the high altar, under a Gothic baldachino, Stefano Maderno's statue of the limp saint is almost modern in style, and shows her incorruptible body as it was found when exhumed in 1599, with three deep cuts in her neck – a fragile, intensely human piece of work that has helped make Cecilia one of the most revered Roman saints. Downstairs, excavations of the baths and the rest of the Roman house are on view in the crypt. But more alluring by far is the singing gallery above the nave of the church (ring the bell to the left of the church door to get in), where Pietro Cavallini's late thirteenth-century fresco of the *Last Judgement* – all that remains of the decoration that once covered the entire church – is a powerful, amazingly naturalistic piece of work for its time, centring on Christ in quiet, meditative majesty, flanked by angels.

Santa Maria in Trastevere

Daily 7am–9pm. In the heart of old Trastevere, Piazza Santa Maria in Trastevere is named after the church in its northwest corner – Santa Maria in Trastevere. Held to be the first Christian place of worship in Rome, it was built on a site where a fountain of oil is said to have sprung on the

▼ SANTA CECILIA IN TRASTEVERE

▲ DOME, SANTA MARIA IN TRASTEVERE

day of Christ's birth. The greater part of the structure now dates from 1140, after a rebuilding by Innocent II, a pope from Trastevere. Nowadays people come for the church's mosaics, which are among the city's most impressive: mostly Byzantine-inspired works depicting a solemn yet sensitive parade of saints thronged around Christ and Mary – the *Coronation of the Virgin* – beneath which are scenes from her life by the Santa Cecilia artist, Pietro Cavallini. Under the high altar on the right, an inscription – "FONS OLEI" – marks the spot where the oil is supposed to have sprung up.

Palazzo Corsini

Via della Lungara 10. Tues–Sun 8.30am–2pm; €4. Housed in the Palazzo Corsini, the **Galleria Nazionale d'Arte di Palazzo Corsini**, sister gallery to the one in Palazzo Barberini (see p.125), is an unexpected cultural attraction on this side of the river, a relatively small collection that only takes up a few rooms of the giant palace. There is a good grouping of Netherlandish paintings, including works by Rubens, Van Dyck and others; a room full of landscapes, including lush scenes by Dughet and a depiction of the Pantheon by Charles Clérisseau, when there was a market held in the piazza outside – though it's a rather fanciful interpretation, squeezing the Pyramid of Cestius and Arch of Janus into the background. There's a famous portrayal of *Salome With the Head of St John the Baptist* by Guido Reni and a painting of *Prometheus* by Salvatore Rosa that is one of the most vivid and detailed expositions of human internal anatomy you'll see. You can also visit the bedchamber of Queen Christina, who renounced Protestantism and, with it, the Swedish throne in 1655, and brought her library and fortune to Rome – she died, here in the palace, in 1689, and is one of only three women to be buried in St Peter's. Also worth a look is the curious Aldobrandini Throne, thought to be a Roman copy of

▲ PALAZZO CORSINI

an Etruscan throne of the second or first century. Made of marble, its back is carved with warriors in armour and helmets, below which is a boar hunt, with wild boars the size of horses pursued by hunters.

The Orto Botanico

Entrance opposite Palazzo Corsini. Tues–Sat 9.30am–6.30pm; €4. The Orto Botanico occupies the eastern side of the Janiculum Hill – after Padua's botanical gardens, the most important in Italy. It's a pleasantly neglected expanse these days, a low-key bucolic treat in the heart of Rome. You can clamber up to high stands of bamboo and ferns cut by rivulets of water, stroll through a wood of century-old oaks, cedars and conifers, and relax in a grove of acclimatized palm trees. There's also a herbal garden with medicinal plants, a collection of orchids that bloom in springtime and early summer, and a garden of aromatic herbs put together for the blind; the plants can be identified by their smell or touch, and are accompanied by signs in braille. The garden also has the distinction of being home to one of the oldest plane trees in Rome, between 350 and 400 years old, situated close by the slightly decrepit monumental staircase.

Villa Farnesina

Via della Lungara 230 Ⓦwww.lincei.it. Mon–Sat 9am–1pm; €5. The early sixteenth-century Villa Farnesina was built by Baldassare Peruzzi for the Sienese banker Agostino Chigi. It's one of the earliest Renaissance villas and its opulent rooms are decorated with frescoes by some of the masters of the period. Most people come to view the Raphael-designed painting of *Cupid and Psyche* in the now glassed-in loggia, completed in 1517 by the artist's assistants. The painter and art historian Vasari claims Raphael didn't complete the work because his infatuation with his mistress – "La Fornarina", whose father's bakery was situated nearby – was making it difficult to concentrate. Nonetheless it's mightily impressive: a flowing, animated work bursting with muscular men and bare-bosomed women, although the only part Raphael is said to have actually completed is the female figure with her back turned on the lunette (to the right of the door leading out to the east). He did, however, apparently manage to finish the Galatea in the room next door – a mixed bag of bucolic country scenes interspersed with Galatea on her scallop-shell chariot and a giant head (once said to have been painted by Michelangelo) in one of the lunettes. The ceiling illustrates Chigi's horoscope constellations, frescoed by the architect of the building, Peruzzi, who also decorated the upstairs Salone delle Prospettive, where trompe l'oeil balconies give views onto contemporary Rome – one of the earliest examples of the technique.

The Janiculum Hill

It's about a fifteen-minute walk up Via Garibaldi from Piazza di Sant'Egidio to the summit of the Janiculum Hill – not one of the original seven hills of Rome, but the one with the best and most accessible views of the centre. Follow Vicolo del Cedro from Via della Scala and take the steps up from the end, cross the main road, and continue on the steps that lead up to **San Pietro in Montorio**, best known – and worth stopping off for – for the Renaissance architect Bramante's little Tempietto in its courtyard. Head up from here to the Passeggiata del Gianicolo and follow the ridge to Piazzale Garibaldi, where there's an equestrian monument to **Garibaldi** – an ostentatious work from 1895. Just below is the spot from which a cannon is fired at noon each day for Romans to check their watches. Further on, the statue of Anita Garibaldi recalls the important part she played in an encounter with the French in 1849 – a fiery, melodramatic work that also marks her grave. Spread out before her are some of the best views over the city.

▲ GARIBALDI MONUMENT, JANICULUM HILL

Shops

The Almost Corner Bookshop

Via del Moro 45. Mon–Sat 10am–1.30pm & 3.30–8pm, Sun 11am–1.30pm & 3.30–8pm. Closed Sun in Aug. Of all Rome's English bookshops, this is perhaps the best bet for picking the very latest titles on your list of must-reads.

Innocenzi

Piazza San Cosimato 66. A great dry goods grocer, with all the usual rice and pasta and Italian goodies but also a great selection of stuff from around the world – tomato ketchup, teas, peanut butter, the works. A good option for homesick ex-pats and foodies alike.

Open Door Bookshop

Via della Lungaretta 23. Mon 4.30–8.30pm, Tues–Fri 10.30am–8.30pm, Sat 10.30am–midnight, Sun noon–6pm. Summer – afternoons and evenings only. Although they do have some new titles, especially on Rome and Roman history, used books dominate the shelves at this friendly bookshop, where you never know what treasures you might turn up. They also have a selection of books in Italian, German, French and Spanish.

Polvere di Tempo

Via del Moro 59. Mon 3.30–8pm, Tues–Sat 10am–1pm & 4–8pm. For that astrolab you've always dreamed of, as well as a huge array of ancient and medieval devices for telling the time, stop by this arcane little shop. Also, alchemists' rings that double as sundials and loads of oddities and curiosities.

Roma-Store

Via della Lungaretta 63. Mon 4–8pm Tues–Sat 9.30am–1.30pm & 4–8pm. Not a football merchandise store but a shop selling classic perfumes – Acqua di Parma, Penhaligons and suchlike – scented soaps, lotions and candles. Only the very finest from Italy, France and England.

Cafés and snacks

Bibli

Via dei Fienaroli 28. Café and bookstore that only has a small selection of English books, but it does have Internet access, and a helpful bulletin board with many ads in English for those looking for work, apartments, and so on. Good food as well.

Gianicolo

Piazzale Aurelia 5. Closed Mon. Quite an ordinary bar, but in a nice location and a bit of a hangout for Italian media stars, writers and academics from the nearby Spanish and American academies. Delicious sandwiches.

Di Marzio

Piazza di Santa Maria in Trastevere 15. Daily 7am–1am. This bar isn't much on the inside, but it's a friendly place that does decent sandwiches and whose terrace bang on Piazza Santa Maria makes it the best people-watching spot in Trastevere.

La Renella

Via del Moro 15. Daily 9am–9pm. Arguably the best bakery in Rome, right in the heart of Trastevere, with great foccaccia and superb *pizza al taglio*. Take a number and be prepared to wait at busy times. You can take away or eat on the premises at the long counter.

Sisini

Via di San Francesco a Ripa 137. Mon–Sat 11am–11pm, closed holidays. Located just half a block from Viale Trastevere, there's no sign outside this *pizza al taglio* hole-in-the-wall, which is ironic as it has perhaps the best pizza by the slice in Rome. Also roast chicken and potatoes, *suppli* and all the usual *rosticceria* fare. Try their unique chopped spicy green olive pizza.

Restaurants

Da Augusto

Piazza de Renzi 15 ☎06.580.3798. Mon–Sat noon–3pm & 8–11pm. Diner-style Trastevere stand-by serving Roman basics in an unpretentious, bustling atmosphere. Not haute cuisine, but decent, hearty Roman cooking.

Ivo

Via di San Francesco a Ripa 158 ☎06.581.7082. Wed–Mon 7.30pm–1am. The Trastevere pizzeria, almost in danger of becoming a caricature, but still good and very reasonable. A nice assortment of desserts, too – try the *monte bianco* for the ultimate chestnut cream and meringue confection. Arrive early to avoid a chaotic queue.

Da Lucia

Vicolo del Mattonato 2 ☎06.580.3601. Tues–Sun noon–3pm & 7.30–11.30pm. Nice old Roman trattoria that is the best place for summer outdoor dining in Trastevere. *Spaghetti cacio e pepe* is the great speciality here – get there early for a table outside.

Ai Marmi

Viale di Trastevere 53/59 ☎06.580.0919. Thurs–Tues 6.30pm–2.30am. Moderately priced restaurant, nicknamed "the mortuary" because of its stark interior and marble tables, and serving unique *suppli al telefono* (so-named because of the string of mozzarella it forms when you take a bite), fresh *baccalà* and some of Rome's best pizza.

Da Olindo

Vicolo della Scala 8 ☎06.581.8835. Mon–Sat noon–3pm & 8–11pm. Great, family-run Trastevere trattoria with traditional Roman fare. There's a small menu of staples, and prices are cheap and easy to remember: *primi* cost €7, *secondi* €9.

Da Paris

Piazza San Callisto 7a ☎06.581.5378. Tues–Sat noon–3pm & 8–11.30pm, Sun noon–3pm. Moderately priced Roman Jewish cookery in one of Trastevere's most atmospheric piazzas. Lots of traditional dishes

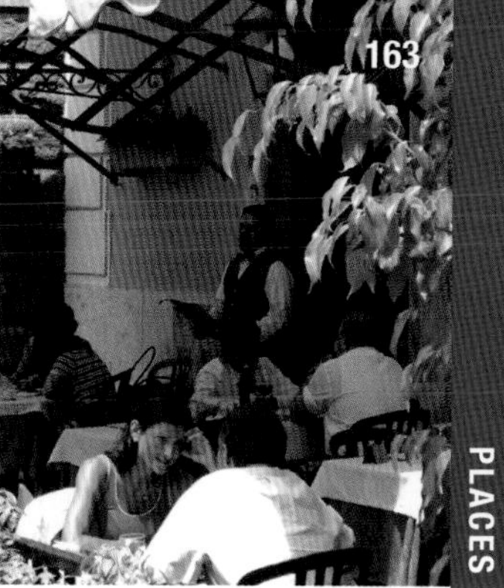

▲ DA PARIS

on the menu: *abbachio*, *carciofi alla giudea* and the like.

Dar Poeta

Vicolo del Bologna ☎06.588.8256. Tues–Sun 7.30pm–1am. A fantastic Trastevere pizzeria, long established, and with a reputation for pizzas that are a tad thicker than the traditional Roman variety. Good beer too, and a nice pubby atmosphere.

Bars

Artú

Largo F. Biondi 5 ☎06.588.0398. Tues–Sun 6pm–2am. Trastevere bar and pub on one of the district's busiest corners. Its terrace is great for watching the world go by, plus there's a full menu if you're peckish.

Fidelio

Via degli Stefaneschi 3/7 ☎06.9784.1585. Daily 6pm–3am. Just behind Piazza Sonino in Trastevere, a creakingly old *vineria* that does good traditional food too.

Freni & Frizioni

Via del Politeama 4/6 ☎06.5833.4210. Daily 4pm–2am. Just off Piazza Trilussa in the pulsing heart of Trastevere's night-scene, this old

▲ OMBRE ROSSE

auto workshop is now home to one of the city's best – and trendiest – bars, with impressive cocktails.

Ombre Rosse

Piazza Sant'Egidio 12 ⓣ06.588.4155. This has become something of a Trastevere institution, especially for a morning cappuccino, but also for interesting light meals. With its outside terrace it's a great place to people-watch.

San Calisto

Piazza San Calisto 4 ⓣ06.583.5869. Mon–Sat 6–2am. An old-guard Trastevere bar which attracts a huge, mixed crowd on late summer nights; the booze is cheap, and you can sit at outside tables for no extra cost. Things are slightly less *demimonde*-ish during the day, when it's simply a great spot to sip a cappuccino, read and enjoy the sun.

Stardust

Vicolo de' Renzi 4. Mon–Sat 3.30pm–2am, Sun noon–2am. One of Trastevere's cosiest night-time haunts, with good food as well as drink, including a buffet brunch on weekends between noon and 4.30pm. Just the place, too, for all-night partying, with regular live jazz.

Clubs and venues

Big Mama

Vicolo San Francesco a Ripa 18 ⓣ06.581.2551, ⓦwww.bigmama.it. Tues–Sat 9pm–2am. Trastevere-based jazz/blues club of long standing, hosting nightly acts. Membership is €8, entry free, except for star attractions (when it's important to book ahead). Doors open 9pm.

The Vatican City

Situated on the west bank of the Tiber, just across from the city centre, the Vatican City has been a sovereign state since 1929, and its 1000 inhabitants have their own radio station, daily newspaper, postal service, and indeed security service, in the colourfully dressed Swiss Guards. It's believed that St Peter was buried in a pagan cemetery on the Vatican hill, giving rise to the building of a basilica to venerate his name and the siting of the headquarters of the Catholic Church here. Stretching north from St Peter's, the Renaissance papal palaces are now home to the Vatican Museums – quite simply, the largest, richest, most compelling and perhaps most exhausting museum complex in the world. The other main Vatican sight worth visiting is the Castel Sant'Angelo on the riverside, a huge fortress which once harboured the popes in times of danger. Apart from visiting the main attractions, you wouldn't know at any point that you had left Rome and entered the Vatican; indeed the area around it, known as the Borgo, is one of the most cosmopolitan districts – full of mid-range hotels, restaurants and scurrying tourists and pilgrims.

Castel Sant'Angelo

Tues–Sun 9am–7.30pm; €8, free guided tours in English Sat & Sun 4.30pm. The great circular hulk of the Castel Sant'Angelo marks the edge of the Vatican, designed and built by Hadrian as his own mausoleum. Renamed in the sixth century (when Pope Gregory the Great witnessed a vision of St Michael here that ended a terrible plague), the papal authorities converted the building for use as a fortress and built a passageway to link it with the Vatican as a refuge in times of siege or invasion. Inside, a spiral ramp leads up into the centre of the mausoleum, over a drawbridge, to the main level at the top, where a small palace was built to house the papal residents in appropriate splendour. Pope Paul III had some especially

▼ CASTEL SANT'ANGELO AND THE PONTE VITTORIO EMANUELE II

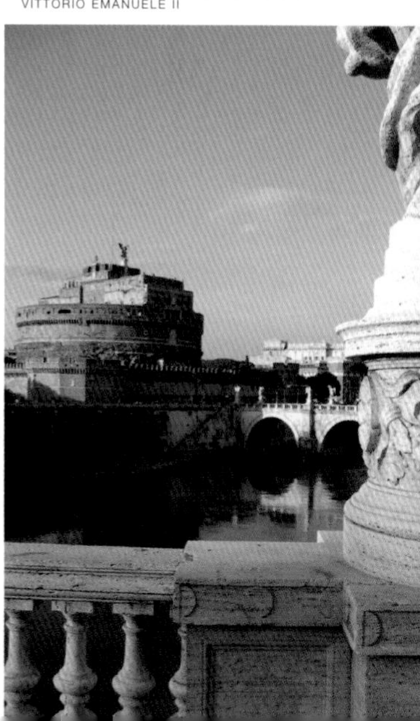

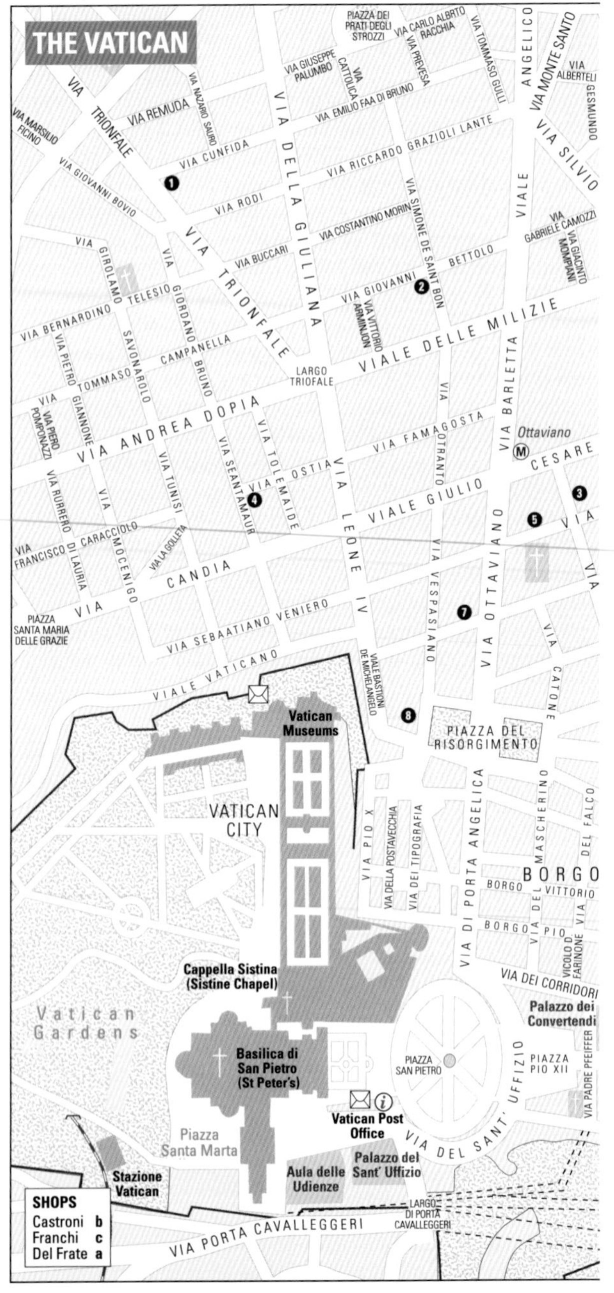

THE VATICAN
Vatican Museums
VATICAN CITY
Cappella Sistina (Sistine Chapel)
Basilica di San Pietro (St Peter's)
Vatican Gardens
Piazza Santa Marta
Stazione Vatican
Aula delle Udienze
Palazzo del Sant' Uffizio
Vatican Post Office
PIAZZA SAN PIETRO
Palazzo dei Convertendi
PIAZZA PIO XII
PIAZZA DEL RISORGIMENTO
BORGO
Ottaviano
VIA TRIONFALE
VIA DELLA GIULIANA
VIALE DELLE MILIZIE
VIA ANDREA DOPIA
VIALE GIULIO CESARE
VIA CANDIA
VIALE VATICANO
VIA LEONE IV
VIA OTTAVIANO
VIA DI PORTA ANGELICA
VIA DEI CORRIDORI
VIA DEL SANT' UFFIZIO
VIA PORTA CAVALLEGGERI
LARGO DI PORTA CAVALLEGGERI
LARGO TRIOFALE
VIALE ANGELICO
SHOPS
Castroni b
Franchi c
Del Frate a

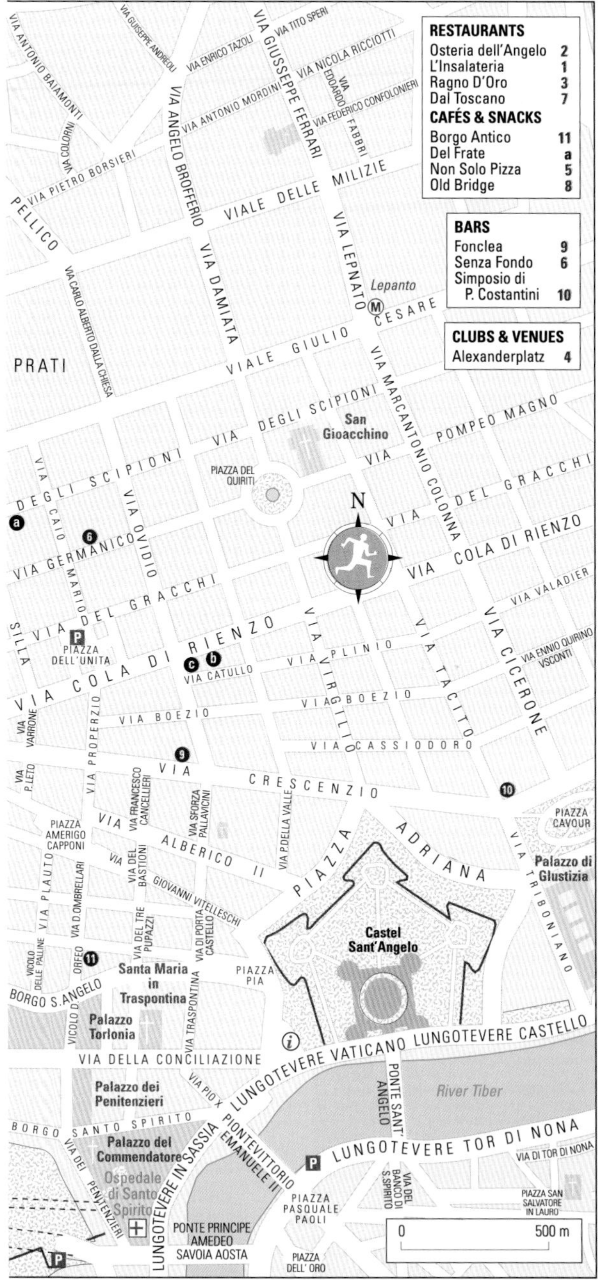
RESTAURANTS
Osteria dell'Angelo 2
L'Insalateria 1
Ragno D'Oro 3
Dal Toscano 7
CAFÉS & SNACKS
Borgo Antico 11
Del Frate a
Non Solo Pizza 5
Old Bridge 8
BARS
Fonclea 9
Senza Fondo 6
Simposio di P. Costantini 10
CLUBS & VENUES
Alexanderplatz 4
PRATI
VIALE DELLE MILIZIE
VIALE GIULIO CESARE
VIA DEGLI SCIPIONI
VIA COLA DI RIENZO
VIA CRESCENZIO
PIAZZA ADRIANA
Castel Sant'Angelo
River Tiber
LUNGOTEVERE CASTELLO
LUNGOTEVERE VATICANO
LUNGOTEVERE TOR DI NONA
LUNGOTEVERE IN SASSIA
VIA DELLA CONCILIAZIONE
BORGO SANTO SPIRITO
BORGO S.ANGELO
Palazzo di Giustizia
PIAZZA CAVOUR
San Gioacchino
PIAZZA DEL QUIRITI
Lepanto
Santa Maria in Traspontina
Palazzo Torlonia
Palazzo dei Penitenzieri
Palazzo del Commendatore
Ospedale di Santo Spirito
PONTE SANT'ANGELO
PONTE PRINCIPE AMEDEO SAVOIA AOSTA
PONTE VITTORIO EMANUELE II
PIAZZA PIA
PIAZZA PASQUALE PAOLI
PIAZZA DELL' ORO
PIAZZA DELL'UNITA
PIAZZA AMERIGO CAPPONI
PIAZZA SAN SALVATORE IN LAURO
0 500 m

fine renovations made, including the beautiful Sala Paolina. The gilded ceiling here displays the Farnese family arms, and you'll also notice Paul III's personal motto, Festina Lenta ("Make haste slowly"), scattered throughout the ceilings and in various corners of all his rooms. Elsewhere, rooms hold swords, armour, guns and the like, while others are lavishly decorated (don't miss the bathroom of Clement VII on the second floor, with its prototype hot and cold water taps and mildly erotic frescoes). Below are dungeons and storerooms which can be glimpsed from the spiralling ramp, testament to the castle's grisly past as the city's most notorious Renaissance prison. From the quiet bar upstairs you'll also get one of the best views of Rome and excellent coffee.

Piazza San Pietro

Perhaps the most famous of Rome's many piazzas, Bernini's Piazza San Pietro doesn't disappoint, although its size isn't really apparent until you're right on top of it, its colonnade arms symbolically welcoming the world into the lap of the Catholic Church. The obelisk in the centre was brought to Rome by Caligula in 36 AD, and was moved here in 1586, when Sixtus V ordered that it be erected in front of the basilica, a task that took four months and was apparently done in silence, on pain of death. The matching fountains on either side are the work of Carlo Maderno (on the right) and Bernini (on the left). In between the obelisk and each fountain, a circular stone set into the pavement marks the focal points of an ellipse, from which the four rows of columns on the perimeter of the piazza line up perfectly, making the colonnade appear to be supported by a single line of columns.

▼ PIAZZA SAN PIETRO

Basilica di San Pietro

Daily: summer 7am–7pm; winter 7am–6pm. Strict dress code – no shorts or bare shoulders. The Basilica di San Pietro, better known to many as **St Peter's**, is the principal shrine of the Catholic Church, built on the site of St Peter's tomb, and worked on by the greatest Italian architects of the sixteenth and seventeenth centuries. Not so long ago you could freely stroll around the piazza and wander into the basilica when you felt like it. Now much of the square is fenced off, and you can only enter St Peter's from the right-hand side (exiting to the left); you also have to go through security first, and the queues can be horrendous unless you get here in early the morning or late afternoon. Once you get close to the basilica, you're channelled through various entrances depending on what you want to see first – all of which is strictly enforced by the unsmiling besuited functionaries that appear at every turn. A carefree experience it is not.

Inside the **basilica**, on the right, is Michelangelo's graceful *Pietà*, completed when he was just 24. Following an attack by a vandal, it sits behind glass, strangely remote from the rest of the building. Further into the church, the dome is breathtakingly imposing, rising high above the supposed site of St Peter's tomb. With a diameter of 41.5m it is Rome's largest dome, supported by four enormous piers, decorated with reliefs depicting the basilica's so-called "major relics": St Veronica's handkerchief, which was used to wipe the face of Christ; the lance of St Longinus, which pierced Christ's side; and a piece of the True Cross. On the right side of the nave is the bronze statue of St Peter, its right foot polished smooth by the attentions of pilgrims. Bronze was also the material used in Bernini's 26m high baldachino, cast out of 927 tonnes of metal removed from the Pantheon roof in 1633. To modern eyes, it's an almost grotesque piece of work, its wild spiralling columns copied from those in the Constantine basilica. Bernini's feverish sculpting decorates the apse too, his bronze *Cattedra* enclosing the supposed chair of St Peter, though his monument to Alexander VII in the south transept is more interesting, its winged skeleton struggling underneath the heavy marble drapes, upon which the Chigi pope is kneeling in prayer.

An entrance off the aisle leads to the steeply priced **Treasury** (daily: summer 9am–6pm;

▲ STATUE OF ST PETER

winter 9am–5pm; €6), while back, outside steps lead down to the **Grottoes** (daily: summer 8am–6pm; winter 7am–5pm), where the majority of the popes are buried. Directly beneath St Peter's baldacchino, the **necropolis** contains a row of Roman tombs with inscriptions confirming that the Vatican Hill was a burial ground in classical times. Whether the tomb claimed as that of St Peter really is the saint's resting place is unclear, although it does tally with some historical descriptions. To be sure of getting a place on the English-language tour, book two or three months in advance via the Scavi office, through the arch to the left of St Peter's (Mon–Sat 9am–3.30pm; ⓣ06.6988.5318; ⓔscavi@fsp.va).

The worthwhile ascent to the **roof and dome** (daily: May–Sept 8am–6pm; Oct–April 8am–5pm; €7 via lift, €4 using the stairs) – is also outside by the entrance to the church. The views from the gallery around the interior of the dome give you a sense of the enormity of the church, and from there the roof grants views from behind the huge statues onto the piazza below, before the (challenging) climb to the lantern at the top of the dome – the views over the city are as glorious as you'd expect.

Vatican Gardens

March–Oct Tues, Thurs & Sat 10am, Nov–Feb Sat 10am; €13.50; visits last about two hours and tickets must be booked in advance on ⓣ06.6988.4466; ⓦwww.vatican.va. It's possible to visit the lovely Vatican Gardens on one guided tour a day – well worth doing for the great views of St Peter's. But you have to be organized and book in advance; you pay when you pick your tickets up on the day. The dress code is as for St Peter's – so no bare knees or shoulders.

Museo Pio-Clementino

Vatican Museums. To the left of the entrance, the Museo Pio-Clementino is home to some

The Vatican Museums

Viale Vaticano 13; March–Oct Mon–Fri 8.45am–3.20pm, Sat 8.45am–12.20pm; Nov–Feb Mon–Sat 8.45am–12.20pm. €12, audio-guides €6. Closed Sun, hols and religious hols, except the last Sun of each month (8.45am–12.20pm) when admission is free; ⓦwww.vatican.va. If you have found any of Rome's other museums disappointing, the Vatican is probably the reason why: so much booty from the city's history has ended up here, and so many of the Renaissance's finest artists were in the employ of the pope, that the result is a set of museums which put most other European collections to shame. As its name suggests, the complex actually holds a number of museums on very diverse subjects – displays of classical statuary, Renaissance painting, Etruscan relics and Egyptian artefacts, not to mention the furnishings and decoration of the building itself. There's no point in trying to see everything, at least not on one visit, and the only features you really shouldn't miss are the Raphael Rooms and the Sistine Chapel. Above all, decide how long you want to spend here, and what you want to see, before you start; you could spend anything from an hour to the better part of a day here, and it's easy to collapse from museum fatigue before you've even got to your main target of interest. Indeed, you should allow a lot of time just to get in – even during the off season the queues stretch far back along the Vatican walls and it's rare to wait less than an hour, even if you get in line before the museums open. Try to avoid Monday – everyone flocks here because Rome's other big museums are all closed.

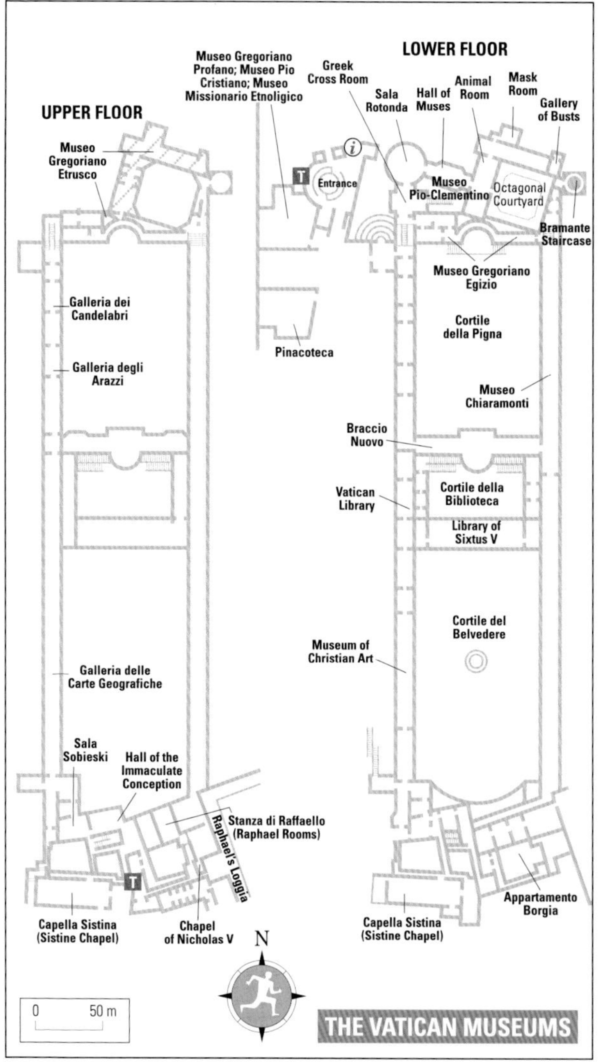

of the Vatican's best classical statuary, including two pieces that influenced Renaissance artists more than any others – the serene *Apollo Belvedere*, a Roman copy of a fourth-century BC original, and the first century BC *Laocoön*. The former is generally thought to be a near-perfect example of male anatomy and was studied by Michelangelo; the latter depicts the prophetic Trojan priest being crushed by serpents for warning of the danger of the Trojan horse, and is perhaps the most famous classical statue of all time. Beyond here there are busts of Roman emperors, the statue of *Venus of Cnidos*, the first known representation of the goddess, the so-called *Belvedere Torso*, found in the Campo de' Fiori during the reign of Julius II, and much, much more sublime classical statuary.

Museo Gregoriano Egizio

Vatican Museums. It may not be one of the Vatican's main highlights, but the Museo Gregoriano Egizio holds a distinguished collection of ancient Egyptian artefacts. These include some vividly painted mummy cases (and two mummies), along with canopi, the alabaster vessels into which the entrails of the deceased were placed. There is also a partial reconstruction of the Temple of Serapis from the Villa Adriana near Tivoli (see p.182), along with another statue of his lover, Antinous, who drowned close to the original temple in Egypt, inspiring Hadrian to build this replica.

Museo Gregoriano Etrusco

Vatican Museums. The Museo Gregoriano Etrusco holds sculpture, funerary art and applied art from the sites of southern Etruria – a good complement to Rome's specialist Etruscan collection in the Villa Giulia (see p.151). Especially worth seeing are the finds from the Regolini-Galassi tomb, from the seventh century BC, discovered near Cerveteri, which contained the remains of three Etruscan nobles, two men and a woman; the breastplate of the woman and her huge fibia (clasp) are of gold. There's also armour, a bronze bedstead, a funeral chariot and a wagon, as well as a great number of enormous storage jars, in which food, oil and wine were contained for use in the afterlife.

Galleria dei Candelabri and Galleria degli Arazzi

Vatican Museums. Outside the Etruscan Museum, a large monumental staircase leads back down to the Galleria dei Candelabri, the niches of which are adorned with huge candelabra taken from Imperial Roman villas. This gallery is also stuffed with ancient sculpture, its most memorable piece being a copy of the famous statue of *Diana of Ephesus*, whose multiple breasts are, according to the Vatican official line, in fact bees' eggs. Beyond here the Galleria degli Arazzi (Tapestries) has Belgian tapestries to designs by the school of Raphael and tapestries made in Rome at the Barberini workshops during the 1600s.

Galleria delle Carte Geografiche

Vatican Museums. The Galleria delle Carte Geografiche (Gallery of Maps) was decorated in the late sixteenth century at the behest of Pope Gregory XIII, to show all of Italy, the major islands in the Mediterranean, the papal possessions in France, as well as the Siege of Malta, the Battle of Lepanto and large-scale maps of the maritime republics of Venice and Genoa. Look also at the ceiling frescoes, illustrating scenes that took place in the area depicted in each adjacent map.

Raphael Rooms

Vatican Museums. The Raphael Rooms (or Stanza di Raffaello) formed the private apartments of Pope Julius II, and when he

▲ GALLERIA DELLE CARTE GEOGRAFICHE

moved in here he commissioned Raphael to redecorate them in a style more in tune with the times. Raphael died in 1520 before the scheme was complete, but the two rooms that were painted by him, as well as others completed by pupils, stand as one of the highlights of the Renaissance. The Stanza di Eliodoro, the first room you come to, was painted by three of Raphael's students five years after his death, and is best known for its painting of the *Mass of Bolsena* which relates a miracle that occurred in the town in northern Lazio in the 1260s, and, on the window wall opposite, the *Deliverance of St Peter,* showing the saint being assisted in a jail-break by the Angel of the Lord. The other main room, the Stanza della Segnatura, or Pope's study, was painted between 1508 and 1511, when Raphael first came to Rome, and comes close to the peak of the painter's art. *The School of Athens*, on the near wall as you come in, steals the show, a representation of the triumph of scientific truth in which all the great minds from antiquity are represented. It pairs with the *Disputation of the Sacrament* opposite, which is a reassertion of religious dogma – an allegorical mass of popes, cardinals, bishops, doctors, and even the poet Dante.

Appartamento Borgia

Vatican Museums. Outside

Julius II and the Sistine Chapel ceiling

The pope responsible for the Sistine Chapel ceiling, Julius II, was an avid collector and patron of the arts, and he summoned to Rome the best artists and architects of the day. Among these was Michelangelo, who, through a series of political intrigues orchestrated by Bramante and Raphael, was assigned the task of decorating the Sistine Chapel. Work commenced in 1508. Michelangelo hadn't wanted to do the work at all: he considered himself a sculptor, not a painter, and was more eager to get on with carving Julius II's tomb (now in San Pietro in Vincoli, see p.136) than the ceiling, which he regarded as a chore. Pope Julius II, however, had other plans, drawing up a design of the Twelve Apostles for the vault and hiring Bramante to design a scaffold to paint from. Michelangelo was apparently an awkward, solitary character: he had barely begun painting when he rejected Bramante's scaffold as unusable, fired all his staff, and dumped the pope's scheme for the ceiling in favour of his own. But the pope was easily his match, and there are tales of the two men clashing while the work was going on – Michelangelo would lock the doors at crucial points, ignoring the pope's demands to see how it was progressing; and legend has the two men at loggerheads at the top of the scaffold one day, resulting in the pope striking the artist in frustration.

the Raphael Rooms, the Appartamento Borgia was inhabited by Julius II's hated predecessor, Alexander VI, and is host to a large collection of modern religious art, although its ceiling frescoes, the work of Pinturicchio between 1492 and 1495, are really the main reason to visit.

Sistine Chapel (Capella Sistina)

Vatican Museums. Steps lead from the Raphael Rooms to the Sistine Chapel, a huge barn-like structure that serves as the pope's official private chapel and the scene of the conclaves of cardinals for the election of each new pontiff. The walls of the chapel were decorated by several prominent painters of the Renaissance – Pinturicchio, Perugino, Botticelli and Ghirlandaio. However they are entirely overshadowed by Michelangelo's more famous **ceiling frescoes**, commissioned by Pope Julius II in 1508, and, together with the painting of the *Last Judgement* on the altar wall, probably the most viewed paintings in the world. They depict scenes from the Old Testament, from the *Creation of Light* at the altar end to *The Drunkenness of Noah* over the door. Julius II lived only a few months after the Sistine Chapel ceiling was finished, but the fame of the work he had commissioned soon spread far and wide. It's staggeringly impressive, all the more so for its restoration, which lifted centuries of accumulated soot and candle grime off the paintings to reveal a much brighter, more vivid painting than anyone thought existed.

The restorers have also been able to chart the progress of Michelangelo as he moved across the vault. Each day a fresh layer of plaster would have been laid, on which Michelangelo would have had around eight hours to paint before it dried. Comparing the different areas of plaster, it seems the figure of Adam, in the key *Creation of Adam* scene, took just four days; God, in the same fresco, took three days. You can also see the development of Michelangelo as a painter when you look at the paintings in reverse order. The first painting, over the door, *The Drunkenness of Noah,* is done in a stiff and formal style, and is vastly different from the last painting he did, *The Creation of Light*, over the altar, which shows the artist as the master of the technique of fresco painting. Look also at the pagan sibyls and biblical prophets which Michelangelo incorporated in his scheme – some of the most dramatic figures in the entire work, and all clearly labelled by the painter, from the sensitive figure of the Delphic Sybil to the hag-like Cumaean Sybil and the prophet Jeremiah – a brooding self-portrait of an exhausted-looking Michelangelo.

The Last Judgement, on the altar wall of the chapel, was painted by Michelangelo more than twenty years later. Michelangelo wasn't especially keen to work on this either, but Pope Paul III, an old acquaintance of the artist, was keen to complete the decoration of the chapel. The painting took five years, again single-handed, and is probably the most inspired and most homogeneous large-scale painting you're ever likely to see. The centre is occupied by Christ, turning angrily as he gestures the condemned to the underworld. St Peter, carrying his keys, looks on in astonishment, while Mary averts her eyes from the scene. Below Christ a group of angels blasts their trumpets to summon the dead from their sleep. On the left, the dead awaken from their graves, tombs and sarcophagi, and are levitating into the heavens or being pulled by ropes and the napes of their necks by angels who take them before Christ. At the bottom right, Charon, keeper of the underworld, swings his oar at the damned souls as they fall off the boat into the waiting gates of hell.

Museum of Christian Art and the Vatican Library

Vatican Museums. After the Sistine Chapel, you're channelled to the exit by way of the **Museum of Christian Art**, which is not of great interest in itself, but does give access to a small room off to the left that contains a number of ancient Roman frescoes and mosaics, among them the celebrated *Aldobrandini Wedding*, a first century BC Roman fresco that shows the preparations for a wedding in touching detail. Back down the main corridor, the **Vatican Library** is home to around a million books, and is decorated with scenes of Rome and the Vatican as it was during his reign. Beyond, the corridor opens out into the dramatic **Library of Sixtus V** on the right, a vast hall built across the courtyard in the late sixteenth century to glorify literature – and of course Sixtus V himself.

Braccio Nuovo and Museo Chiaramonti

Vatican Museums. The Braccio Nuovo and Museo Chiaramonti both hold classical sculpture, although be warned that they are the Vatican at its most overwhelming – close on a thousand statues crammed into two long galleries. The Braccio Nuovo was built in the early 1800s to display prized classical statuary, and it contains, among other things, probably the most famous extant image of Augustus, and a bizarre-looking statue depicting the Nile, whose yearly flooding was essential to the fertility of the Egyptian soil. The 300-metre-long Chiaramonti gallery is especially unnerving, lined as it is with the chill marble busts of hundreds of nameless, blank-eyed ancient Romans, along with the odd deity. It pays to have a leisurely wander, for there are some real characters here: sour, thin-lipped matrons with their hair tortured into pleats, curls and spirals; kids, caught in a sulk or mid-chortle; and ancient old men, their flesh sagging and wrinkling to reveal the skull beneath.

The Pinacoteca

Vatican Museums. The Pinacoteca is housed in a separate building on the far side of the Vatican Museums' main spine, and is among Rome's picture galleries, with works from the early to high Renaissance and right up to the nineteenth century. Among early works, there is an amazing *Last Judgement* by Nicolo and Giovanni from the twelfth century, the stunning *Simoneschi* triptych by Giotto, painted in the early 1300s for the old St Peter's, and fragments of Melozzo de Forli's *Musical Angels*, painted for the church of Santi Apostoli. Further on are the rich backdrops and elegantly clad figures of the Umbrian School painters, Perugino and

Pinturicchio. Raphael has a room to himself, where you'll find his *Transfiguration*, which he had nearly completed when he died in 1520, *The Coronation of the Virgin*, done when he was only 19 years old, and, on the left, the *Madonna of Foglino*, showing SS John the Baptist, Francis of Assisi and Jerome. Leonardo's *St Jerome*, in the next room, is a remarkable piece of work with Jerome a rake-like ascetic torn between suffering and a good meal, while Caravaggio's *Descent from the Cross*, two rooms on, is a warts-and-all canvas that unusually shows the Virgin Mary as a middle-aged mother grieving over her dead son. Take a look too at the most gruesome painting in the collection, Poussin's *Martyrdom of St Erasmus,* which shows the saint stretched out on a table with his hands bound above his head in the process of having his small intestine wound onto a drum – basically being "drawn" prior to "quartering".

Musei Gregoriano Profano, Pio Cristiano and Missionario Etnologico

Vatican Museums. Next door to the Pinacoteca, the Museo Gregoriano Profano holds more classical sculpture, mounted on scaffolds for all-round viewing, including mosaics of athletes from the Baths of Caracalla and Roman funerary work, notably the Haterii tomb friezes, which show backdrops of ancient Rome and realistic portrayals of contemporary life. The adjacent Museo Pio Cristiano has intricate early Christian sarcophagi and, most famously, an expressive third-century AD statue of the Good Shepherd. The Museo

▲ FRANCHI

Missionario Etnologico displays art and artefacts from all over the world, collected by Catholic missionaries.

Shops

Castroni

Via Cola di Rienzo 196. Mon–Sat 8am–8pm. Huge, labyrinthine food store with a large selection of Italian treats as well as hard-to-find international favourites – plus a café with coffee, cakes and sandwiches. There's another branch nearby at Via Ottaviano 55 and one just off Via Nazionale, on Via delle Quattro Fontane, both of which also have cafés.

Franchi

Via Cola di Rienzo 200. Mon–Sat 8am–9pm. One of the best delis in Rome – a triumph of cheeses and sausages with an ample choice of cold or hot food to go, including delicious *torta rustica* and roast chicken. They'll make up customized lunches for you, and they have the wines to go with it.

Del Frate

Via degli Scipioni 118/124 ☎06.321.1612. Mon–Sat 8am–8pm. This large wine and spirits shop is located on a quiet street near the Vatican, and has all the Barolos and Chiantis you could want, alongside shelves full of *grappa* in all shapes and sizes. See also below.

Cafés and snacks

Borgo Antico

Borgo Pio 21. Tues–Sat noon–3pm & 7.30–10.30pm. Sun noon–3pm. Great old-fashioned wine bar right by Piazza San Pietro that does (mainly cold) food and great wine.

Del Frate

Via degli Scipioni 118/124. Mon–Sat 1–3pm & 7.30pm–midnight. This large wine and spirits shop is a wine bar, too, with a great selection of cheeses and cold meats as well as regular pasta dishes and main courses. Very handy for the Vatican, whether for lunch or at the end of the day.

Non Solo Pizza

Via degli Scipioni 95–97. Tues–Sun 8.30am–10pm. Pizza by the slice, as well as *suppli*, *olive ascolane*, *fiori di zucca*, *crocchette*, etc, and a complete selection of hot dishes. From 7pm they offer made-to-order round pizzas, too. No extra charge to sit, inside or out.

Old Bridge

Via dei Bastioni di Michelangelo 5. Daily 10–2am. The *gelato* here is some of the city's best, and the queues – which rival those of the Vatican Museums across the street – are proof.

Restaurants

Osteria dell'Angelo

Via G. Bettolo 24 ☎06.372.9470. Mon–Sat 8–11.15pm, plus Tues & Fri 12.45–2.30pm. Above-average traditional Roman food, in a very popular restaurant run by an ex-rugby player. Booking advisable. Reasonable prices.

L'Insalatiera

Via Trionfale 94 ☎06.3974.2975. Mon–Sat noon–3.30pm & 7pm–midnight. Moderately priced vegetarian restaurant specializing in regional Italian cuisine. Everything is home-made, including the wonderful desserts.

Ragno d'Oro

Via Silla 26 ☎06.321.2362. This family-run restaurant not only has great Roman cooking and good service, but it's also just five minutes' walk from the Vatican. Decent prices too.

Dal Toscano

Via Germanico 58/60 ☎06.3972.5717. Tues–Sun 12.30–3pm & 8–11pm. This

▼ DAL TOSCANO

restaurant specializes in *fiorentine* (the famous thick Tuscan T-bone steaks), perfectly grilled on charcoal; also does delicious *pici* (thick home-made spaghetti) and *ribollita* (veg & bread soup) – all at reasonable rates.

Bars

Fonclea

Via Crescenzio 82a ⓣ06.689.6302. Daily 7pm–2am. This historic basement joint is loaded both with devoted regulars and visitors who have happily discovered that there is life in the Vatican's sometimes somnolent Borgo and Prati area. Live music adds to the excitement.

Senza Fondo

Via Germanico 168 ⓣ06.321.1415. Open daily 9pm–3am. Convivial Prati basement pub with a good choice of beers and decent food. Sometimes live music, too.

Simposio di Piero Costantini

Piazza Cavour 16 ⓣ06.321.1502. Mon–Sat 12.30–2.30pm & 7.30–11pm. On the corner of Piazza Cavour right behind the Castel Sant'Angelo, this old-fashioned wine bar and restaurant has a fine and authentic Art Nouveau feel. Good food.

Clubs and venues

Alexanderplatz

Via Ostia 9 ⓣ06.5833.5781, ⓦwww.alexanderplatz.it. Daily 8am–2am. Rome's top live jazz club/restaurant with reasonable membership (€10) and free entry, except when there's star-billing. Reservations recommended. Performances start around 9pm.

Day-trips

You may find there's quite enough in Rome to keep you occupied during your stay. But it can be a hot, oppressive city, and its churches, museums and ruins are sometimes intensely wearying – so if you're around long enough it's well worth getting out to see something of the countryside. Two of the main attractions visitable on a day-trip are, admittedly, more ancient Roman sites, but just the process of getting to them can be energizing. Tivoli, about an hour by bus northeast of Rome, is a small provincial town famous not only for the travertine quarries nearby, but also for two villas – one Renaissance, one Roman, both complete with landscaped gardens and parks. Southwest of Rome, Ostia is the city's busiest seaside resort, but more importantly was the site of the port of Rome in classical times, the ruins of which – Ostia Antica – are well preserved and worth seeing. If you're after a day by the sea, you're best off skipping Ostia and travelling south to Anzio or Nettuno: both have decent beaches and good seafood restaurants.

Tivoli

Buses leave Rome for Tivoli every 20min from Ponte Mammolo metro station (line B); journey time 1hr. Perched high on a hill, with fresh mountain air and a pleasant position on the Aniene River, Tivoli has always been a retreat from the city. In classical days it was a retirement town for wealthy Romans; during the Renaissance it again became the playground of the moneyed classes, attracting some of the city's most well-to-do families and their new-built villas. Nowadays the leisured classes have mostly gone, but Tivoli does very nicely on the fruits of its still-thriving marble business and supports a small, airy centre that preserves a number of relics from its ritzier days. To do justice to the gardens and villas – especially if Villa Adriana is on your list – you'll need time: set out early.

Villa d'Este

Piazza Trento, Tivoli. Summer daily 9am–1hr before sunset; winter Tues–Sun 9am–1hr before sunset; €6.50. Tivoli's major sight is the

▼ VILLA D'ESTE

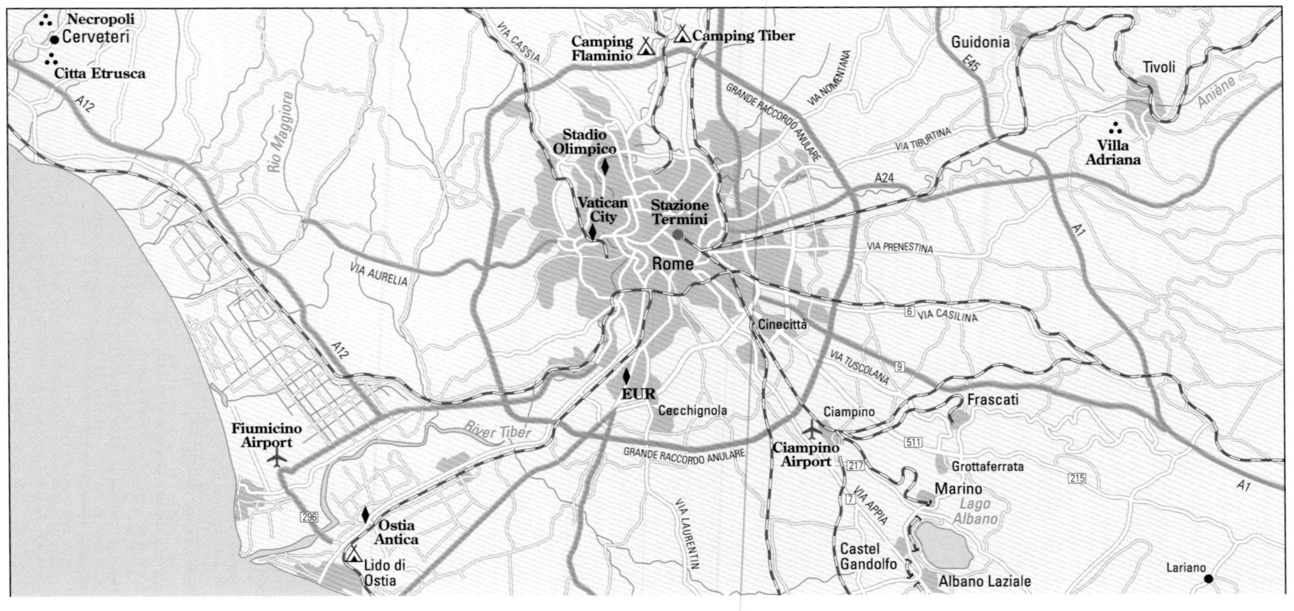

Necropoli
Cerveteri
Citta Etrusca
A12
Rio Maggiore
VIA CASSIA
Camping Flaminio
Camping Tiber
VIA NOMENTANA
GRANDE RACCORDO ANULARE
Guidonia
E45
Tivoli
Aniene
Villa Adriana
Stadio Olimpico
VIA TIBURTINA
A24
Vatican City
Stazione Termini
Rome
VIA AURELIA
VIA PRENESTINA
A1
6
VIA CASILINA
Cinecittà
A12
VIA TUSCOLANA
9
EUR
Cecchignola
Frascati
Ciampino
Fiumicino Airport
River Tiber
Ciampino Airport
GRANDE RACCORDO ANULARE
511
217
Grottaferrata
215
A1
296
Marino
Lago Albano
VIA LAURENTIN
7
VIA APPIA
Ostia Antica
Lido di Ostia
Castel Gandolfo
Albano Laziale
Lariano

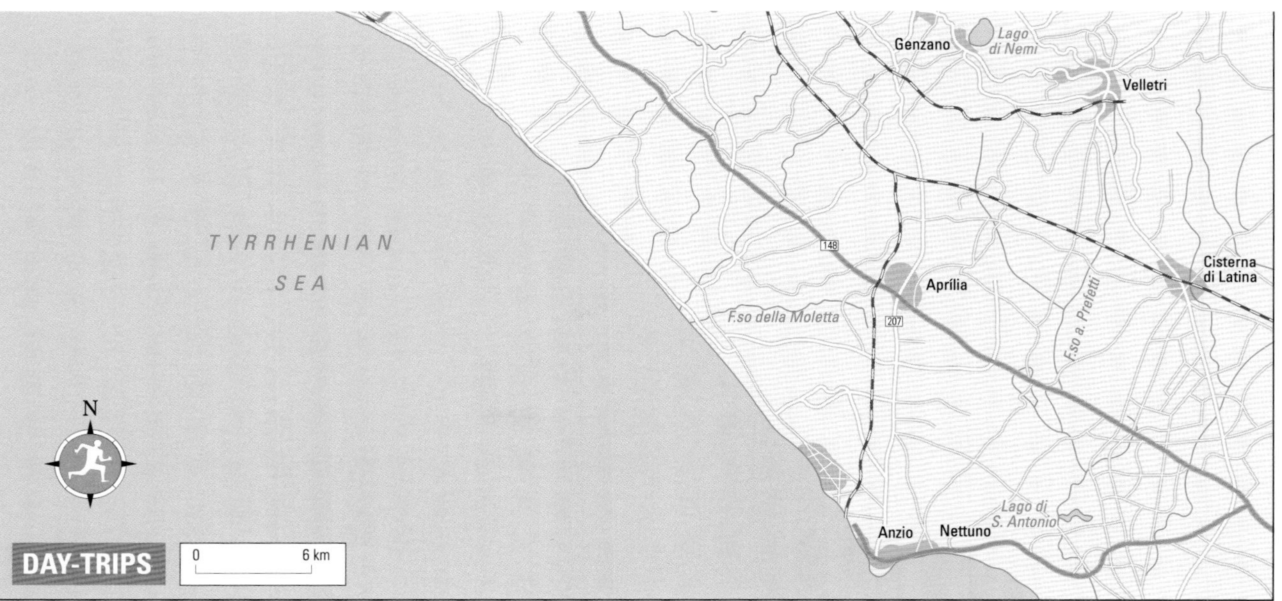
Genzano
Lago
di Nemi
Velletri
TYRRHENIAN
SEA
148
Aprília
Cisterna
di Latina
F.so della Moletta
207
F.so a. Prefetti
N
Lago di
S. Antonio
Anzio
Nettuno
DAY-TRIPS
0
6 km

Villa d'Este, across the main square of Largo Garibaldi. This was the country villa of Cardinal Ippolito d'Este, and has been restored to its original state. Beautiful Mannerist frescoes in its seven rooms show scenes from the history of the d'Este family in Tivoli, but it's the gardens that most people come to see, peeling away down the hill in a succession of terraces, their carefully tended lawns, shrubs and hedges interrupted by one playful fountain after another. In their day they were quite amazing – one was a water organ, the air for the pipes being forced by water valves, another imitated the call of birds. Among the other surviving fountains, the central, almost Gaudí-like Fontana del Bicchierone, by Bernini, is one of the simplest and most elegant; on the far left, the Rometta, or "Little Rome", has reproductions of the city's major buildings and a boat holding an obelisk; while perhaps the best is the Fontana dell'Ovato on the opposite side of the garden, fringed with statues, behind which is a rather dank arcade, in which you can walk.

Villa Gregoriana

April–Oct daily 10am–6.30pm; €4. Tivoli's other main attraction, the **Villa Gregoriana** was created when Pope Gregory XVI diverted the flow of the river here to ease the periodic flooding of the town in 1831. At least as interesting and beautiful as the d'Este estate, it remains less well-known and less visited, and has none of the latter's conceits – its vegetation is lush and overgrown, descending into a gorge over 60m deep. There are two main waterfalls – the larger Grande Cascata on the far side, and a small Bernini-designed one at the neck of the gorge. The path winds down to the bottom of the canyon, passing ruined Roman resting pavilions and scaling the drop on the other side past two grottoes, where you can get right up to the roaring falls. It's harder work than the Villa d'Este but is in many ways more rewarding; the path leads up on the far side to an exit and the substantial remains of a **Temple of Vesta**, which you'll have seen clinging to the side of the hill.

Villa Adriana

6km southwest of Tivoli. Ask the Rome–Tivoli bus to drop you off or take the local CAT #4 bus from Largo Garibaldi in Tivoli. Daily 9am–1hr before sunset; €6.50. Probably the largest and most sumptuous villa in the Roman Empire, Villa Adriana, just outside Tivoli, was the retirement home of the Emperor Hadrian for a short while between 135 AD and his death three years later. Hadrian was a great traveller and a keen architect, and parts of the enormous site were inspired by buildings he had seen around the world. The massive Pecile, for instance, through which you enter, is a reproduction of a building in Athens; the Canopus, on the opposite side of the site, is a copy of the sanctuary of Serapis near Alexandria, its long, elegant channel of water fringed by sporadic columns and statues leading up to a temple of Serapis at the far end. Near the Canopus, a museum displays the latest finds from the ongoing excavations here, though most of the discoveries have found their way to museums in Rome. Back towards the entrance there

▲ VILLA ADRIANA

are the remains of two bath complexes, a fishpond with a cryptoporticus (underground passageway) underneath, marked with the names of the seventeenth- and eighteenth-century artists who visited here, and finally the Teatro Marittimo, with its island in the middle of a circular pond – the place to which it's believed Hadrian would retire for a siesta.

Ostia Antica

Regular trains from Roma–Lido di Ostia (next door to Piramide metro station, on line B); journey time 30min. Also reachable by bus #23. April–Oct Tues–Sun 8.30am–6pm, March 8.30am–5pm, Nov–Feb 8.30am–4pm; €4. The excavations of the Roman port of Ostia – Ostia Antica – constitute one of the finest ancient Roman sites you'll see anywhere – and easily merits a half-day journey out. Until its harbour silted up and the town was abandoned during the fourth century, Ostia was Rome's principal port and a thriving commercial centre. Over the centuries the sand and mud of the Tiber preserved its buildings incredibly well and the excavations here are an evocative sight: it's much easier to visualize a Roman town here than from any amount of pottering around the Forum – or even Pompeii. From the entrance the Decumanus Maximus, the main street of Ostia, leads west, past the Baths of Neptune on the right (where there's an interesting mosaic) to the town's commercial centre, known as the Piazzale delle Corporazioni. Shops and offices here specialized in enterprises from all over the ancient world, and the mosaics just in front denote their trade – grain merchants, ship-fitters, ropemakers and the like.

▲ OSTIA ANTICA

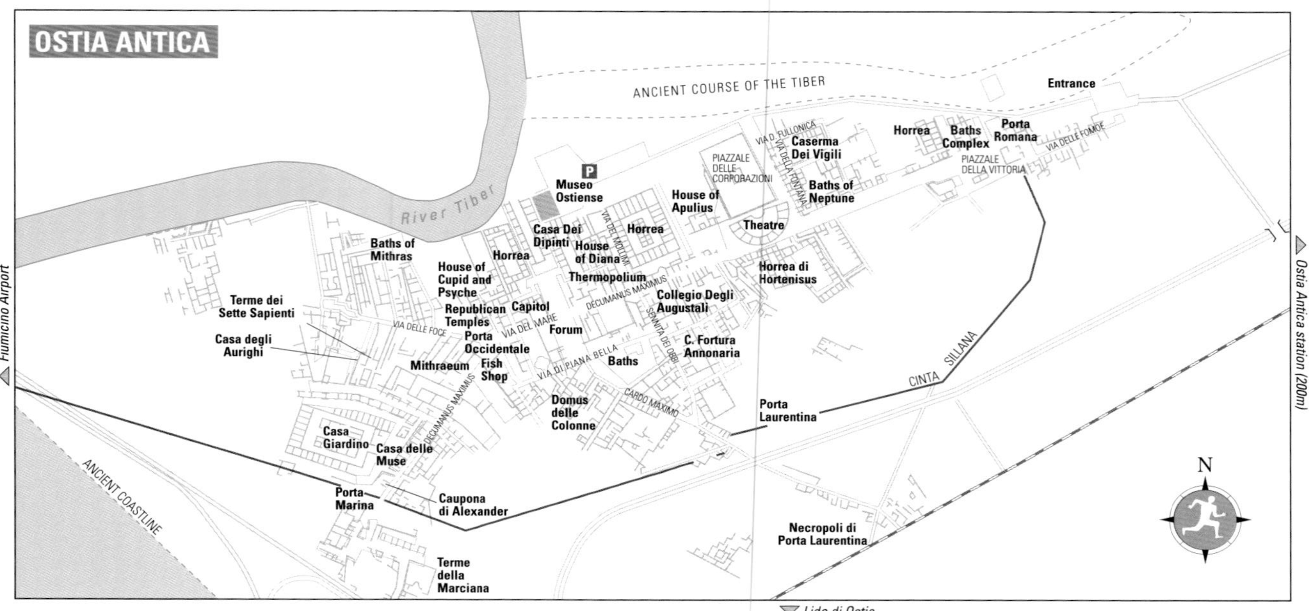
OSTIA ANTICA
ANCIENT COURSE OF THE TIBER
Entrance
Horrea
Baths Complex
Porta Romana
VIA DELLE TOMBE
PIAZZALE DELLA VITTORIA
VIA D. FULLONICA
VIA DELLA FONTANA
Caserma Dei Vigili
Baths of Neptune
PIAZZALE DELLE CORPORAZIONI
River Tiber
P
Museo Ostiense
House of Apulius
Theatre
Casa Dei Dipinti
House of Diana
VIA DEL MOLINI
Horrea
Baths of Mithras
Horrea
House of Cupid and Psyche
Thermopolium
DECUMANUS MAXIMUS
Horrea di Hortenisus
Collegio Degli Augustali
Terme dei Sette Sapienti
Republican Temples
Capitol
VIA DELLE FOCE
VIA DEL MARE
Forum
Porta Occidentale
SEMITA DEI CIPPI
C. Fortura Annonaria
Casa degli Aurighi
Mithraeum
Fish Shop
VIA DI PIANA BELLA
Baths
CINTA SILLANA
DECUMANUS MAXIMUS
Domus delle Colonne
CARDO MAXIMO
Porta Laurentina
Casa Giardino
Casa delle Muse
ANCIENT COASTLINE
Porta Marina
Caupona di Alexander
N
Necropoli di Porta Laurentina
Terme della Marciana
Fiumicino Airport
Ostia Antica station (200m)
Lido di Ostia

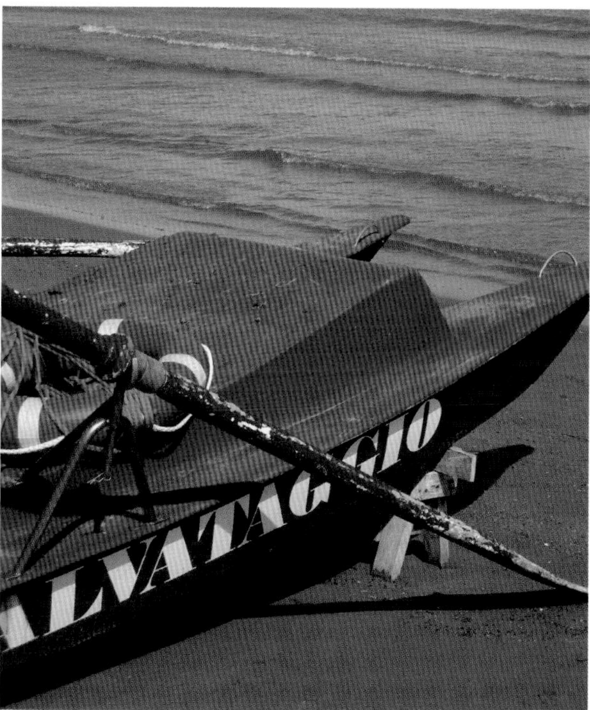

▲ THE BEACH AT ANZIO

Flanking one side of the square, Ostia's theatre has been much restored and sometimes hosts performances of classical drama during summer. On the left of the square, the House of Apulius preserves mosaic floors and, beyond, a dark-aisled Mithraeum with more mosaics illustrating the cult's practices. Behind here, the House of Diana is probably the best-preserved private house in Ostia, with a dark, mysterious set of rooms around a central courtyard, and another Mithraeum at the back. You can climb up to its roof for a fine view of the rest of the site, afterwards crossing the road to the Thermopolium – an ancient Roman café, complete with seats outside, a high counter, display shelves and even wall paintings of parts of the menu. North of the House of Diana, the museum holds a variety of articles from the site, including wall paintings depicting domestic life in Ostia and some fine sarcophagi and statuary, notably one of *Mithras Slaying the Bull* from one of Ostia's Mithraeums. Left from here, the Forum centres on the Capitol building, reached by a wide flight of steps, and is fringed by the remains of baths and a basilica.

Anzio and Nettuno

Hourly trains from Termini station; journey time around 1hr. About 40km south of Rome, and easily seen on a day-trip, Anzio spreads along the coast and focuses on a lively central square. Much of the town was damaged during a difficult Allied landing here on January 22, 1944, to which two military cemeteries (one British, another, at nearby Nettuno, American) bear testimony. But despite a pretty thorough rebuilding it's a likable resort, still depending as much on fish as tourists for its livelihood. The town's seafood restaurants, which crowd together along the harbour and are relatively good value, are reason enough to come – try *Pierino* at Piazza C. Battisti 3 (closed Mon) – while the beaches, which edge the coast on either side, don't get unbearably thronged outside of August. Hydrofoils leave daily in summer for the lovely, small island of **Ponza** – ask for a timetable at the tourist office on Piazza Pia 19 (daily 10am–12.30pm; winter 4–6pm; summer 5–7pm; ⓣ06.984.5147).

Nettuno, a couple of kilometres down the coast (and walkable by the coast road), is more of the same, but with slightly less beach space and water that's not quite so clear and calm. Again it's a mostly modern town, but there's a well-preserved old quarter, still walled, with a couple of trattorias on the main square.

Accommodation

Hotels

As you might expect, there is plenty of accommodation in Rome, and for much of the year you can expect to find something without too much trouble. Many of the city's **cheaper options** are located conveniently close to Termini, and you could do worse than end up in one of these, as long as you can tolerate the district's relative seediness, which in any case has improved dramatically in recent years. If you want to stay somewhere more central and alluring, there are many hotels in the centro storico and around Campo de' Fiori; some of them are not that expensive, but they fill quickly. For more **luxurious surroundings**, the city's prime hunting-ground for premium accommodation is the Tridente and the area east of Via del Corso, towards Via Veneto and around the Spanish Steps, although there are still a few affordable options by Piazza di Spagna. You should also consider staying across the river in Prati, a pleasant neighbourhood nicely distanced from the hubbub of the city centre and handy for the Vatican and St Peter's. Also on the west bank of the river, Trastevere boasts many new options, all located within easy walking distance of the centre of town and all the sights.

We've listed the price you're likely to pay for a **double room** at most times during the year, but bear in mind that rates are very much driven by demand. They could be higher during peak times and are often lower if the hotel is quiet – in August, for example, when deals abound. Never be afraid to ask for a better rate; they can only say no.

Centro storico

Albergo del Senato Piazza della Rotonda 73 ⓣ06.678.4343, ⓦwww.albergodelsenato.it. A classy choice next door to the Pantheon, with friendly service and knockout views of the city from the roof and the Pantheon from some of the rooms. Prices can soar in the high season but you can't beat the location. From €140 for a double.

Due Torri Vicolo del Leonetto 23 ⓣ06.6880.6956, ⓦwww.hotelduetorriroma.com. This fine little hotel was once a residence for cardinals, after which it served as a brothel. Recently completely renovated, it retains a homely feel yet is very near Piazza Navona and many of the city's greatest sights. Some rooms have private terraces with rooftop views. Doubles from €172, and apartments from €235.

Booking hotels

You should **book in advance** if you want to snag a bargain, especially when the city is at its busiest. As well as contacting the hotel direct it's worth doing an internet search for discount deals – and going to ⓦwww.venere.com (ⓣ00800.8363.7300), which has lots of deals on Italian hotels. If you arrive without having booked anything, the Enjoy Rome office is your best bet (see p.205), while the Free Hotel Reservation Service (daily 8am–10pm; ⓣ06.699.1000), has multilingual staff who will check out vacancies for you. The rooms offered by the touts at Termini are rarely a good deal, and should only be used as a last resort.

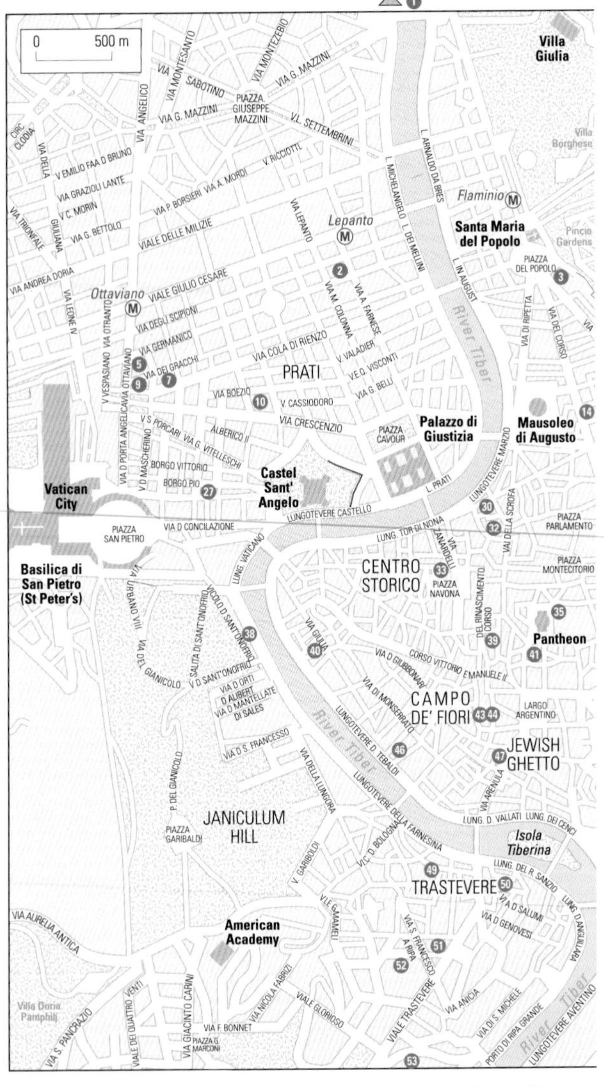

HOTELS

Hotel	No.	Hotel	No.	Hotel	No.	Hotel	No.
Albergo del Senato	35	Cisterna	51	Firenze	26	Navona	39
Aleph	15	Colors	10	Forty Seven	48	Palazzetto	8
Alpi	16	Condotti	11	Gerber	2	Plaza	14
Amalia	5	Dei Consoli	7	Grifo	36	Piazza di Spagna	12
Des Artistes	18	Daphne	19	Hassler Villa Medici	13	Portrait Suites	17
Beehive	25	Duca D'Alaba	45	Homs	23	Portoghesi	32
Dei Borgognoni	29	Due Torri	30	Hotel Art	4	Radisson SAS	37
Bramante	27	Erdarelli	28	D'Inghilterra	22	Raphael	33
Campo de' Fiori	43	Fawlty Towers	31	Modigliani	20	La Residenza	6

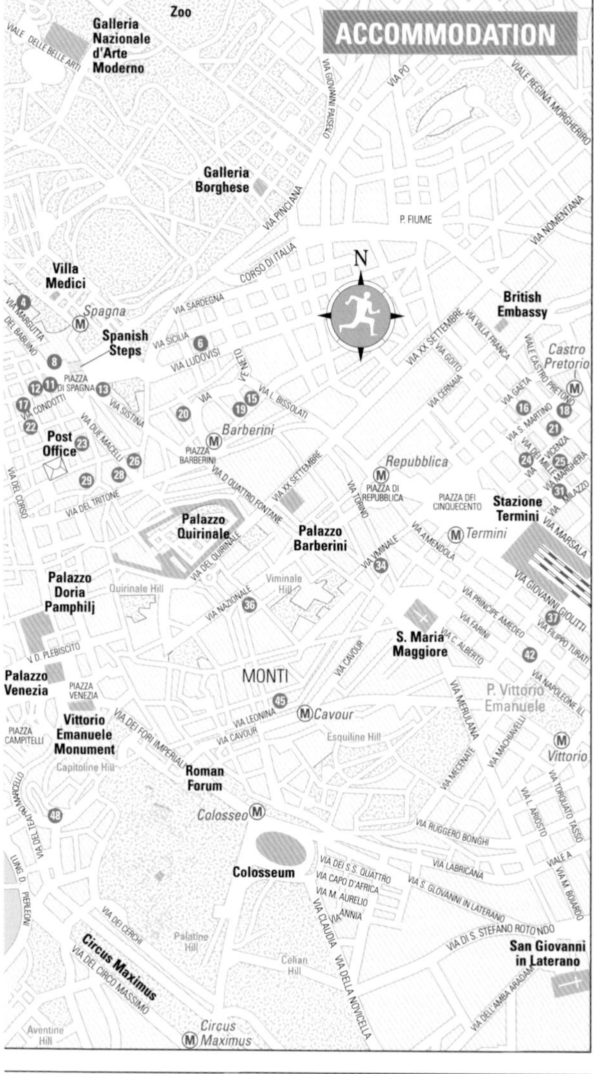

				HOSTELS & CONVENTS	
Residenza Farnese	46	Trastevere	52	Alessandro Downtown	42
Ripa	53	Villa delle Rose	24	Alessandro Palace Hostel	21
La Rovere	38	Zanardelli	34	Casa di Santa Brigida	44
De Russie	3			Casa di Santa Francesca Romana	50
Santa Chiara	41			Ostello del Foro Italico	1
Santa Maria	49			Ottaviano	9
Smeraldo	47			YWCA	34
St George	40				
Sole	44				

Renting an apartment

A few hotels rent out apartments, and a number of agencies specialize in short lets. One of the best is At Home, Via del Babuino 56 (☎06.3212.0102, ⓦwww.at-home-italy.com), which has great service and perhaps the city's best choice of centrally located apartments.

Navona Via dei Sediari 8 ☎06.686.4203, ⓦwww.hotelnavona.com. Once a *pensione* and now a hotel, this place is housed in a building that dates back to the first century AD. It's a fairly welcoming place, and the location, very close to Piazza Navona, is great. Double rooms €135–160.

Portoghesi Via dei Portoghesi 1 ☎06.686.4231, ⓦwww.hotelportoghesiroma.com. Decent and well-equipped – if slightly characterless – modern rooms five minutes from most centro storico attractions. Breakfast (included) is served on the roof terrace upstairs. Doubles go for €190, although the junior suites for €220 are good value.

Raphael Largo Febo 2 ☎06.682.831, ⓦwww.raphaelhotel.com. In a quiet square just off Piazza Navona, the Raphael is filled with antiques and modern art, including an entire floor designed by architect Richard Meier, and the refined atmosphere is matched by professional and efficient service. Try to identify all of Rome's domes over a cocktail in the roof-top bar and restaurant. Doubles go for around €400, but are much cheaper in July and Aug.

Santa Chiara Via Santa Chiara 21 ☎06.687.2979, ⓦwww.albergosantachiara.com. A friendly and stylish hotel on a quiet piazza behind the Pantheon. Nice rooms too, some of which overlook the church of Santa Maria sopra Minerva. Doubles €200–250.

Zanardelli Via G. Zanardelli 7 ☎06.6821.1392, ⓦwww.hotelnavona.com/zanardelli. Run by the same family as the *Navona* (see above) – to which it is the more lavish alternative. Located just north of Piazza Navona, the building used to be a papal residence and has many original fixtures and furnishings. The rooms are elegant, but still decently priced. €145–185.

Campo de' Fiori and the Ghetto

Campo de' Fiori Via del Biscione 6 ☎06.6880.6865, ⓦwww.hotelcampodefiori.com. A friendly place in a nice location close to Campo de' Fiori with clean rooms in all shapes and colours. The large sixth-floor roof terrace has some great views and the hotel owns a number of small apartments nearby if you're keen to self-cater. Rates vary wildly depending on the room, starting at €120 and going right up to €260 for the best grade room at the most expensive time; apartments cost €180 for two, €260 for four.

Residenza Farnese Via del Mascherone 59 ☎06.6821.0980, ⓦwww.residenzafarneseroma.it. Situated on a quiet side street right by the massive Palazzo Farnese, this hotel boasts tastefully appointed rooms and very helpful staff. The location can't be bettered – its great for both the centro storico and Trastevere, just across the water by way of the Ponte Sisto footbridge. Do ask, though, for a decent room – they vary a lot and some can be on the small side. Around €250 a night for a double.

Forty Seven Cia Petroselli 47 ☎06.678.7816, ⓦwww.fortysevenhotel.com. Simple and elegant rooms above the ancient cattle market just outside the Ghetto. Within perfect striking distance of the Forum, Trastevere and the Ghetto, it has a fitness centre too. Doubles around €400.

Smeraldo Via dei Chiodaroli 9–11 ☎06.687.5929, ⓦwww.smeraldoroma.com. Clean and comfortable hotel with a slightly bland modern interior and recently renovated rooms with shiny new baths, televisions and a/c. The location is perfect, there's a terrace, and some rooms have lovely views over Rome's rooftops. Breakfast is not included in the price but is available for €7. Doubles €125–150.

Sole Via del Biscione 76 ⓣ06.687.9446, ⓦwww.solealbiscione.it. There are two hotels of this name, and both enjoy enviable locations, with this one – the cheaper of the pair – almost overlooking Piazza del Campo de' Fiori. It has pleasant rooms with TV and phone, and a small roof terrace with a spectacular view of the domed churches of San Andrea delle Valle and San Carlo ai Catinari. Doubles cost €120–160, but there are one or two rooms with shared bathroom which go for less.

St George Via Giulia 62 ⓣ06.686.611, ⓦwww.stgeorgehotel.it. Modern design, technology and style are the trademarks at this new five star on one of Rome's most enchanting streets. Relax in style after a tough day's sightseeing in the decadent spa. From €450.

The Tridente and Via Veneto

Aleph Via di San Basilio 15 ⓣ06.422.901, ⓦwww.boscolohotels.com. Almost the epitome of Rome's recent hotel makeover, the Aleph exudes cool, understated luxury, with all the facilities you could need, including a lovely top floor terrace bar and restaurant. Double rooms start at around €330.

The Beehive Via Marghera 8 ⓣ06.4470.4553, ⓦwww.the-beehive.com. "Hotel, Café, Art, Yoga" is the slogan of this ecological – and economical – hotel run by an American couple. There is free Internet access, a yoga studio, and a restaurant that serves organic breakfast and dinner daily. Basic but very well decorated doubles go for €75, more spartan dorms for €22 a head, and you can also stay in one of three nearby apartments for €35 per person.

Dei Borgognoni Via del Bufalo 126 ⓣ06.6994.1505, ⓦwww.hotelborgognoni.it. Nicely situated four star that has pleasant, well-renovated big rooms. A surprisingly large hotel, considering its location down a side street not far from Piazza di Spagna, and handy for this part of town and for the centro storico, though rates are on the high side. From about €280 a double.

Condotti Via Mario de Fiori 37 ⓣ06.679.4661, ⓦwww.hotelcondotti.com. A cosy and inviting three star, with comfortable rooms equipped with satellite TV and minibars. It's a bit devoid of personality, although this is somewhat compensated for by the cheery and welcoming staff. Not a bad price for the location, with doubles starting at €180.

Daphne Via San Basilio 55 and Via degli Avigonesi 20 ⓣ06.8745.0087, ⓦwww.daphne-rome.com. Two wonderfully welcoming *pensioni* run by an American woman and her Roman husband. Bright, beautifully renovated modern rooms in two great locations close to Piazza Barberini, and as much advice as you need on how to spend your time in Rome. Some rooms have shared bathrooms (€90–130), some are en suite (€130–200).

Erdarelli Via due Macelli 28 ⓣ06.679.1265, ⓦwww.erdarelliromehotel.com. A rather plain hotel with no-frills rooms, but good value, given it's just round the corner from the Spanish Steps. Doubles go for €120–150, although a few rooms have shared baths and are cheaper.

Firenze Via due Macelli 106 ⓣ06.679.4988, ⓦwww.hotelfirenzeroma.it. A reasonable three star, recently renovated, with large if not characterful rooms, each with TV and minibar. Good value at €100–160 a double.

Hassler Villa Medici Trinità dei Monti 6 ⓣ06.699.340, ⓦwww.hotelhasslerroma.com. You can't get much closer to the heart of Rome than this – and you certainly can't get a much better view. Situated right at the top of the Spanish Steps, this luxury hotel has elegant rooms and every convenience a guest could possibly require. The so-called "classic" rooms start at €550.

Homs Via della Vite 71/72 ⓣ06.679.2976, ⓦwww.hotelhoms.it. Perfectly located for the Spanish Steps, Trevi Fountain and all the elegant shops around, this boutique hotel boasts a roof terrace with marvellous views, rooms that have recently been refurbished, and a friendly atmosphere – something that's not always guaranteed in the hotels of this neighbourhood. €200–250.

Hotel Art **Via Margutta 56, no phone, ⓦwww.hotelartrome.com.** Tucked away on Via Margutta, this luxury hotel – an expanded church chapel – features contemporary art and innovative design. Has a wide range of amenities, including a Turkish bath, gym, spa, and a cathedral-like bar. Doubles around €400.

D'Inghilterra **Via Bocca di Leone 14 ⓣ06.699.811, ⓦwww.hoteldinghilterraroma.it.** This old favourite, formerly the apartments of the princes of Torlonia, does not disappoint and is surprisingly good value compared to what you'll pay for similar pampering elsewhere in the city. Intimacy, opulence, exquisite antiques, frescoed rooms, and all the delights of the ancient city centre on your doorstep. Doubles from €400.

Modigliani **Via della Purifacazione 42 ⓣ06.6938.0742, ⓦwww.hotelmodigliani.com.** A young artist couple run this tastefully modern hotel on a quiet street just off Piazza Barberini. Rooms are comfortable, and all have a/c and a minibar. The staff are friendly and helpful. Doubles €155–190.

Palazzetto **Vicolo del Bottino 8 ⓣ06.699.0878, ⓦwww.ilpalazzettoroma.com.** This elegant hotel runs courses on wine and hosts a distinguished restaurant and rooftop bar (Aug & Sept 7.30pm–1am), and even rents out some of its sumptuously decorated rooms to the International Wine Academy. Not especially quiet (the rooms open onto the Spanish Steps), but the location just off Piazza di Spagna is great, and it fully merits its prices. Doubles €200–300, breakfast included.

Piazza di Spagna **Via Mario de' Fiori 61 ⓣ06.679.3061, ⓦwww.hotelpiazzadispagna.it.** This small hotel, just minutes' walk from the Spanish Steps, is a good alternative to the opulent palaces that dominate the area. Rooms are comfortable, and all have a/c, minibar and phone. Friendly staff too. €180–250.

Plaza **Via del Corso 126 ⓣ06.6992.1111, ⓦwww.grandhotelplaza.com.** One of the most sumptuous hotels in Rome, with huge rooms furnished with antiques and a fantastic lobby that's worth dropping into even if you're not staying here. The rooms have been updated and have everything you might need, including Wi-Fi. Rates go for from €370 for a double – not bad for the atmosphere and location.

Portrait Suites **Via di Bocca di Leone 23 ⓣ06.6938.0742, ⓦwww.lungarnohotels.com.** A newcomer to the luxury hotel circuit, this converted town house with 14 suites, owned and designed by the Salvatore Ferragamo group, is a bastion of luxury and comfort. You pay for it though – €500 or so for one of their superbly appointed suites.

La Residenza **Via Emilia 22–24 ⓣ06.488.0789, ⓦwww.laresidenza.hotelinroma.com.** A great option in the overpriced Via Veneto area, this place combines the luxuries and atmosphere of a grand hotel with the easy-going comforts and intimacy of a private home. It's set off the busy main drag and is very tranquil. Doubles €160–220.

De Russie **Via del Babuino 9 ⓣ06.328.881, ⓦwww.hotelderussie.it.** Coolly elegant and gorgeously understated, this hotel's emphasis on comfort and quality, not to mention its stellar location just off Piazza del Popolo, make it first choice for the hip traveller spending someone else's money – it's popular among visiting movie stars. €580 and up for a double.

The Quirinale, Termini and Monti

Alpi **Via Castelfidardo 84 ⓣ06.444.1235, ⓦwww.hotelalpi.com.** One of the more peaceful hotels close to Termini, recently renovated, and within easy walking distance of the easyJet bus stop. Its pleasant (if somewhat small) rooms with bathrooms go for around €150 a double, with a great buffet breakfast – much better than you would normally expect in a hotel in this bracket.

Des Artistes **Via Villafranca 20 ⓣ06.445.4365, ⓦwww.hoteldesartistes.com.** One of the better-value hotels in the Termini area. Exceptionally good value, spotlessly clean and with a wide range of rooms, including dorm beds for around €25, although be aware that the location is on the far side of the Termini area. You can eat breakfast or recover from a long day of sightseeing on a breezy roof terrace. Doubles go for around €150, with en-suite facilities.

Residenza Cellini Via Modena 5 ☎06.4782.5204. The rooms here are comfortable and large, and, for the price, the location is great. From €145 for a double, and not a lot more for one of their spacious junior suites.

Duca d'Alba Via Leonina 14 ☎06.484.771, ⓦwww.hotelducadalba .com. A reliable three star in the heart of Monti, just steps from the district's best restaurants and nightlife. All rooms have en-suite bathrooms, a/c and satellite TV and some have balconies. Doubles can be had for around €100.

Fawlty Towers Via Magenta 39 ☎06.445.4802, ⓦwww.fawltytowers .org. This playfully named place has dorm beds for around €25 and comfortable hotel rooms, some with private baths, for €45–55.

Grifo Via del Boschetto 144 ☎06.487.1395, ⓦwww.hotelgrifo .com. A new addition to the Monti district, with crisply functional decor and a terrace overlooking a scene of medieval Rome at its most picturesque. Doubles cost between €145 and €170.

Radisson SAS Via F. Turati 171 ☎06.444.841, ⓦwww.rome .radissonsas.com. Launched a few years ago as one of Rome's new designer hotels, and still something of a flagship for the redevelopment of Termini, the rooms here are cool and stylish – much like the rooftop bar and spa. A snip at €200 for a double room.

Villa delle Rose Via Vicenza 5 ☎06.445.1788, ⓦwww.villadellerose .it. This centuries-old aristocratic villa sits amidst its own tranquil rose gardens, belying the fact that it's only a block from Termini station. Newly done up, it's quiet, pleasant and appealingly decorated, with very friendly staff. Doubles start at €150.

Trastevere

Cisterna Via della Cisterna 7–9 ☎06.581.7212, ⓦwww.cisternahotel.it. Friendly two star with a homely feel, bang in the middle of Trastevere. Twelve rooms, some with colourful tiled floors and wooden beamed ceilings, and all with private bathrooms. Doubles from €100.

Ripa Via degli Orti di Trastevere 3 ☎06.58.611, ⓦwww.ripahotel.com. One of the latest additions to Rome's burgeoning bevy of designer hotels, the Ripa is situated in Trastevere's lower and less attractive reaches but makes up for it with the effortless style of its rooms and lobby. Whether you want to pay €200–270 a double to stay down here is another matter.

Santa Maria Vicolo dei Piede 2 ☎06.589.4626, ⓦwww .hotelsantamaria.info. A few yards off Piazza Santa Maria in the heart of Trastevere, the rooms of this small three star surround a garden filled with orange trees, giving the feel of a place far removed from the city. Doubles €180–250.

Trastevere Via Luciano Manara 24a/25, ☎06.581.4713. Another good place to come if you want to be in the heart of Trastevere, with nicely decorated doubles for around €100, quads for €150, and apartments to rent with rooms for up to five people.

Prati

Amalia Via Germanico 66 ☎06.3972.3356, ⓦwww.hotelamalia .com. Located on an attractive corner not far from the Vatican, this place provides four-star amenities and three-star prices, with nicely renovated double rooms for €150–200. Don't be misled by the website though – it's nowhere near the Spanish Steps!

Bramante Vicolo delle Palline 24 ☎06.6880.6426, ⓦwww.hotelbramante .com. This little hotel, located right next to the ancient wall running from the Vatican to Castel Sant'Angelo, has recently been restored, and its rooms are charmingly decorated with original wood-beam ceilings and antiques. Doubles are a reasonable €150–200.

Colors **Via Boezio 31 ⓣ06.687.4030, ⓦwww.colorshotel.com.** Run by the friendly people from Enjoy Rome, this is a smaller version of their popular Fawlty Towers (see p.195). A hostel/hotel in a quiet neighbourhood near the Vatican, Colors provides kitchen facilities, a lounge with satellite TV and a small terrace. Dorm beds €25, doubles with shared facilities €80, ensuite doubles €100; the same organization rents out apartments for €80–120 a night with two people sharing.

Dei Consoli **Via Varrone 2d ⓣ06.6889.2972, ⓦwww.hoteldeiconsoli.com.** From the elegantly welcoming entrance to the thoughtfully designed rooms, this is an excellent choice near the Vatican. The decor on each floor is inspired by old masters and double rooms cost around €260.

Gerber **Via degli Scipioni 241 ⓣ06.321.6485 ⓦwww.hotelgerber.it.** A friendly staff and elegant, comfortable rooms make this hotel great value. Has a convenient location on a quiet street not far from the Vatican. Doubles €100–155.

La Rovere **Vicolo San Onofrio 4–5 ⓣ06.6880.6739, ⓦwww.hotellarovere.com.** Just across the bridge from Piazza Navona, this attractive, newly refurbished boutique hotel is tucked away from Rome's bustle, and offers a terrace garden and antique-filled setting for its guests to relax in. Good value at €130–230.

Hostels and convents

Rome has more options than most cities for people travelling alone or on a tight budget. Many of its convents once specialized in putting up solo female visitors, although these days many also accept men, and there are a handful of privately run hostels alongside the official Hostelling International locations. Bear in mind, too, that some of the hotels listed in this chapter offer dorm accommodation.

Alessandro Palace Hostel **Via Vicenza 42 ⓣ06.446.1958, ⓦwww.hostelsalessandro.com.** This place has been voted one of the top hostels in Europe, and it sparkles with creative style. Pluses include no lock-out or curfew, a good bar with free pizza every night, and Internet access and satellite TV. Beds cost €22–30, doubles €70, with bath €90. A few blocks away on the other side of Termini, the Alessandro Downtown, Via C.Cattaneo 23 (ⓣ06.4434.0147), is run by the same owners.

Casa di Santa Brigida **Piazza Farnese 96 ⓣ06.6889.2596, ⓦwww.brigidine.org.** Located right on a Renaissance square, this convent is hard to beat – clean and comfortable, with no curfew. All rooms have their own facilities and breakfast is included. Single rooms €105, double €190. If they're full then the same order has other locations in Rome.

Casa di Santa Francesca Romana **Via dei Vascellari 61 ⓣ06.581.2125, ⓦweb.tiscali.it/sfromana/.** This former medieval convent has been newly restructured as a refined and cheerful accommodation option in the quieter half of Trastevere. Although the rooms are fairly institutional, the central courtyard is very inviting, and the curfew is not until 2am, with no lock-out during the day. Breakfast included. Single rooms €70, doubles €100.

Ostello del Foro Italico **Viale delle Olimpiadi 61 ⓣ06.323.6267, ⓦwww.ostellionline.org.** Rome's official youth hostel, though not especially central or easy to reach from Termini – take bus #32, 69, 224, 280 and ask the driver for the "ostello". You can call ahead to check out availability, but they won't take phone bookings. You can join here if you're not a HI member already. Beds cost €18, including breakfast.

Ottaviano Via Ottaviano 6 ⓣ06.3973.8318, ⓦwww.pensioneottaviano.com. A simple *pensione*-cum-hostel near to the Vatican that is very popular with backpackers; book well in advance. Fluent English spoken. Dorm beds €20, doubles €50 with shared bath.

YWCA Via C. Balbo 4 ⓣ06.488.0460. Open to women and men, and conveniently situated just ten minutes' walk from Termini, although the market outside may get you up earlier than you intended. A range of singles to quadruples. Singles from €50, doubles €80, triples and quads €26 per person. Breakfast included. Curfew 11pm.

Essentials

Arrival

Arriving in Rome is a painless experience if you're travelling by air, by train or even by bus, although negotiating the city's outskirts by car is something you might want to avoid.

By air

Rome has two **airports**: Leonardo da Vinci, better known simply as Fiumicino, which handles most scheduled flights, and Ciampino, where you'll arrive if you're travelling on a charter or with one of the low-cost European airlines. **Taxis** for the half-hour journey to and from the airports now have a flat fee: €40 for Fiumicino, €30 for Ciampino.

Fiumicino airport

Fiumicino is connected to the centre of Rome by direct trains, which make the thirty-minute ride to Termini for €11; services begin at 6.37am and leave every half-hour until 11.37pm. Alternatively, there are more frequent trains to Trastevere, Ostiense and Tiburtina stations, each on the edge of the city centre, roughly every twenty minutes from 6.27am to 11.27pm; tickets to these stations cost less (€5.50) and Tiburtina and Ostiense are just a short (€1) metro ride from Termini, making it a cheaper (and not necessarily much slower) journey. You also can catch city bus #175 from Ostiense, or city bus #492 or #649 from Tiburtina, to the centre of town (again €1).

Ciampino airport

There is no direct public transport between **Ciampino** and the city centre. If you're travelling with one of the low-cost airlines, easyJet or Ryanair, the best thing to do is take one of the Terravision shuttle buses to Termini (they pull up on Via Marsala), which leave half an hour after each arrival – costs are around €8 single, €14 return. Otherwise ATRAL buses run every half an hour from the airport to the Anagnina metro station, at the end of line A – a twenty-minute journey (€1), from where it's a twenty-minute ride into the centre (a further €1).

By train

Most Italian and international trains arrive in Rome at **Stazione Termini**, centrally placed for all parts of the city and the meeting point of the two metro lines and many city bus routes. Among **other rail stations**, Tiburtina is a stop for some north–south intercity trains, selected routes around Lazio are handled by the Regionali platforms of Stazione Termini (a further five-minute walk from the regular platforms), and the Roma-Nord line station on Piazzale Flaminio runs to Viterbo.

By bus

Arriving by **bus** can leave you in any one of a number of bus/metro stations around the city. However, most national and international services stop at **Tiburtina**, Rome's second railway terminal after Termini, which is connected to the city centre by metro line B or buses #492 or #649. **Other bus stations,** mainly serving the Lazio region, include Ponte Mammolo (trains from Tivoli and Subiaco), Lepanto (Cerveteri, Civitavecchia, Bracciano area), EUR Fermi (Nettuno, Anzio, southern Lazio coast) and Anagnina (Castelli Romani); all of these stations are on a metro line.

By car

Driving into Rome can be quite confusing and is best avoided unless you're used to driving in Italy and know where you're going to park (see p.208). Bear in mind that non-residents aren't allowed to drive in the centro storico area. It's usually best to get on the Grande Raccordo Anulare (GRA), which circles Rome and is connected with all of the major arteries into the city centre – the Via Cassia from the north, Via Salaria from the northeast, Via Tiburtina or Via Nomentana from the east, Via Prenestina and Via Casilina or Via Cristoforo Colombo from the southeast, Via Appia Nuova and the Pontina from the south, and Via Aurelia from the northwest. From Ciampino, either follow Via Appia Nuova into the centre or join the GRA at junction 23 and follow the signs to the centre. From Fiumicino, just follow the A12 motorway into the city centre; it crosses the river just north of EUR, from where it's a short drive north up Via Cristoforo Colombo to the city walls and, beyond, to the Baths of Caracalla.

City transport

The best way to get around is to **walk** – you'll see more and will better appreciate the city. Rome wasn't built for motor traffic, and it shows in the jams, the pollution, and the bad tempers of its drivers. However, it has good public transport on the whole – a largely efficient blend of buses, a few trams and a small two-line metro.

Tickets and information

ATAC (*Agenzia dei Transporti Autoferrotranviari del Commune di Roma*) runs the city's bus, tram and metro service. There's an **information office** in the centre of Piazza dei Cinquecento and a toll-free **enquiries line** (Mon–Sat 8am–8pm; ⓣ 800.431.784 – as with most Italian numbers, you may struggle to find someone who speaks English), or try their website, ⓦ www.atac.roma.it, which has tourist info in English and a route planner. Flat-fare **tickets** cost €1 each and are good for any number of bus and tram rides and one metro ride within 75 minutes of validation. Buy them from tobacconists, newsstands and ticket machines located in all metro stations and at major bus stops, and validate them in the yellow machines on buses, trams and the entrance to metro stations. You can also get a **day pass**, valid on all city transport until midnight on the day purchased, for €4, a **three-day pass** for €11, or a **seven-day pass** for €16. Finally, it's worth knowing that there are hefty spot **fines** (€50–100) for fare-dodging, and pleading a foreigner's ignorance will get you nowhere.

Buses and trams

The **bus and tram service**, "trambus" (ⓦ www.trambus.com), is pretty good – cheap, reliable and as quick as the clogged streets allow (see box opposite for useful bus routes). Remember to board through the rear doors and punch your ticket as you enter. There is also a small network of electric minibuses that negotiate the narrow backstreets of the old centre. Around midnight, **nightbuses** click into service, accessing most parts of the city through to about 5am; they don't sell tickets on board so be sure to have one before boarding; they are easily identified by the owl symbol above the "bus notturno" schedule.

Metro

Rome's **metro** or "Met.Ro" as it calls itself (ⓦ www.metroroma.it), runs from 5.30am to 11.30pm, though it's not as useful as you might think, since its two lines – A (red) and B (blue) don't cover large parts of the city centre. Nonetheless, there are a few useful city-centre stations: Termini is the hub of both lines, and there are stops at the Colosseum, Piazza Barberini and Piazza

Useful bus routes

#3 Tram Stazione Trastevere–Via Marmorata–Piramide–Circo Massimo–Colosseum–San Giovanni–San Lorenzo–Via Nomentana–Parioli–Viale Belle Arti.

#23 Piazza Clodio–Piazza Risorgimento–Ponte Vittorio Emanuele II–Ponte Garibaldi–Via Marmorata–Piazzale Ostiense–Centrale Montemartini–Basilica di S. Paolo.

#30 Express Piazza Clodio–Piazza Mazzini–Piazza Cavour–Corso Rinascimento–Largo Argentina–Piazza Venezia–Luntotevere Aventino–Via Marmorata–Piramide–Via C.Colombo–EUR.

#40 (Express) Termini–Via Nazionale–Piazza Venezia–Largo Argentina–Piazza Pia.

#62 Piazza Bologna–Via Nomentana–Porta Pia–Piazza Barberini–Piazza San Silvestro–Via del Corso–Piazza Venezia– Corso V.Emanuele II–Borgo Angelico–Piazza Pio.

#64 Termini–Piazza della Repubblica–Via Nazionale–Piazza Venezia–Largo Argentina–Corso Vittorio Emanuele II–Stazione S. Pietro.

#75 Via Poerio (Monteverde)–Via Induno–Porta Portese–Testaccio–Piramide–Circo Massimo–Colosseo–Via Cavour–Termini–Piazza Indipendienza.

#116 Porta Pinciana–Via Veneto–Via del Tritone–Piazza di Spagna–Piazza San Silvestro–Corso Rinascimento–Campo de' Fiori–Piazza Farnese–Lungotevere Sangallo–Terminal Gianicolo.

#117 San Giovanni in Laterano–Piazza Celimontana–Via Due Macelli–Via del Babuino–Piazza del Popolo–Via del Corso–Piazza Venezia–Via Nazionale–Via dei Serpenti–Colosseo–Via Labicana.

#119 Piazza del Popolo–Via del Corso–Piazza Venezia–Largo Argentina–Via del Tritone–Piazza Barberini–Via Veneto–Porta Pinciana–Piazza Barberini–Piazza di Spagna–Via del Babuino–Piazza del Popolo.

#175 Termini–Piazza Barberini–Via del Corso–Piazza Venezia–Colosseo–Circo Massimo–Aventine–Stazione Ostiense.

#271 S. Paolo–Via Ostiense–Piramide–Viale Aventino–Circo Massimo–Colosseo–Piazza Venezia–Ponte Sisto–Castel Sant'Angelo–Via Vitilleschi–Piazza Risorgimento–Ottaviano–Foro Italico.

#492 Stazione Tiburtina–Piazzale Verano–Termini–Piazza Barberini–Via del Corso–Piazza Venezia–Largo Argentina–Corso del Rinascimento–Piazza Cavour–Piazza Risorgimento–Cipro.

#590 Same route as metro line A but with access for disabled; runs every 90 minutes.

#660 Largo Colli Albani–Via Appia Nuova–Via Appia Pignatelli–Via Appia Antica.

#714 Termini–Santa Maria Maggiore–Via Merulana–San Giovanni in Laterano–Viale Terme di Caracalla–EUR.

#910 Termini–Piazza della Repubblica–Via Piemonte–Via Pinciana (Villa Borghese)–Piazza Euclide–Palazetto dello Sport–Piazza Mancini.

di Spagna. They're working on line C, projected for completion in 2011.

Tourist buses

Three main tourists buses circle Rome and its major sights. They're in competition with each other, but all start from outside Termini, and you can get combined tickets for two of them. Information on each is available at Ⓦ www.trambusopen.com or from Ⓣ 800.281.281.

Bus #110 Good for general orientation and a quick glance at the sights, this ATAC-run open-top bus has a guided commentary. It leaves from Piazza dei Cinquecento outside Stazione Termini and stops at all the major sights, including Piazza di Spagna, Castel Sant'Angelo, the Vatican and Via Appia Antica. The whole round trip takes two hours, and in summer departures are every twenty minutes from 8.40am until 8.20pm daily, including holidays and Sundays. Tickets cost €13 and allow you to get on wherever you like and hop on and off throughout the day. Combined #110 and Archeobus tickets cost €20. Tickets can be bought on board, or before you get on at Piazza dei Cinquecento.

Archeobus The Archeobus is another hop-on-hop-off service, linking some of the most compelling monuments on and around the Via Appia Antica. Like the other tourist lines, it starts at Piazza dei Cinquecento, in front of Termini, before heading down to the southern edge of the city via Piazza Venezia, Piazza Bocca della Verità, Circo Massimo–Terme di Caracalla and the Porta San Sebastiano. On Via Appia, there are stops at Domine Quo Vadis–Catacombe di S. Callisto, Catacombe di S. Sebastiano, Circo di Massenzio, Casal Rotundo–Aquedotti Romani and the Villa dei Quintili. Buses run daily every hour between 9am and 4pm. Tickets cost €8, and integrated tickets are available, including the #110 bus and various museums and so on, with different lengths of validity. They can be bought on board, or at Piazza dei Cinquecento.

Christian Rome The Vatican's tourist bus service links Rome's major basilicas and other Christian sights, starting, like the others, in front of Termini on Piazza dei Cinquecento. Services run daily every thirty minutes between 8.30am and 7.30pm, and tickets cost €13 for the day (€20 for two days, €28 for three); they can be bought on board, at Piazza dei Cinquecento or at the Info Points on Piazza Pio XII, next to St Peter's Square, and San Giovanni in Laterano. More information at Ⓦwww.orpnet.org.

Taxis

The easiest way to get a **taxi** is to find the nearest taxi stand (*fermata dei taxi*) – central ones include Termini, Piazza Venezia, Piazza San Silvestro, Piazza di Spagna, Piazza Navona, Piazza San Pietro and Piazza Barberini. Alternatively, you can call a taxi (Ⓣ06.3570, Ⓣ06.4994, Ⓣ06.6645, or Ⓣ06.88.177), but remember that you'll pay for the time it takes to get to you. You will be given a call number for the car, usually a city and number, "Roma 10", "Verona 34", etc. Only take licensed white cabs with the "Comune di Roma" insignia clearly marked on the door, and make sure the meter is switched on; a card in every official taxi explains – in English – the extra charges for luggage, late-night, Sundays and holidays, and airport journeys. To give you a rough idea of how much taxis cost, you can reckon on a journey from one side of the city centre to another costing around €10, if the traffic isn't too bad, or around €15 on Sunday or at night.

Bicycle and scooter rental

Appia Antica Visitor Center Via Appia Antica 58/60. Ⓣ06.512.6314, Ⓦwww.parcoappiaantica.org. Cycle along Rome's first highway and through the Caffarella Valley on Sun – €3/hr or €10/day. Good information in English about suggested routes.

Scooter Hire Via Cavour 80 Ⓣ06.481.5669, Ⓦwww.scooterhire.it. Bike, scooter and motorcycle rental – €12/day for bicycles, €30/day for scooters and €90 /day for motorcycles.

Treno e Scooter Rent Stazione Termini, near Track 1. Ⓣ06.4890.5823, Ⓦwww.trenoescooter.191.it. Scooter and bicycle rental – €10/day for bikes, €37–60/day for mopeds or scooters.

Information

There are **tourist information booths** in Terminal B at Fiumicino (daily 8.15am–7pm; ⓣ06.6595.4471), and in Piazza dei Cinquecento at Termini station (daily 8am–9pm; ⓣ06.4890.6300), although the long queues that often develop at both of these mean you're usually better off heading straight for the main **tourist office** at Via Parigi 5 (Mon–Sat 9am–7pm; ⓣ06.488.991, ⓦwww.romaturismo.it), ten minutes' walk from Termini. They have free maps that should – together with our own – be ample for finding your way around, and plenty of other printed information. There are also **information kiosks** in key locations around the city centre (see below). They, too, have general information and are useful for free maps, directions and up-to-the-minute information (opening times, for example) about nearby sights – the staff usually speak English.

There's also an unofficial source of information: **Enjoy Rome** (Via Marghera 8a; Mon–Fri 8.30am–7pm, Sat 8.30am–2pm; ⓣ06.445.1843, ⓦwww.enjoyrome.com), whose English-speaking staff also run a free room-finding service, organize tours, have a left-luggage service and run shuttle buses to the airport. Their information is often more up-to-date and reliable than that handed out by the various tourist offices, and they will also advise on where to eat, drink and party, if you so wish.

For what's-on information, the city's best source of **listings** is perhaps *Romac'è* (€1, Thursdays), which has a helpful section in English giving information on tours, clubs, restaurants, services and weekly events. The expat bi-weekly, *Wanted in Rome* (€1.50 every other Wednesday), which is entirely in English, is also a useful source of information, especially if you're looking for an apartment or work. If you understand a bit of Italian, the daily arts pages of the Rome **newspaper**, *Il Messaggero*, lists movies, plays and major musical events, and can be found in most bars for the customers to read, or at newsstands for €0.90. The newspaper *La Repubblica* also includes the "Trova Roma" section in its Thursday edition, another handy guide to current offerings.

Information kiosks

Piazza di Spagna Largo Goldoni ⓣ06.6813.6061. 9am–6pm.
San Giovanni Piazza San Giovanni in Laterno ⓣ06.7720.3535. 9am–6pm.
Via Nazionale Palazzo delle Esposizioni ⓣ06.4782.4525. 9am–6pm.
Piazza Navona Piazza delle Cinque Lune ⓣ06.6880.9240. 9am–6pm.
Castel Sant'Angelo Piazza Pia ⓣ06.6880.9707. 9am–6pm.
Fori Imperiali Piazza del Tempio della Pace ⓣ06.6992.4307. 9am–6pm.
Trastevere Piazza Sonnino ⓣ06.5833.3457. 9am–6pm.

Sights and museums

Most **museums and galleries** are closed on Mondays. **Opening hours** for state-run museums are generally from 9am until 7pm, Tuesday to Sunday. Most other museums roughly follow this pattern too, although they are more likely to close for a couple of hours in the afternoon, and have shorter opening hours in winter. Some museums also run late-night openings in summer (till 10pm or later Tues–Sat, or 8pm on Sun).

In restauro

You may find buildings of all kinds closed for restoration (**chiuso per restauro**), and it's usually pretty uncertain when they might reopen. If there's something you really want to see, and you don't know when you might be back in Rome, it might be worth trying to persuade a workman, priest or curator to show you around, even if there's scaffolding everywhere.

There is no **museum pass** that will get you into all the main attractions in Rome, but some sights are grouped together, making it easier and cheaper to visit them. Much of Rome's ancient sculpture, alongside other artifacts, has been gathered together into the Museo Nazionale Romano, which operates on four main sites: Palazzo Massimo, the Terme di Diocleziano, the Crypta Balbi and Palazzo Altemps. You can buy a ticket (at each branch) that grants entry to all four locations for just €7 and is valid for three days. As for the **ancient sites**, the Colosseum and Palatine Hill are visitable on a combined ticket. There's also the **Roma Pass** (€20), a three-day ticket that gives free entry to two state-run attractions and discounts to others as well as a three-day public transport pass – probably the city's best bargain.

The **opening times** of ancient sites are more flexible: most are open every day, including Sunday, from 9am until late evening – frequently specified as one hour before sunset, and thus changing according to the time of year. In winter, times are drastically cut, if only because of the darker evenings; 4pm is a common closing time.

Churches

Rome is very used to tourists, but the rules for visiting **churches** are much as they are all over Italy. Dress modestly, which usually means no shorts, short skirts or bare shoulders, and try to avoid wandering around during a service. We've given **opening hours** throughout the guide, but most major Roman churches – and most of the ones written up in this book – open in the early morning, at around 7am or 8am, and close around noon, opening up again at 4pm and closing at 6pm or 7pm.

Public holidays

Many sights will be closed on the following days:

January 1 (New Year's Day)
January 6 (Epiphany)
Pasquetta (Easter Monday)
April 25 (Liberation Day)
May 1 (Labour Day)
August 15 (*Ferragosto*; Assumption of the Blessed Virgin Mary)
November 1 (*Ognissanti*; All Souls' Day)
December 8 (*Immacolata*; Immaculate Conception of the Blessed Virgin Mary)
December 25 (*Natale*; Christmas)
December 26 (*Santo Stefano*; St Stephen's Day)

Directory

Airlines Air Canada ☎06.6501.0991; Alitalia ☎06.2222; American Airlines ☎06.6605.3169; British Airways ☎199.712.266; Delta ☎800.477.999; easyJet ☎848.887.766; Ryanair ☎899.88.99.73.
Airport enquiries Fiumicino ☎06.65951, Ⓦwww.adr.it; Ciampino ☎06.65951, Ⓦwww.adr.it.
Car rental All the usual suspects have desks at Fiumicino, Ciampino, Termini and elsewhere in the city. Avis ☎199.100.133, Termini ☎06.481.4273, Ciampino ☎06.7934.0368, Fiumicino ☎06.6501.1531; Europcar ☎800.014.410, Termini ☎06.488.2854, Ciampino ☎06.7934.0387, Fiumicino ☎06.6501.0879; Hertz ☎199.112.211, Termini ☎06.474.0389, Ciampino ☎06.7934.0616, Fiumicino ☎06.6501.1553; Maggiore ☎848.867.067, Termini ☎06.488.0049, Ciampino ☎06.7934.0368, Fiumicino ☎06.6501.0678; Sixt ☎800.900.666, Termini ☎06.474.0014, Ciampino ☎06.7934.0838, Fiumicino ☎06.6595.3547.
Dentist Dr Andrea Chiantini at Absolute Dentistry, Via G. Pisanelli 1/3, has a 24-hour emergency service ☎06.3600.3837 or 339.250.7016.
Disabled travellers Although changes are in the works, Rome can be quite a challenge for those with disabilities. Contact the Cooperative Integrate Onlus (CO.IN), Via Enrico Giglioli 54a (☎06.712.9011, toll free in Italy ☎800.271.027), who have English-speaking 24hr information on their phone line, and produce a guide, *Roma Accessible*, which contains information on major sites, museums, hotels and restaurants. Ⓦwww.coinsociale.it/tourism has additional information. Another resource about access in Rome can be found on the Emerging Horizons web site, Ⓦwww.emerginghorizons.com.
Doctors AlphaMed, Via Zanardelli 36 ☎06.6830.9493, Mon–Fri 9am–8pm, is an ultra-central medical practice with English-speaking doctors. Tobias Wallbrecher, Via Domenico Silveri 30 ☎06.638.0569, Mon–Fri 9am–1pm & 4–7pm, is a general English-speaking family doctor close to the Vatican.
Electricity 220 volts. If coming from the US, buy an adaptor before you come, as they are more expensive once you get here.
Embassies Australia Via Bosio 5 ☎06.852.721; Britain Via XX Settembre 80a ☎06.4220.0001; Canada Via G.B. de Rossi 30 ☎06.445.981; Ireland Piazza Campitelli 3 ☎06.697.9121; New Zealand Via Zara 28 ☎06.441.7171; USA Via Veneto 119a ☎06.46.741.
Emergencies Police ☎113; Carabinieri ☎112; Fire ☎115; Ambulance ☎118.
Exchange American Express, Piazza di Spagna 38 (Mon–Fri 9am–5.30pm, Sat 9am–12.30pm); Thomas Cook, Piazza Barberini 21a (Mon–Sat 9am–8pm, Sun 9.30am–5pm), and Via della Conciliazione 23 (Mon–Sat 8.30am–7.30pm, Sun 9.30am–5pm). Post offices will exchange American Express travellers' cheques and cash commission-free.
Hospital The most central hospitals with emergency facilities are: Fatebenefratelli, Isola Tiberina ☎06.683.7299; Rome American Hospital, Via E. Longoni 81 ☎06.22.551 – a private multi-speciality hospital with bilingual staff and a 24hr emergency line; San Giovanni Via A. Aradam 8 ☎06.49.971; Santo Spirito Lungotevere in Sassia 1 ☎06.68.351, near the Vatican.
Internet cafés Bibli, Via dei Fienaroli 28 (Mon 5.30pm–midnight, Tues–Sun 11am–midnight); Easy Internet Café, Via Barberini 2 (daily 7am–1am); Internet Train, Piazza Sant'Andrea delle Valle 3 (Mon–Fri 10am–11pm, Sat 10am–8pm, Sun noon–8pm); Internet Café, Via Cavour 213 (daily 9am–1am; ☎06.4782.3051; Pole2Pole, Via Santa Maria Maggiore 129 (daily 9am–11pm).
Left luggage Termini station (daily 6am–midnight; €3.80 per piece for 5hr, €0.60 for each additional hour, ☎06.4782.5543), no plastic bags; the Enjoy Rome office (see p.205) will also look after its customers' luggage.
Lost credit cards American Express ☎06.7290.0347; MasterCard ☎800.870.866; Visa ☎800.877.232.
Lost property For property lost on a train call ☎06.4730.6682 (daily 7am–11pm); on a bus ☎06.6769.3214 (Mon–Fri 8.30am–1pm, Tues–Thurs 3–5pm); on

Fly Less – Stay Longer!

Rough Guides believes in the good that travel does, but we are deeply aware of the impact of fuel emissions on climate change. We recommend taking fewer trips and staying for longer. If you can avoid travelling by air, please use an alternative, especially for journeys of under 1000km/600miles. And always offset your travel at ⓦwww.roughguides.com/climatechange.

the Metro A ⓣ06.487.4309 (Mon, Wed, Fri 9.30am–12.30pm), on the Metro B ⓣ06.5753.2265 (Mon–Sat 7am–7pm).

Parking You can park on the street for around €1/hr (8am–8pm), or there are parking garages in the Villa Borghese (around €1/hr) in front of Stazione Termini (€5/2hr, then €1.50/hr). There are also car parks next to the terminal metro stations, from where it's easy to get into the city centre.

Pharmacies The following pharmacies are open 24hr, year-round: Farmacia della Stazione, Piazza dei Cinquecento 51 ⓣ06.488.0019; Internazionale, Piazza Barberini 49 ⓣ06.482.5456; Piram, Via Nazionale 228 ⓣ06.488.0754.

Police ⓣ113. Both the police (Polizia Statale) and the *carabinieri* (who wear military-style uniforms) have offices in Termini. Otherwise the most central police station is off Via del Corso in Piazza del Collegio Romano 3, and there's a carabinieri office in Piazza Venezia to the right of Via del Corso. Theft should be reported to the Polizia Statale.

Post offices Piazza San Silvestro 12 ⓣ06.6976.6320; Corso Vittorio Emanuele II 330 ⓣ06.6840.2920; Largo Brancaccio82 (Via Marmorata) ⓣ06.4890.3635; Via Arenula 4 ⓣ06.684.0501; Via Cavour 277 ⓣ06.462.0741; Via Giolitti 14 ⓣ06.488.8741; Via del Quirinale 30 ⓣ06.474.0226; Via Milano 18 (Via Nazionale) ⓣ06.474.5631; Via della Scrofa 61 ⓣ06.6840.9220.

Summer venues Rome's monuments and parks become the backdrop for performances in the summer. The opera season moves to the Baths of Caracalla (ⓣ06.4816.0287 & 800.907.080, ⓦwww.operaroma.it). From June to Oct there are classical concerts at the Theater of Marcellus (ⓣ06.8713.1590, ⓦwww.tempietto.org). The Villa Celiamontana, near the Colosseum, has nightly jazz performances from July to Sept (ⓣ06.589.7807, ⓦwww.villaceliamontanajazz.com).

Time Rome is one hour ahead of GMT, six hours ahead of Eastern Standard Time, and nine hours ahead of Pacific Standard Time in North America.

Train enquiries For general enquiries about schedules and prices ⓣ892.021 (24hr), ⓦwww.trenitalia.it.

Travel agents For discount tickets try the CTS offices at Via Genova 16 ⓣ06.462.0431 and Corso Vittorio Emanuele II 297 ⓣ06.687.2672, both open on Sat until 1pm, when all the other travel agents are closed. Other good places to try are Viaggiare, Via San Nicola da Tolentino 15 ⓣ06.421.171 (Mon–Fri 9am–6.30pm), who have some English-speaking staff, and Tiuk Travel, Via Cavour 151 ⓣ06.481.5464 (Mon–Fri 9am–5.30pm).

Wireless hotspots There are now dozens of free wireless hotspots throughout the city including the Circus Maximus, Villa Borghese, Piazza Navona, Largo Argentina, Trevi Fountain, and the Spanish Steps. See ⓦwww.romawireless.com.

Chronology

Rome chronology

9th century BC ▸ Iron Age village founded on the Palatine Hill.

753 BC ▸ Romulus kills Remus and becomes the city's first ruler.

616–579 BC ▸ Tarquinius Priscus is Rome's first Etruscan king.

6th century BC ▸ The Cloaca Maxima, one of the world's earliest sewerage systems, is built, and the first buildings appear on the Capitoline Hill.

509 BC ▸ Tarquinius Superbus, the last Etruscan king, is deposed and the Roman Republic is established.

474 BC ▸ Final defeat of the Etruscan tribes.

390 BC ▸ The Gauls capture Rome.

378 BC ▸ The Servian Wall is built to protect the city from invasion.

343–290 BC ▸ Wars against the Samnites.

264–146 BC ▸ Punic Wars against Carthage.

218 BC ▸ Hannibal invades Italy but spares Rome.

201 BC ▸ Scipio Africanus captures North Africa.

146 BC ▸ Sack of Carthage by Roman forces.

87 BC ▸ Civil War breaks out between Marius and Sulla.

82 BC ▸ Sulla becomes dictator of Rome.

78 BC ▸ Sulla dies and the city enters another unsettled period, culminating in a slave revolt led by Spartacus in 73 BC.

65–63 BC ▸ Marius's nephew, Julius Caesar, establishes a formidable military reputation and occupies some of the most influential posts in the Republic.

60 BC ▸ Triumvirate of Julius Caesar, Crassus and Pompey rules Rome.

58–51 BC ▸ Caesar colonises Gaul.

49–45 BC ▸ Caesar heads back south, crosses the Rubicon river and marches on Rome, sparking off a new civil war between him and Pompey, eventually leading to Pompey's murder in Egypt and a subsequent triumphant return to Rome.

44 BC ▸ Caesar's pride and ambition lead to his assassination in Pompey's Theatre on March 15.

43 BC ▸ Leadership of Rome is assumed by a triumvirate of Antony, Octavian and Lepidus.

42 BC ▸ Caesar's assassins, Cassius and Brutus, are killed at Philippi.

40 BC ▸ Antony marries Octavian's sister, Octavia.

31 BC ▸ Octavian defeats Antony and Cleopatra at the Battle of Actium. The pair would commit suicide less than a year later.

27 BC ▸ Octavian becomes sole ruler as Augustus, presiding over the city's first Imperial era and heralding the Augustan dynasty.

14 AD ▸ Tiberius, Augustus's stepson, assumes power and marries Augustus's daughter, Julia, who gives birth to Caligula, the next emperor.

41 AD ▸ Caligula is assassinated after four disinterested and chaotic years in power. Caligula's uncle, Claudius, reluctantly takes over the reigns and proves to be a wiser ruler.

54 AD ▸ Claudius is succeeded by his stepson, Nero, whose reign is marred by more corruption and excess, typified by the construction of the monstrous Domus Aurea (Golden House) after a huge fire in 64 AD.

69 AD ▸ The emperor Vespasian restores order to Rome and is the first ruler of the Flavian dynasty. Committed to obliterating all traces of Nero, he deliberately builds the Colosseum in the grounds of the Domus Aurea.

81 AD ▸ After a reign of just two years, Vespasian's son Titus is succeeded by Domitian, who is eventually murdered in 96 AD, but not before he built the stadium that forms the foundations of today's Piazza Navona.

98 AD ▸ Trajan becomes emperor and expands the borders of the empire to the east. He presides over a city that is as prosperous and peaceful as it has ever been, growing to a population of around a million.

117 ▸ Trajan is succeeded by Hadrian, who continues the expansionist agenda, and proves a similarly wise and resourceful emperor, ruling over what many see as the empire's golden age.

138–192 ▸ Trajan is succeeded first by Antonius Pius, then Marcus Aurelius, who continues to rule a stable city and a rich empire, though one that was at constant threat from tribes to the northeast. The Antonine line fizzles out when Marcus Aurelius's son, the cruel and autocratic Commodus, is strangled by the Praetorian Guard.

193 ▸ Septimius Severus becomes the first emperor of the Severan dynasty. Rome's true decline begins when his son Caracalla murders his brother and assumes power for himself in 211.

238 ▸ There are six emperors in one year, as the city becomes more threatened, and more violent.

275 ▸ The emperor Aurelian builds his namesake walls around the city's seven hills to keep it safe from invaders.

284 ▸ Diocletian inherits a safer city, and proceeds to stabilize Rome, bring the army under control and divide the empire into east and west. He also gains a name as a ruthless persecutor of Christians, before retiring to his native Croatia in 305.

306 ▸ Constantine sees a vision of a cross in the sky and converts to Christianity. The next day he defeats his rival Maxentius at the Battle of Ponte Milvio to claim the Western Empire.

325 ▸ The empire's first Christian emperor, Constantine shifts the seat of power east to Byzantium, renaming it Constantinople.

410 ▸ Rome is captured by Alaric and the Visigoths, the first time a foreign invader has held the city for 800 years.

455 ▸ The city is pillaged again by the Vandals.

5th century ▸ The city declines to a population of around 30,000.

590 ▸ Gregory I becomes pope and takes the name Pontifex Maximus, after the high priests of ancient times, revitalising the city with new basilicas and converting ancient Roman structures like the Pantheon and the Castel Sant'Angelo.

753 ▸ The Lombards besiege Rome.

800 ▸ Charlemagne visits Rome and is crowned ruler of the Holy Roman Empire. The city is restored under Pope Hadrian I.

850–1300 ▸ The city becomes the focus of struggles between the papacy, successive Holy Roman Emperors and its own aristocracy.

1305 ▸ Clement V transfers the papal court to Avignon, France.

1347 ▸ Cola di Rienzo seizes power and re-establishes Rome's Republic for seven years.

1376 ▸ The pope returns to Rome but the schism continues, with a rival anti-pope still based in Avignon.

1417 ▸ Martin V consolidates papal power in Rome.

1475 ▸ Pope Sixtus IV commissions the Sistine Chapel.

1503 ▸ Julius II becomes pope and commissions some frescoes for the ceiling of the papal chapel from a then little-known sculptor, Michelangelo, as well as the decoration of his own apartments by Raphael.

1513 ▸ Leo X assumes the papal throne and continues Julius's role as patron of the city's greatest artists and architects.

1527 ▸ Holy Roman Emperor Charles V captures Rome and Pope Clement VII flees to the Castel Sant'Angelo, where he is confined for a year.

1534 ▸ Alessandro Farnese is elected pope as Paul III. Michelangelo completes his Sistine Chapel painting of the Last Judgement and various last works – Piazza di Campidoglio, Palazzo Farnese and the initial plans for the new church of St Peter's.

1585 ▸ Sixtus V undertakes widespread construction works, ploughing roads through the city centre and creating grand vistas and new squares.

1605 ▸ St Peter's is completed under the Borghese pope, Paul V.

1623 ▸ Urban VIII ascends the papal throne and becomes the greatest patron of the Baroque era's most dominant figure, Gianlorenzo Bernini – a patronage continued by his successors Paul V and Innocent X, under whom the colonnade of St Peter's was completed.

1700 ▸ The population of Rome is now 150,000, but visitors number over half as much again – the era of tourism is beginning to dawn, and Rome becomes an essential stop on any traveller's Grand Tour.

1798 ▸ French forces commanded by Napoleon occupy the city and the reigning pope, Pius VI, is taken prisoner in France.

1815 ▸ Papal rule is restored under Pius VII.

1849 ▸ The Unification movement is building, and Giuseppe Mazzini forces Pope Pius IX to leave Rome and declares the city a republic. However, the papacy is restored four months later by Napoleon III.

1859–64 ▸ Unification forces gather strength throughout the Italian peninsula and Florence becomes the capital of the new kingdom of Italy.

1870 ▸ Italian forces take Rome and declare the city the capital of the new state under Victor Emmanuele II. Pope Pius IX is confined to the Vatican. Agostino Depretis becomes first prime minister of Italy, remaining in power until 1887.

1922 ▸ Mussolini marches on Rome, at first occupying the Palazzo del Viminale but eventually taking up residence in the Palazzo di Venezia.

1922–42 ▸ Mussolini oversees the construction of numerous public works – Via della Conciliazione, Via dei Fori Imperiali, Foro Italico and, finally, EUR.

1929 ▸ The Lateran Pact is signed by Italy and the Vatican, recognising the sovereignty of Vatican City, together with key basilicas and papal palaces.

1946 ▸ King Victor Emmanuele III is forced to abdicate and a republic is declared under Alcide de Gasperi.

1960 ▸ Fellini releases *La Dolce Vita*, a film that would define the Sixties in Rome – and, indeed, everywhere else.

1970s ▸ The *anni piombi*, or "years of lead", when like other Italian cities Rome became a focus for violent protest and terrorism. The period culminated with the brutal murder of Aldo Moro and the dumping of his body in the city centre.

1980s ▸ The population of the city reaches three million.

1990s ▸ A series of corruption scandals named *tangentopoli*, or "bribesville", in national and local government leads to a series of show trials and the reconfiguration of the entire Italian political landscape, the so-called "Mani Puliti" shakeout, which results in the effective demise of the three main parties.

1993 ▸ Francesco Rutelli is elected mayor of Rome after resigning on principle as a government minister during the *tangentopoli* scandal. He becomes the most popular mayor for years.

2000 ▸ Under Rutelli's guidance, Rome spruces itself up for the Church's millennium jubilee, instigating a series of positive changes to the city's infrastructure that continue to the present-day.

2001 ▸ Walter Veltroni is elected mayor of Rome, and proves a charismatic leader. He is re-elected five years later and oversees a series of prestigious public works.

2006 ▸ Ancient meets modern Rome as the new Richard Meier-designed building to house the Augustan Altar of Peace finally opens after years of controversy, along with the city's new Auditorium – itself perhaps the biggest symbol of Rome's revitalisation.

Language

Italian

Speaking some Italian, however tentatively, can mark you out from the hordes of tourists in Rome, and having a little more can open up the city no end. What follows is a brief pronunciation guide, some useful words and phrases, and a food and drink glossary. For more detail, get *Italian: The Rough Guide Phrasebook*, which has a huge and accessible vocabulary, a detailed menu reader and conversational examples to get you through most situations.

Pronunciation

Italian **pronunciation** is very simple – all words are stressed on the penultimate syllable unless an accent (` or ´) denotes otherwise. The only difficulties you're likely to encounter are the few consonants that are different from English:

c before e or i is pronounced as in church, while ch before the same vowels is hard, as in cat.

The same goes with g – soft before e or i, as in geranium; hard before h, as in garlic.

sci or sce are pronounced as in sheet and shelter respectively.

gn has the ni sound of onion.

gl in Italian is softened to something like li in English, as in stallion.

h is not aspirated, as in honour.

Words and phrases

Basic words and phrases

Buongiorno	Good morning
Buonasera	Good afternoon/ evening
Buonanotte	Good night
Ciao (informal; to strangers use phrases above)	Hello/goodbye
Arrivederci	Goodbye
Si	Yes
No	No
Per favore	Please
Grazie (molte/ mille grazie)	Thank you (very much)
Prego	You're welcome
Va bene	All right/that's OK
Come stai/sta? (informal/formal)	How are you?
Bene	I'm fine
Parla inglese?	Do you speak English?
Non ho capito	I don't understand
Non lo so	I don't know
Mi scusi	Excuse me
Permesso (in a crowd)	Excuse me
Mi dispiace	I'm sorry
Sono qui in vacanza	I'm here on holiday
Sono inglese	I'm English
scozzese	Scottish
gallese	Welsh
irlandese	Irish
americano/a (masculine/ feminine)	American
australiano/a (masculine/ feminine)	Australian
neozelandese	a New Zealander

Oggi	Today
Domani	Tomorrow
Dopodomani	Day after tomorrow
Ieri	Yesterday
Adesso	Now
Più tardi	Later
Aspetta!	Wait a minute!
Andiamo!	Let's go!
Di mattina	In the morning
Nel pomeriggio	In the afternoon
Di sera	In the evening
Qui/Là	Here/There
Buono/Cattivo	Good/Bad
Grande/Piccolo	Big/Small
Economico/Caro	Cheap/Expensive
Presto/Tardi	Early/Late
Caldo/Freddo	Hot/Cold
Vicino/Lontano	Near/Far
Velocemente/Lentamente	Quickly/Slowly
Con/Senza	With/Without
Più/Meno	More/Less
Basta	Enough, no more
Signor/Signora/Signorina	Mr/Mrs/Miss

Numbers

uno	1
due	2
tre	3
quattro	4
cinque	5
sei	6
sette	7
otto	8
nove	9
dieci	10
undici	11
dodici	12
tredici	13
quattordici	14
quindici	15
sedici	16
diciassette	17
diciotto	18
diciannove	19
venti	20
ventuno	21
ventidue	22
trenta	30
quaranta	40
cinquanta	50
sessanta	60
settanta	70
ottanta	80
novanta	90
cento	100
centuno	101
centodieci	110
duecento	200
cinquecento	500
mille	1000
cinquemila	5000
diecimila	10,000
cinquantamila	50,000

Some signs

Entrata/Uscita	Entrance/Exit
Ingresso libero	Free entry
Signori/Signore	Gentlemen/Ladies
Vietato fumare	No smoking
Gabinetto/Bagno	WC/Bathroom
Aperto/Chiuso	Open/Closed
Chiuso per restauro	Closed for restoration
Chiuso per ferie	Closed for holidays
Tirare/Spingere	Pull/Push
Cassa	Cash desk

Transport

Autostazione	Bus station
Stazione ferroviaria	Train station
Un biglietto a ...	A ticket to ...
Solo andata/andata e ritorno	One-way/return
Mi può dire dove scendere?	Can you tell me when to get off?
A che ora parte?	What time does it leave?
Da dove parte?	Where does it leave from?

Accommodation

Albergo	Hotel
C'è un albergo qui vicino?	Is there a hotel nearby?
Ha una camera ...	Do you have a room ...
per una/due/tre persona/e	for one/two/three person/people
per una/due/tre notte/i	for one/two/three night/s
per una/due settimana/e	for one/two week/s
con un letto matrimoniale	with a double bed
con due letti	with twin beds
con una doccia/un bagno	with a shower/bath
con balcone	with a balcony

con acqua calda/ fredda	with hot/cold water
Quanto costa?	How much is it?
È caro	It's expensive
È compresa la prima colazione?	Is breakfast included?
Ha qualcosa che costa di meno?	Do you have anything cheaper?
Pensione completa/ mezza pensione	Full/half board
Posso vedere la camera?	Can I see the room?
La prendo	I'll take it
Vorrei prenotare una camera	I'd like to book a room
Ho una prenotazione	I have a booking

Questions and directions

Dove? (Dov'è/Dove sono ... ?)	Where? (where is/where are ... ?)
Quando?	When?
Cosa? (Cos'è?)	What? (what is it?)
Quanto/Quanti?	How much/many?
Perché?	Why?
C'è ... ?	It is/there is (is it/is there ...)?
Che ore sono?	What time is it?
Per arrivare a ... ?	How do I get to ... ?
Quant'è lontano ... ?	How far is it to ... ?
A che ora apre?	What time does it open?
A che ora chiude?	What time does it close?
Quanto costa?	How much does it cost?
(Quanto costano?)	(... do they cost?)
Come si chiama in italiano?	What's it called in Italian?

Food and drink terms

Basics and snacks

Aceto	Vinegar
Aglio	Garlic
Biscotti	Biscuits
Burro	Butter
Caramelle	Sweets
Cioccolato	Chocolate
Formaggio	Cheese
Frittata	Omelette
Marmellata	Jam
Olio	Oil
Olive	Olives
Pane	Bread
Pepe	Pepper
Riso	Rice
Sale	Salt
Uova	Eggs
Yoghurt	Yoghurt
Zúcchero	Sugar
Zuppa	Soup

Starters (antipasti) and fried snacks (fritti)

Antipasto misto	Mixed cold meats and cheese (and a selection of other things in this list)
Arancini	Fried rice balls with mozzarella and tomato
Caponata	Mixed aubergine, olives, tomatoes and celery
Caprese	Tomato and mozzarella salad
Insalata di mare	Seafood salad
Insalata di riso	Rice salad
Melanzane in parmigiana	Fried aubergine in tomato and parmesan cheese
Mortadella	Salami-type cured meat
Pancetta	Bacon
Peperonata	Grilled green, red or yellow peppers stewed in olive oil
Pomodori ripieni	Stuffed tomatoes
Prosciutto	Ham
Salame	Salami
Suppli	Fried rice balls with mozzarella

Soups (zuppa)

Brodo	Clear broth
Minestrina	Any light soup
Minestrone	Thick vegetable soup
Pasta e fagioli	Pasta soup with beans
Pastina in brodo	Pasta pieces in clear broth
Stracciatella	Broth with egg

Pasta

Bucatini	Thick, hollow spaghetti-type pasta very common in Rome. Sometimes known as tonarelli
Cannelloni	Large, stuffed pasta tubes
Farfalle	Literally "bow"-shaped pasta; the word also means "butterflies"
Fettuccine	Flat ribbon egg noodles
Gnocchi	Small potato and dough dumplings
Paccheri	Large tubes of pasta
Pasta al forno	Pasta baked with minced meat, eggs, tomato and cheese
Penne	The most common variety of tubed pasta, deriving its name from the word for "quill"
Ravioli	Small packets of stuffed pasta
Rigatoni	Large, curved and ridged tubes of pasta – larger than penne but smaller than paccheri
Spaghettini	Thin spaghetti
Strozzapreti	Literally "strangled priests" – twisted flat noodles
Tagliatelle	Flat ribbon egg noodles, slightly thinner than fettucini
Vermicelli	Thin strand pasta often served in soup – literally "little worms"

Pasta sauces

Aglio e olio	With just garlic and oil
Amatriciana	With tomato and guanciale
Arrabbiata	Spicy tomato sauce, with chillies ("Angry")
Alla Carbonara	Pasta with beaten eggs, cubes of pan-fried guanciale or bacon, and pecorino cheese
Alla Gricia	With pecorino and guanciale
Cacio e pepe	Pasta with pecorino and ground black pepper
Maccheroni alla ciociara	With slices of sausage, prosciutto and tomato
Panna	Cream
Parmigiano	Parmesan cheese
Pasta al pajata	With calf's intestines – a very Roman dish
Peperoncino	Olive oil, garlic and fresh chillies
Pomodoro	Tomato sauce
Puttanesca	Tomato, anchovy, olive oil and oregano ("whorish")
Ragù (or Bolognese)	Meat sauce
Vongole	With baby clams

Meat (carne)

Abbacchio	Milk-fed lamb roasted to melting tenderness with rosemary, sage and garlic
Agnello	Lamb
Bistecca	Steak
Carpaccio	Slices of raw beef
Cervello	Brain, usually calves'
Cinghiale	Wild boar
Coda alla vaccinara	Oxtail stewed in a rich sauce of tomato and celery
Coniglio	Rabbit

Costolette	Cutlet, chop
Coratella	Lamb's heart, liver, lungs and spleen cooked in olive oil with lots of black pepper and onions
Fegato	Liver
Guanciale	Unsmoked bacon made from pigs' cheeks
Maiale	Pork
Manzo	Beef
Milza	Spleen – sometimes served as a pâté on toasted bread
Ossobuco	Shin of veal
Pajata	The intestines of an unweaned calf
Pancetta	Bacon
Pollo	Chicken
Polpette	Meatballs
Porchetta	Pork stuffed with herbs and roasted on a spit
Rognoni	Kidneys
Salsiccia	Sausage
Saltimbocca alla Romana	Veal cooked with a slice of prosciutto and sage on top, served plain or with a Marsala sauce
Scottadito	Grilled lamb chops, eaten with the fingers
Spezzatino	Stew
Testerelle d'abbacchio	Lamb's head baked in the oven with herbs and oil
Trippa	Tripe
Vitello	Veal

Fish (pesce) and shellfish (crostacei)

Acciughe	Anchovies
Anguilla	Eel
Aragosta	Lobster
Baccalà	Cod, best eaten Jewish-style, deep-fried: rather like British fish and chips without the chips
Calamari	Squid
Cefalo	Grey mullet
Cozze	Mussels
Dentice	Sea bream
Gamberetti	Shrimps
Gamberi	Prawns
Granchio	Crab
Merluzzo	Cod
Ostriche	Oysters
Pesce spada	Swordfish
Polpo	Octopus
Rospo	Monkfish
Sampiero	John Dory
Sarde	Sardines
Sogliola	Sole
Tonno	Tuna
Trota	Trout
Vongole	Clams

Vegetables (contorni) and salad (insalata)

Asparagi	Asparagus
Carciofi…	Artichokes
…alla Romana	Stuffed with garlic and Roman mint and stewed
…alla guidea	Flattened and deep fried in olive oil
Carciofini	Artichoke hearts
Cavolfiori	Cauliflower
Cavolo	Cabbage
Cipolla	Onion
Fagioli	Beans
Fagiolini	Green beans
Fiori di zucca	Batter-fried squash or courgette blossom stuffed with mozzarella and a sliver of marinated anchovy
Finocchio	Fennel
Funghi	Mushrooms
Insalata verde /mista	Green salad /mixed salad
Lenticchie	Lentils
Melanzane	Aubergine
Patate	Potatoes
Peperoni	Peppers
Piselli	Peas
Pomodori	Tomatoes
Radicchio	Red salad leaves
Spinaci	Spinach

Useful terms

Alla brace	Barbecued
Alla griglia	Grilled

Alla milanese	Fried in egg and breadcrumbs
Allo spiedo	On the spit
Al dente	Firm, not overcooked
Al ferri	Grilled without oil
Al forno	Baked
Al sangue	Rare
Arrosto	Roast
Ben cotto	Well done
Bollito/lesso	Boiled
Cotto	Cooked (not raw)
Crudo	Raw
Fritto	Fried
In umido	Stewed
Pizzaiola	Cooked with tomato sauce
Ripieno	Stuffed
Stracotto	Braised, stewed

Cheese (formaggi)

Dolcelatte	Creamy blue cheese
Fontina	Northern Italian cheese, often used in cooking
Gorgonzola	Soft, strong, blue-veined cheese
Mozzarella	Soft white cheese, traditionally made from buffalo's milk
Pecorino	Strong, hard sheep's cheese
Provola/Provolone	Smooth, round mild cheese, made from buffalo's or sheep's milk, sometimes smoked
Ricotta	Soft, white sheep's cheese

Fruit (frutta) and nuts (noce)

Ananas	Pineapple
Anguria/Coccomero	Watermelon
Arance	Oranges
Banane	Bananas
Ciliegie	Cherries
Fichi	Figs
Fichi d'India	Prickly pears
Fragole	Strawberries
Limone	Lemon
Mandorle	Almonds
Mele	Apples
Melone	Melon
Pere	Pears
Pesche	Peaches
Pignoli	Pine nuts
Pistacchio	Pistachio nut
Uva	Grapes

Desserts (dolci)

Amaretti	Macaroons
Cassata	Ice-cream cake with candied fruit
Gelato	Ice cream
Macedonia	Fruit salad
Torta	Cake, tart
Zabaglione	Dessert made with eggs, sugar and Marsala wine
Zuppa Inglese	Trifle

Drinks

Acqua minerale	Mineral water
Acqua del rubinetto	Tap water
Aranciata	Orangeade
Bicchiere	Glass
Birra	Beer
Bottiglia	Bottle
Caffè	Coffee
Cioccolata calda	Hot chocolate
Ghiaccio	Ice
Granita	Iced drink, with coffee or fruit
Latte	Milk
Limonata	Lemonade
Selz	Soda water
Spremuta	Fresh fruit juice
Spumante	Sparkling wine
Succo	Concentrated fruit juice with sugar
Tè	Tea
Tónica	Tonic water
Vino	Wine
Rosso	Red
Bianco	White
Rosato	Rosé
Secco	Dry
Dolce	Sweet
Litro	Litre
Mezzo	Half
Quarto	Quarter
Caraffa	Carafe
Salute!	Cheers!

Travel store

ROUGH GUIDES Complete Listing

UK & Ireland
Britain
Devon & Cornwall
Dublin **D**
Edinburgh **D**
England
Ireland
The Lake District
London
London **D**
London Mini Guide
Scotland
Scottish Highlands & Islands
Wales

Europe
Algarve **D**
Amsterdam
Amsterdam **D**
Andalucía
Athens **D**
Austria
Baltic States
Barcelona
Barcelona **D**
Belgium & Luxembourg
Berlin
Brittany & Normandy
Bruges **D**
Brussels
Budapest
Bulgaria
Copenhagen
Corfu
Corsica
Costa Brava **D**
Crete
Croatia
Cyprus
Czech & Slovak Republics
Denmark
Dodecanese & East Aegean Islands
Dordogne & The Lot
Europe
Florence & Siena
Florence **D**
France
Germany
Gran Canaria **D**
Greece
Greek Islands
Hungary
Ibiza & Formentera **D**
Iceland
Ionian Islands
Italy
The Italian Lakes
Languedoc & Roussillon
Lanzarote & Fuerteventura **D**
Lisbon **D**
The Loire Valley
Madeira **D**
Madrid **D**
Mallorca **D**
Mallorca & Menorca
Malta & Gozo **D**
Menorca
Moscow
The Netherlands
Norway
Paris
Paris **D**
Paris Mini Guide
Poland
Portugal
Prague
Prague **D**
Provence & the Côte D'Azur
Pyrenees
Romania
Rome
Rome **D**
Sardinia
Scandinavia
Sicily
Slovenia
Spain
St Petersburg
Sweden
Switzerland
Tenerife & La Gomera **D**
Turkey
Tuscany & Umbria
Venice & The Veneto
Venice **D**
Vienna

Asia
Bali & Lombok
Bangkok
Beijing
Cambodia
China
Goa
Hong Kong & Macau
Hong Kong & Macau **D**
India
Indonesia
Japan
Kerala
Laos
Malaysia, Singapore & Brunei
Nepal
The Philippines
Rajasthan, Dehli & Agra
Singapore
Singapore **D**
South India
Southeast Asia
Sri Lanka
Taiwan
Thailand
Thailand's Beaches & Islands
Tokyo
Vietnam

Australasia
Australia
Melbourne
New Zealand
Sydney

North America
Alaska
Baja California
Boston
California
Canada
Chicago
Colorado
Florida
The Grand Canyon
Hawaii
Honolulu **D**
Las Vegas **D**
Los Angeles
Maui **D**
Miami & South Florida
Montréal
New England
New Orleans **D**
New York City
New York City **D**
New York City Mini Guide
Orlando & Walt Disney World® **D**
Pacific Northwest
San Francisco
San Francisco **D**
Seattle
Southwest USA
Toronto
USA
Vancouver
Washington DC
Washington DC **D**
Yellowstone & The Grand Tetons
Yosemite

Caribbean & Latin America
Antigua & Barbuda **D**
Argentina
Bahamas
Barbados **D**
Belize
Bolivia
Brazil
Cancùn & Cozumel **D**
Caribbean
Central America
Chile
Costa Rica
Cuba
Dominican Republic
Dominican Republic **D**
Ecuador
Guatemala
Jamaica
Mexico
Peru
St Lucia **D**
South America
Trinidad & Tobago
Yúcatan

Africa & Middle East
Cape Town & the Garden Route
Dubai **D**

Available from all good bookstores D: Rough Guide DIRECTIONS

Egypt
Gambia
Jordan
Kenya
Marrakesh **D**
Morocco
South Africa, Lesotho & Swaziland
Syria
Tanzania
Tunisia
West Africa
Zanzibar

Travel Specials
First-Time Africa
First-Time Around the World
First-Time Asia
First-Time Europe
First-Time Latin America
Travel Health
Travel Online
Travel Survival
Walks in London & SE England
Women Travel
World Party

Maps
Algarve
Amsterdam
Andalucia & Costa del Sol
Argentina
Athens
Australia
Barcelona
Berlin
Boston & Cambridge
Brittany
Brussels
California
Chicago
Chile
Corsica
Costa Rica & Panama
Crete
Croatia
Cuba
Cyprus
Czech Republic
Dominican Republic
Dubai & UAE
Dublin
Egypt
Florence & Siena
Florida
France
Frankfurt
Germany
Greece
Guatemala & Belize
Iceland
India
Ireland
Italy
Kenya & Northern Tanzania
Lisbon
London
Los Angeles
Madrid
Malaysia
Mallorca
Marrakesh
Mexico
Miami & Key West
Morocco
New England
New York City
New Zealand
Northern Spain
Paris
Peru
Portugal
Prague
Pyrenees & Andorra
Rome
San Francisco
Sicily
South Africa
South India
Spain & Portugal
Sri Lanka
Tenerife
Thailand
Toronto
Trinidad & Tobago
Tunisia
Turkey
Tuscany
Venice
Vietnam, Laos & Cambodia
Washington DC
Yucatán Peninsula

Dictionary Phrasebooks
Croatian
Czech
Dutch
Egyptian Arabic
French
German
Greek
Hindi & Urdu
Italian
Japanese
Latin American Spanish
Mandarin Chinese
Mexican Spanish
Polish
Portuguese
Russian
Spanish
Swahili
Thai
Turkish
Vietnamese

Computers
Blogging
eBay
iPhone
iPods, iTunes & music online
The Internet
Macs & OS X
MySpace
PCs and Windows
PlayStation Portable
Website Directory

Film & TV
American Independent Film
British Cult Comedy
Chick Flicks
Comedy Movies
Cult Movies
Film
Film Musicals
Film Noir
Gangster Movies
Horror Movies
Kids' Movies
Sci-Fi Movies
Westerns

Lifestyle
Babies
Ethical Living
Pregnancy & Birth
Running

Music Guides
The Beatles
Blues
Bob Dylan
Book of Playlists
Classical Music
Elvis
Frank Sinatra
Heavy Metal
Hip-Hop
Jazz
Led Zeppelin
Opera
Pink Floyd
Punk
Reggae
Rock
The Rolling Stones
Soul and R&B
Velvet Underground
World Music (2 vols)

Popular Culture
Books for Teenagers
Children's Books, 5-11
Conspiracy Theories
Crime Fiction
Cult Fiction
The Da Vinci Code
His Dark Materials
Lord of the Rings
Shakespeare
Superheroes
The Templars
Unexplained Phenomena

Science
The Brain
Climate Change
The Earth
Genes & Cloning
The Universe
Weather

For more information go to www.roughguides.com

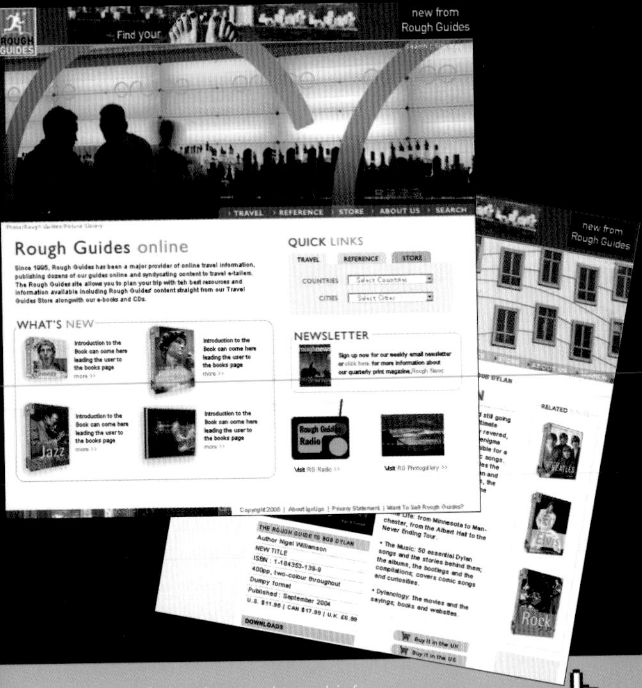

small print & Index

A Rough Guide to Rough Guides

In 1981, Mark Ellingham, a recent graduate in English from Bristol University, was travelling in Greece on a tiny budget and couldn't find the right guidebook. With a group of friends he wrote his own guide, combining a contemporary, journalistic style with a practical approach to travellers' needs. That first Rough Guide was a student scheme that became a publishing phenomenon. Today, Rough Guides include recommendations from shoestring to luxury and cover hundreds of destinations around the globe, including almost every country in the Americas and Europe, more than half of Africa and most of Asia and Australasia. Millions of readers relish Rough Guides' wit and inquisitiveness as much as their enthusiastic, critical approach and value-for-money ethos. The guides' ever-growing team of authors and photographers is spread all over the world.

In the early 1990s, Rough Guides branched out of travel, with the publication of Rough Guides to World Music, Classical Music and the Internet. All three have become benchmark titles in their fields, spearheading the publication of a range of more than 350 titles under the Rough Guide name, including phrasebooks, waterproof maps, music guides from Opera to Heavy Metal, reference works as diverse as Conspiracy Theories and Shakespeare, and popular culture books from iPods to Poker. Rough Guides also produce a series of more than 120 World Music CDs in partnership with World Music Network.

Visit www.roughguides.com to see our latest publications.

Rough Guide travel images are available for commercial licensing at www.roughguidespictures.com

Publishing information

This second edition published March 2008 by **Rough Guides Ltd**, 80 Strand, London WC2R 0RL.
345 Hudson St, 4th Floor, New York, NY 10014, USA.

Distributed by the Penguin Group
Penguin Books Ltd, 80 Strand, London WC2R 0RL
Penguin Group (USA), 375 Hudson Street, NY 10014, USA
14 Local Shopping Centre, Panchsheel Park, New Delhi 110017, India
Penguin Group (Australia), 250 Camberwell Road, Camberwell, Victoria 3124, Australia
Penguin Group (Canada), 10 Alcorn Avenue, Toronto, ON M4V 1E4, Canada
Penguin Group (NZ), 67 Apollo Drive, Mairangi Bay, Auckland 1310, New Zealand
Typeset in Bembo and Helvetica to an original design by Henry Iles.

Cover concept by Peter Dyer.

Printed and bound in China

240pp includes index

A catalogue record for this book is available from the British Library

ISBN 978-1-85828-444-6

1 3 5 7 9 8 6 4 2

Help us update

We've gone to a lot of effort to ensure that the second edition of **ROME DIRECTIONS** is accurate and up-to-date. However, things change – places get "discovered", opening hours are notoriously fickle, restaurants and rooms raise prices or lower standards. If you feel we've got it wrong or left something out, we'd like to know, and if you can remember the address, the price, the phone number, so much the better.

We'll credit all contributions, and send a copy of the next edition (or any other DIRECTIONS guide or Rough Guide if you prefer) for the best letters.

Everyone who writes to us and isn't already a subscriber will receive a copy of our full-colour thrice-yearly newsletter. Please mark letters: "**ROME DIRECTIONS Update**" and send to: Rough Guides, 80 Strand, London WC2R 0RL, or Rough Guides, 4th Floor, 345 Hudson St, New York, NY 10014. Or send an email to **mail@roughguides.com**

Have your questions answered and tell others about your trip at **www.roughguides.atinfopop.com**

Rough Guide credits

Text editors: James Smart and Lucy White
Layout: Jessica Subramanian
Photography: James McConnachie
Cartography: Swati Handoo
Picture editor: Mark Thomas
Proofreader: Anne Burgot
Production: Vicky Baldwin
Cover design: Chloë Roberts

The author

Martin Dunford is one of the founders of the Rough Guide series and today works as the Publishing Director, responsible for all Rough Guides' travel publishing. In addition to Rome, he has authored Rough Guides to Italy, Amsterdam, the Netherlands, Brussels, Belgium & Luxembourg and New York.

Acknowledgements

Thanks to James (and Lucy) for calm, creative and efficient support throughout; to Katie Parla for bang up-to-date suggestions and reviews; to Flo for books, historical updates and shared enthusiasms; and above all to Caroline, Daisy and Lucy – all-round Rome playmates for years to come.

The editors would also like to thank Jessica Subramanian, Swati Handoo, Mark Thomas, Joanna Kirby and Kathryn Lane.

Readers' letters

Thanks to all those readers who wrote in with suggestions and updates: Antoinette Sutto, Mark Lloyd, Martin Oldsberg, Andrew Young, Martin Kenzie, Dr René Brouwer, Douglas Smith, Jeffrey Robson, J Plumtree, Denise Cookson, Craig Wright, Michelle Villeneau, Alison Harris, G Tillson, Jonathan Sidaway, Bill and Margaret Gray, James Bigus and Kimberley Lomax, Gary Elflett, Miranda Gardner, Kay and Enda Bannon, Michael Upshall, Roger Hunter, Iain Baker, Maria Laffey, John Newton, Judy Wood, Stephanie Kull, Phillip Melville, Bill and Carolyn Thomas, Emma Jones and Chris Wilkinson, Ana Belén Martin, Anita Mokarram, Joanne Carter, Peter Lawton, Bruno and Jelbrich Forment, Hans Kleinen Hammans, Rosemary O'Connor, Michael Wyatt, Helen Ryan.

Photo credits

All photography © Rough Guides except the following:

p.1 Piazza del Popolo © Mark Thomas
p.2 Basilica di San Pietro © Mark Thomas
p.5 Man on scooter, Piazza Venezia © Mark Thomas
p.6 Frieze outside Piazza del Campidoglio © Mark Thomas
p.8 The Spanish Steps © Mark Thomas
p.10 Head of Nero, Museo Nazionale Romano © 1990 Photo Scala, courtesy of the Ministero Bedni e Att Culturali
p.11 Apollo and Daphne, Villa Borghese, John Heseltine © Dorling Kindersley, courtesy of the Museo e Galleria Borghese
p.14 Mosaic floor in Ostia Antica © Araldo de Luca/Corbis
p.18 Mosaic with fish, Museo Nazionale Romano © 1990 Photo Scala, courtesy of the Ministero Bedni e Att Culturali
p.21 Neo-classical temple of Diana, Villa Borghese, Kim Sayer © Dorling Kindersley
p.26 Fragment of the colossal statue of Constantine, Museo Capitolini © 1990 Photo Scala
p.26 Scarcophagus of the bride and groom, Museo di Villa Giulia © 1990 Photo Scala
p.27 Caravaggio, Michelangelo Merisi da (1573–1610): David and Goliath, Galleria Borghese © 1990 Photo Scala
p.27 Relief of flute player on the Ludovici throne, Museo Nazionale Romano © 1990 Photo Scala courtesy of the Ministero Bedni e Att Culturali
p.27 Raphael (1483–1520): La Fornarina (The Baker Girl), Galleria Nazionale d'Arte Antica © 2003 Photo Scala

p.27 Portrait of Pope Innocent X by Diego Rodriguez de Silva y Velasquez (1599-1660) © Galleria Doria Pamphilj, Rome/Bridgeman Art Library
p.34 Room in the Daphne, photo courtesy of the Daphne Hotel
p.35 Suite in the d'Inghilterra, photo courtesy of the d'Ingilterra Hotel
p.35 Pool in the Radisson SAS, photo courtesy of the Radisson SAS
p.35 View from a room, photo courtesy of the Hotel de Russie
p.38 Museo Pio-Clementino © Danita Delimont/ Alamy
p.39 Sistine Chapel celing © Vatican Musums, Vatican City/Bridgeman Art Library
p.39 School of Athens from the Stanza della Segnatura by Raphael (1483–1520) © Vatican Museums, Vatican City/Bridgeman Art Library
p.39 Leonardo da Vinci (1452–1519): Saint Jerome, Vatican, Pinacoteca © 1990 Photo Scala
p.40 Titian (1477/89-1576): Portrait of Julius II © 1990 Photo Scala, courtesy of the Ministero Beni e Att Culturali
p.40 Augustus of Via Labicana, Rome, Museo Nazionale Romano © 2003 Photo Scala, courtesy of the Ministero Bedni e Att Culturali
p.41 Francesco Totti © Christophe Simon/Getty Images
p.41 Mussolini © Bettmann/Corbis
p.41 Valentino © David Benett/Getty Images
p.41 Carravaggio, Michelangelo Merisi da (1573–1610): Sick Bacchus, Galleria Borghese © 1990 Photo Scala, courtesy of the Ministero Bedni e Att Culturali
p.43 Dying Galatian, Mike Dunning © Dorling Kindersley, Courtesy of Roma Musei Capitolini
p.43 Laocoön, Vatican, Museo Pio-Clementino © 1990 Photo Scala
p.45 Loggia of Cupid and Psyche, Villa Farnesia, John Heseltine © Dorling Kindersley
p.51 Catacombe di San Callisto © Richard T Nowitz/Corbis
p.51 Mosaic from the necropolis below St Peter's © Visual Arts Library/Alamy
p.54 Baroque corridor, Stanze di Sant'Ignazio, John Heseltine © Dorling Kindersley
p.55 Bernini, Giovanni Lorenzo (1598–1680): Self portrait at a mature age, Galleria Borghese © Photo Scala, courtesy of the Ministero Beni e Att Culturali
p.55 Borromini, Francesco (1599–1667): Self portrait, church of San Calo alle Quattro Fintane © 1990 Photo Scala
p.56 Belly of an Architect (1987) Brian Dennehy © Movie Store Collection
p.56 Anita Ekberg plays Sylvia from La Dolce Vita, directed by Federico Fellini © John Kobal Foundation/Getty Images
p.57 Gladiator (2000) Russell Crowe © Moviestore Collection Ltd
p.57 Roman Holiday (1953) Audrey Hepburn, Gregory Peck © Moviestore Collection Ltd
p.57 The Talented Mr Ripley (2000) Matt Damon © Moviestore Collection Ltd
p.58 The Trevi Fountain © Mark Thomas
p.60 The Colosseum © Mark Thomas
p.150 Bernini's David © Dorling Kindersley, courtesy of the Museo e Galleria Borghese
p.151 Votive offering, Villa Giulia © Dorling Kindersley
p.170 The Momo staircase in the Vatican © Jim Holmes/Axiom
p.173 Galleria delle Carte Geografiche © Doug McKinlay/Axiom
p.183 Villa Adriana © Dorling Kindersley
p.183 Ostia Antica © Massimo Borchi/Corbis

Index

Maps are marked in colour

a

b

c

d

e

f

g

h

i

j

k

l

m

n

INDEX

o

p

q

r

s

t

V